# The *Soul*
## of
# *Development*

RELIGION IN AMERICA SERIES
Harry S. Stout, General Editor

# The *Soul*
## *of*
# *Development*

Biblical Christianity and
Economic Transformation
in Guatemala

AMY L. SHERMAN

New York    Oxford
Oxford University Press
1997

Oxford University Press

Oxford   New York

Athens   Auckland   Bangkok   Bogota   Bombay   Buenos Aires
Calcutta   Cape Town   Dar es Salaam   Delhi   Florence   Hong Kong
Istanbul   Karachi   Kuala Lumpur   Madras   Madrid   Melbourne
Mexico City   Nairobi   Paris   Singapore   Taipei   Tokyo   Toronto

and associated companies in
Berlin   Ibadan

Copyright © 1997 by Amy L. Sherman

Published by Oxford University Press, Inc.
198 Madison Avenue, New York, New York 10016

Oxford is a registered trademark of Oxford University Press

Library of Congress Cataloging-in-Publication Data
Sherman, Amy L., 1965–
The soul of development : Biblical Christianity and economic
transformation in Guatemala / Amy L. Sherman.
p.   cm. — (Religion in America series)
Includes bibliographical references and index.
ISBN 0-19-510671-7
1. Protestant churches—Guatemala—History—20th century.
2. Evangelicalism—Guatemala—History—20th century.   3. Economic
development—Religious aspects—Christianity.   4. Guatemala—Church
history—20th century.   5. Guatemala—Economic policy.
6. Guatemala—Economic conditions—1945–   I. Title.   II. Series
Religion in America series (Oxford University Press)
BX4834.G9S48   1997
305.6'04407281—dc20      96-10378

Author and publisher wish to thank the following publications for allowing
us to reproduce articles by Amy L. Sherman that appeared previously
in these publications, sometimes in a slightly different form:
"The Evangelical Explosion in Latin America," reprinted (in somewhat altered form)
from Rutherford, May 1994, by permission, all rights reserved.
"Evangelicals and Politics in Latin America," reprinted (in somewhat altered form) from
terra nova, Summer 1992, by permission, all rights reserved.

1 3 5 7 9 8 6 4 2

Printed in the United States of America
on acid-free paper

FOR
GABRIELA MICHELLE SAMAYOA VELASCO
*a jewel of Guatemala and my special friend*

# *Preface*

## Of Fires and Tremors

I nearly killed myself (accidentally, of course) in the north-central mountains of Guatemala. I was taking a bath. Not any sort of bath, though, but a Mayan Indian "sweat bath" or *tuk*. Grimy from a three-hour tortuously slow "crawl" up a muddy mountain trail from the town of Uspantan to the hamlet of Las Pacayas, I was ready for *any* kind of a bath. From the outside, the *tuk* looked a little like an oversized wooden doghouse. Inside, its essential elements were an open fire with a large, black "witches' brew" kettle of boiling water suspended over it and a small three-legged stool. You sit on the stool, relaxing in the steamy, sauna-like atmosphere, letting your anxieties float up with the hot vapors seeping through the multiple cracks in the roof.

Unless you get in too soon, while the fire is still smoldering. Then you flatten yourself against the dirt floor, gasping for breath, groping for the door in a wild, desperate attempt to escape asphyxiation. The teenage Mayan domestic who had prepared the *tuk* had told me (I'd thought) that "the water wasn't ready." I'd misinterpreted, dashed in and felt the water in the pot—plenty hot!—and told her the temperature was fine. (She'd actually said that the *bath* wasn't ready.) Twenty minutes later, the homeowner stared down incredulously at me as I lay limply in bed, coughing and clearing my throat. Rolling her eyes at this greenhorn *gringa*, she blurted out: "You NEVER go in until the smoke has totally cleared!"

It's likely that some people who read this book will have an attitude similar to that of my hostess from Las Pacayas. I am, after all, trying to analyze the consequences of a phenomenon—the "explosion" of Evangelical Protestantism in Guatemala—that is still under way. The fires of revival are still smoking, and, in the thick of the event itself, it is difficult to assess what its impact will be. Scholars may argue (with some legitimacy) that it is premature to analyze the social, economic, and political consequences of the dramatic Evangelical explosion under way in Guatemala; that the smoke produced from this explosion is still too thick, hindering our ability to discern the effects of this still-in-process religious revolution.

Such an objection is difficult to answer. Ideally, a book about the socioeconomic consequences of the Protestant revival in Guatemala would base its conclusions on years of research and longitudinal surveys tracing the effects of conversion from one generation to another. But the ideal is not always possible. Moreover, though the smoke from the fires of Evangelical revival has not yet cleared in Guatemala, enough time has passed to allow for at least some tentative conclusions.

## Historical Background

Protestantism was introduced into Guatemala, after all, over 100 years ago. The Protestant community grew slowly but steadily in the early years. During the first 35 years of this century, according to one history of Protestantism in Latin America, the Evangelical movement in Guatemala "experienced extraordinary progress."[1] From the mid-1930s to the mid-1960s, the number of Protestant converts in Central America more than quadrupled. The number of Protestants relative to nonconverts, though, was still small. In Guatemala, Evangelicals constituted just under 3 percent of the population in 1950.[2] Missionary fervor in Guatemala and the novel Evangelization in Depth campaigns in the 1960s sponsored by the Latin American Mission (which included door-to-door evangelization) stimulated a heightened pace of growth.[3] From 1967, annual growth of the Protestant community averaged over 10 percent.[4]

The real explosion of Protestantism in Guatemala, though, began around 1976, after a massive earthquake registering 7.5 on the Richter scale shook the country. Scores of Evangelical relief and development agencies, churches, and "para-church" organizations (mission agencies, associations of Christian schools, Christian radio stations, Christian student organizations, etc.) came into Guatemala to help with reconstruction efforts following the disaster. After the clean up, many organizations decided either to stay, or at least to establish national partner organizations in the country in order to have a continuing presence

there. Such groups combined evangelism with their relief and development efforts and won many converts. Even more important, indigenous
Pentecostal churches were extremely active in evangelism, and, perhaps
because people were more open to spiritual matters in the aftermath of
the suffering caused by the earthquake, these churches multiplied.[5] The
translation of some parts of the Bible into the indigenous Mayan languages, and the emphasis put on preaching in those languages, rather
than in Spanish, further spurred the growth of the Evangelical movement. Today over half of Guatemalan Evangelicals are Pentecostal and
nearly 40 percent of the Protestant community is indigenous.[6]

The wrenching political violence in Guatemala during the late 1970s
and early 1980s also encouraged large numbers of conversions. Many
people had their lives tragically turned upside down by the war, and
they found in the Evangelical churches a spiritual solace they had not
known previously. Traditional Mayan "Cristo-pagan" religion (a syncretistic blending of animism and Catholic ritual) had already begun to
erode by the late 1970s under the combined influences of political
change, modernization, and urbanization, thus paving the way for
adoption of new beliefs. Moreover, the traditional religious leaders
were unable to explain the violence that ripped apart poor communities
in the highlands, and many Mayans lost faith as the old customs and
sacrifices did not lead to a relenting of their suffering. Many people in
this difficult climate, in short, were ripe for conversion. By 1981, 20
percent of the population of Guatemala called itself Evangelical; now,
this small nation has the highest per capita representation of Evangelicals in Latin America.[7] Today, estimates of the size of its Protestant
community range from 25 to 35 percent of the population.

## Defining "Evangelicals"

By way of definition, it should be noted that in the Guatemalan context
"Evangelical" is basically synonymous with "Protestant"—in common
conversation it denotes a non-Catholic. The Guatemalan Evangelical
community can be divided, simplistically, into three main branches. The
first is the historic mission churches ("mainline" denominations such
as, for example, the Methodists, Presbyterians, and Nazarenes). The
second is the Pentecostals, including both formal denominations (such
as the Assemblies of God, Church of God, and the Prince of Peace, to
name some of the major ones) and independent churches with no over-
arching denominational authority structure. The third is the neo-
Pentecostal denominations. These are generally younger than the Pentecostal groups, have greater membership among urban middle- and
upper-class Ladinos, have varying ties with North American counter-
points, and, broadly speaking, are less pietistic and more concerned

about the church's role in political, educational, and cultural issues facing the nation than are the Pentecostals.

All three branches share a common affirmation of certain central doctrines of historic, orthodox Christianity: monotheism; the divine inspiration and authority of Scripture; the divinity of Christ; the veracity of the various miracles of Christ; Christ's historical, actual, physical death on a cross, and his resurrection; the Trinitarian Godhead; the reality of original sin and the subsequent need for redemption; the necessity of faith in Christ for salvation; and the idea of Christ as the only way to eternal life.[8] They differ on such theological matters as church authority, organization, and governance; eschatology; baptism; and the gifts of the Holy Spirit; and on such Christian living issues as the appropriate role of the church in Guatemalan society and standards of Christian dress and practice. In many places in the book I use the terms "orthodox Christian," "Evangelical," "Pentecostal," and "Protestant" interchangeably, and where distinctions among these terms are necessary, I identify them.

## Impact of the Growth of the Evangelical Community

In reflecting on the impact of Evangelical conversion in Guatemala, I am reminded of a large suspension bridge in zone three of Guatemala City. During the 1976 mega-earthquake, the Puente Martín Prado was damaged. I was reminded of this fact every time my Guatemalan translator/chauffeur and I drove over the bridge. The roadway authorities have put a number of speed bumps on the bridge to slow the traffic passing over it, for apparently this reduces the stress on the weakened bridge. At the decreased speed, you can crane your neck and get a good look at the rocky valley several hundred feet below. Large, 6-inch-wide cracks are visible in the concrete slabs adjacent to the guardrails on the sides of the bridge, a frightening testimony to the awesome power of the titanic earthquake that shook this bridge nearly two decades ago. Crossing the bridge was particularly disconcerting whenever my Guatemalan translator's six-year-old son, little Nagib, was in the car, since he would inevitably ask, "Papa, is this the bridge that is going to fall down one day? Do we have to go over it, Papa?"

The cracks in the Puente Martín Prado are clear, visible, and significant. The bridge has been unmistakably altered by the earthquake, but the potential meaning of this change for the future is uncertain. The cracks may never widen any further, but this seems unlikely: my translator reports that he has seen a gradual enlargement in them over time. It is possible that, one sad day, the bridge will collapse. In this sense, the cracks are now partial, suggestive, and anticipatory.

Like the cracks in the Puente Martín Prado, evidence of the socio-economic impact of Evangelical conversion is now visible and significant. This book describes the attitudes and behaviors that are correlated with Christian orthodoxy and the sorts of changes induced by Evangelical conversion. The changes that conversion has brought, however, again like the fissures in the bridge, are partial, suggestive, and anticipatory. It will take time to determine what the fruits of conversion will be as Evangelical faith is passed down from generation to generation. In the meantime, though, a veritable religious "revolution" is underway in Guatemala. The tremors and ripple effects of this revolution can be felt now, even if the ultimate consequences of the aftershocks are not yet discernible.

*Charlottesville, Virginia*                                                   A.L.S.

# Acknowledgments

My best thanks are due to the many wonderful friends I made in Guatemala, who housed, guided, critiqued, and encouraged me. I am deeply indebted to Nancy Armstrong, my faithful companion on many a "chicken bus" ride, who traveled light, reminded me of the ever-important credo "Don't panic," and cheerfully and accurately translated hour upon hour of interviews. Sheny and Estuardo Salazar and Erwin and Margarita Marroquin, despite the bad luck I brought to their cars, always got me where I needed to be. I am delighted and blessed to call them friends and thank them for their translation work and thoughtful insights about the Guatemalan Evangelical community. Steve and Cindy Antosh gave me a "home away from home," provided invaluable logistical support, prayerful encouragement, and steadfast friendship. The hard-working staff and associates of the Summer Institute of Linguistics (SIL)—especially Paul Townsend, Dwight and Sue Jewett, Vilma Luz Avila, Pablo Mo, Stan and Margot McMillan, Abby and Nate Kugler, and Merietta Johnson—served variously as hosts, tour guides, interpreters, book providers, and invaluable resources during my "initiation" into Mayan culture. I have learned much from them not only about the complexities and beauties of rural Guatemala but about faithfulness to and sacrifice for Christ's Kingdom. Ray and Helen Elliott, also with SIL, were gracious hosts in Nebaj and critical, helpful commentators on Protestant history in the Ixil region. The staff from Fundación Contra el Hambre were similarly invaluable in arranging lodging and transportation. My special and warm thanks go to Porfirio

Chavez and Victor Hugo Alvarado. The pilots of MAF/AGAPE spared me the rigors of hours-long bus rides and safely transported me about the highlands. Marco Tulio Cajas, Alfred Kaltschmitt, Guillermo Mendez, and Virgilio Zapata were exceptionally informed commentators on the intersection of religion and public life in Guatemala and gave generously of their time.

I would be remiss not to mention as well the generosity of so many Evangelical pastors in villages throughout Guatemala who gave me their time and their opinions. I am particularly indebted to Jorge and Ani Serritos in Coban and Cesar Menjivar Cartegena in Almolonga, who went above and beyond the call of duty during my visits to their towns. Numerous pastors in Guatemala City also granted me interviews, as did leaders of various Evangelical organizations. I am thankful as well for the willing participation of the one thousand Guatemalans who took the time to be interviewed for the Worldview and Development Survey.

Roger Murillo supervised the fieldwork and interviewing for the survey and was a competent, efficient, helpful, and valuable partner in the not-so-easy task of gathering public opinion data in rural Guatemala. Tom Guterbock and Joe Spear of the Center for Survey Research patiently explained to me the mysteries of Statistical Package for the Social Sciences (SPSS) and carefully analyzed and helped me to interpret the tidal wave of raw data I carried back from Guatemala. Carol Mullen Sargeant kept my office running while I was away, diligently guarded my prose, and provided creative, thoughtful editorial help and efficient research and clerical help. Jeffrey Leach also provided research assistance, was a helpful traveling companion during initial fieldwork, and often served as a sounding board. Herb and Terry Schlossberg listened to lengthy recitations of my adventures in Guatemala, read chapters in draft, and helped me sort through and make sense of what I uncovered. Members of the Villars Committee on Relief and Development encouraged me and provided helpful feedback at various stages. David Jordan, James Hunter, Whittle Johnston, and Stephen Rhoads of the University of Virginia supervised my dissertation, from which this book emerged. They provided numerous comments at various stages of the research, gave me freedom to pursue politically incorrect subjects, suggested helpful books, and helped me clarify my avenues of inquiry. I thank them for the role they have played in my intellectual development. As the pages ahead show, I owe an intellectual debt as well to David Martin, Peter Berger, and Lawrence Harrison.

Finally, this work would have been impossible without the generous support of the Smith Richardson Foundation, the Fieldstead Institute, and the Earhart Foundation. The worth of the book is theirs to share.

# Contents

# Glossary

| | |
|---|---|
| *aanhel* | angel-like figures with magical powers in the Ixil cosmology |
| *Accionístas* | those who are members of Catholic Action |
| *aldeas* | hamlets |
| *brujos* | witches |
| *cargo* | office or burden |
| *casados* | legally, formally married |
| *Catholic Action* | a lay Catholic movement begun in the 1950s (with the blessing of Roman authorities) to purge the syncretistic elements of the Mayans' Catholic faith |
| *campos* | small, informal fellowship gatherings |
| *cofrades* | members of *cofradias* |
| *cofradia* | religious brotherhoods |
| *commerciántes* | businessmen, merchants |
| *costumbre* | offering sacrifices and performing certain rituals to appease the gods |
| *"counting the days"* | the practice of interpreting life's events according to the powerful influence of the various gods of certain days |
| *curandero* | witch doctor/shaman |
| *cuerda* | unit of land |
| *daykeeper* | Mayan diviner |
| *dios del mundo* | "earth god" or god of the Sacred World |

| | |
|---|---|
| *dueño* | "spirit-owner" |
| *hermano* | brother |
| *indígenas* | indigenous Maya |
| Ladino | those with Spanish ancestry, or Mayans who adopt the Spanish language and Western-style dress and customs |
| *mal de ojo* | the "evil eye" |
| *mayordomo* | the highest ranked member of a *cofradia* |
| *medicina naturala* | natural, herbal medicines |
| *milpa* | small plot of land on which corn and beans are grown |
| *mozo* | agricultural day laborer |
| *naguale* | an animal co-spirit into which certain humans may change |
| *principales* | the oldest, highest ranking members of the *cofradias*, or alumni of these positions |
| *quetzales* | the currency of Guatemala; financial figures in the book are calculated at an exchange rate of Q5.25 to $1.00 (which prevailed during most of the six months of field research) |
| *Renovacionístas* | orthodox Catholics who belong to the so-called Catholic renovation fellowships that stress Bible study and faithful attendance at mass |
| *susto* | paralyzing fright |
| *taxistas* | drivers |
| *tiendas* | tiny, traditional stores selling basic foodstuffs, soda pop, toiletries |
| *tuk* | Guatemalan sweat bath |
| *unidos* | when a man and woman live together under an informal, common-law arrangement |

# The *Soul*
of
# *Development*

# Introduction

*There were a lot of people at the graveyard. On this farm, only a shaman had the right to perform ceremonies for all other people. When the people living there saw that Señor Martín was a shaman, they began to ask him to do them the favor of making ceremonies for their own dead. They wanted him to do this because it helps the spirit of the dead person because the spirit does not know where it is. So to help the spirit feel satisfied and happy for a little while, they have a shaman perform a ritual for it. . . . According to the beliefs of the people, if the shaman is not used, the spirit becomes sad and will cry because it does not have protection. Some believe that if a shaman did not perform a ceremony for the deceased spirit's protection, those who are still alive would get sick or would suffer much poverty or their children would die because they didn't help the dead spirit.*

*[The shaman] claimed that the reason we are having earthquakes is that the people in this day and age have forgotten to perform the* costumbres *[rituals] to the Sacred World. They no longer burn myrrh, incense, and candles. For that reason, the God of the Sacred World is angry. In fury he moves the earth because his children do not remember to give him offerings.*

—Ignacio, a Tzutuhil Mayan Indian of Guatemala,
in *Son of Tecún Umán*[1]

*To live in [peasant] villages, even temporarily, is to suspend one's disbelief in the supernatural; indeed, seemingly supernatural occurrences are part of everyday life.*

—Richard Critchfield in *Villages*

*As long as there is poverty there will be gods.*

—Will Durant

Will Durant's formulation of the connection between economic life and religion symbolizes the dominant view among social scientists that religious conviction is something that has to be explained, rather than—as for most religious adherents themselves—something that explains. According to Durant's phrase, belief in the existence of gods is the result of objective socioeconomic factors—that is, poverty is the independent variable and religious belief the dependent variable. Though several scholars have asserted that religious worldview actually influences economic life, rather than only being influenced by it, they have been in the minority.

Max Weber may not have been the first, but he was probably the best-known analyst to suggest the unorthodox way of looking at religion and economics. In landmark works—such as his essays on the sociology of religion and his famous book *The Protestant Ethic and the Spirit of Capitalism*—Weber asserted that the complicated mixture of Protestant thinking (rational and forward-looking), Protestant behavior (ascetic and morally strict), and Protestant associational life (probationary and legitimizing) gave rise to a "spirit of capitalism" in northern Europe. Weber granted that there were "feedbacks" in the linkage between religion and economics; in addition to affecting, Protestantism also was affected by the spirit of capitalism it birthed. Nonetheless, in his view religion did have causal significance.

Nineteenth-century England experienced what sociologist David Martin calls the "second wave" of Protestant revivalism.[2] A few analysts have suggested that this wave, like the earlier Calvinist one which interested Weber, also led to notable socioeconomic changes. The French historian Élie Halévy, for example, speaking of the English Methodists of the 1820s and 1830s, argued "[W]e must . . . be always on the alert to detect the silent influence exercised over the nation by these independent Churches of the lower middle class, an influence which their very number and diversity render it more difficult to define."[3] Importantly, Halévy recognized that Evangelical religion's public influence went beyond the specific pieces of social legislation it encouraged (William Wilberforce's triumph in ending the British slave trade being the premier example) to the *cultural transformation* it brought about. Historian Herbert Schlossberg notes that even scholars generally unsympathetic to religion admit that the Methodist and Evangelical revivals changed British society. For instance, Schlossberg explains that J. L. and Barbara Hammond, probably the best-known historians of Victorian England,

> generally have a rather negative view of the influence of religion; nevertheless, they report with a dogged kind of honesty what elsewhere they seem to disbelieve. "Wesley and his disciples," the Hammonds write,

"converted whole districts . . . from a life of dissipation and plunder to devout and orderly habits."[4]

A "third wave" of Protestant revival, which has been labeled the Pentecostal wave or "Evangelical explosion," is currently under way across the globe.[5] It is growing with particularly dramatic force in Latin America, and, within that region, especially in the small nation of Guatemala. The principal question animating this book is whether this "Pentecostal wave" of Protestant revival will have any socioeconomic effects of the sort produced by the earlier waves. I argue in the pages that follow that it is likely that it will; indeed, it already has.

## Religion's Political Influence

The prevailing wisdom in academia has not only been reluctant to acknowledge the causal significance of religious worldview on *economic* life, but it also has been slow to admit religion's influence on *political* life. Princeton sociologist Robert Wuthnow suggests that the three theories dominating discussions of religion and politics—modernization theory, world-system theory, and critical theory—are, in this regard, painfully inadequate:

> In seeking to make empirical predictions, each of the three theories . . . focuses on the broad dynamics of economic and political systems as the determining forces in the modern world. All three regard religion as something that wiggles when these controlling puppeteers pull the strings. None of the three take religion seriously.[6]

Wuthnow goes on to assert that these theories do not take religious actors seriously either; they "do not recognize the sway religious leaders may hold over their followers or the role of faith in motivating people to take political action."[7] This insight was brought home to me most powerfully in a story once related by a university professor concerning the fall of the shah of Iran. Apparently, in the midst of the crisis, members of the Carter administration were trying desperately to find out "who is this Ayatollah Khomeini anyway?" Political scientists neglect the role of religious leaders at their own peril.

Perhaps more important, Wuthnow contends that the prevailing theories about religion and politics fail to understand the religious meaning of important contemporary events.[8] For me, the clearest example of this emerged during the collapse of communism in Eastern Europe in 1989 and 1990. As James F. Pontuso, author of *Solzhenitsyn's Political Thought*, noted in a recent interview, most commentators focused on the socioeconomic failings of communism rather than its fatal flaw—namely, its attempts to crush the human spirit:

> If you look at the way the West has reported the defeat of Marxism, it
> said the reasons why Marxism has been defeated is because there [were]
> not enough material goods in the East. Now that certainly is important.
> But why would someone sacrifice his life because he didn't have a dish-
> washer? Some of those people stood in the streets and took their lives in
> their hands. And they didn't know whether the guy next to them was a
> police informant, or a spy. There was a lot of bravery in those [Eastern
> European] countries during those revolts. Why would people do these
> things for a dishwasher or an electric toothbrush? There has to be some-
> thing more to human beings, something which elevates their spirit, which
> makes them sacrifice.[9]

The economic failure of communism undoubtedly contributed to its
demise. The political failure of communism did, too. But communism's
spiritual failure—its attempt to replace the transcendent with the state,
to deny the existence of any meaning or authority outside of the Communist Party—was certainly a crucial factor as well. Because social
scientists frequently lack an appreciation for the political significance of
religious belief, many of them failed to see this.

Not wishing to repeat the errors Wuthnow identifies, I include in this
volume a consideration of the political implications of Evangelical conversion in Guatemala. (I do not give nearly as much attention to this
question, however, as I do to the issue of conversion's economic effects.) In the course of my research in Guatemala, I discovered that a
person's religious worldview was correlated with his or her political
beliefs and participation. As described in chapters 6 and 7, individuals
with orthodox Christian convictions tended to be more sympathetic
toward the institutions and norms of democratic capitalism than did
individuals with animist or pagan beliefs.

Religious conviction, to sum up, is powerful and should not be dis-
missed. It affects how people think and behave. It provides the eye-
glasses through which some people see and interpret the world. In this
sense, religion is the "root" or "heart" of what we call culture—that
complex of beliefs, values, attitudes, customs, and social institutions.
Thus, religion has serious, systematic social, economic, and political
consequences. This book examines those consequences among the poor
of Guatemala. It assumes that religion is neither dead nor impotent. It
argues that religion can be an independent variable, an agent of change.
It suggests that there is some degree of truth in a reversal of Will
Durant's formulation quoted at the outset of this chapter—that it is
accurate to say that because there are gods, there is poverty. And it
asserts that Guatemalan converts' escape from belief in gods (animism),
and their embrace of belief in God (orthodox Christianity), has helped
them to begin to climb out of poverty.

## Getting Beyond Nominal Affiliation

As the quotation from Richard Critchfield at the beginning of this chapter suggests, belief in the supernatural is alive and well in the peasant villages of the Third World. It is certainly alive and well in the villages of Guatemala I visited. Predictably, religion in the impoverished highlands is "highly propitiatory; the gods are to be served and appeased."[10] This, however, may not be immediately evident to the researcher who visits Guatemala's *altiplano*, for the villagers there call themselves Catholics rather than animists. I discovered that it is extremely important to be careful about names in Guatemala, for sometimes words do not mean what we might think.

A humorous incident my (North American) Spanish translator and I experienced during my first research trip to Guatemala imprinted this lesson. Standing around our pickup truck in a small village in Guatemala's Alta Verapaz department (province), we were reviewing a list of pastors' names with our local informants. They had been helping us to locate the different men's homes, and we had spent the whole day walking back and forth from one end of the community to the other. The last man we wished to interview lived far in the outskirts of the village, and since we were tired, my translator suggested that we *vamos en coche*—an innocent request which we thought meant, "Let's take the car." The look of astonishment on our companions' faces, and their outburst of laughter, indicated we had miscommunicated. We'd said, "Let's go by pig!" My colleague and I had both been taught Mexican Spanish, but in Guatemala the natives use the word *carro* for "car" and *coche* for "pig." Some of them also use the term "Catholic" for what would more accurately be labeled "Cristo-pagan"—a syncretistic blending of traditional Mayan animism with a thin overlay of Catholic ritual.

There are fewer Cristo-pagans in Guatemala now than a generation ago, but I still encountered adherents to this worldview in my visits to 15 villages. Some Cristo-pagans carry on the ancient Mayan tradition of "counting the days"; that is, interpreting life's events according to the powerful influence of the various gods of certain days identified in the 260-day Mayan calendar. Cristo-pagans may also believe that some humans, especially *curanderos* (witch doctors) or *brujos* (witches) can transform themselves into animal forms. (These special humans, it is believed, have an animal co-spirit called a *naguale*, into which they change.)[11] Cristo-pagans serve in religious brotherhoods called *cofradias* that protect and take care of the (usually wooden) images of local saints. Once again, digging through to the real meaning of terms is important in understanding the word "saint," for the "Catholic saint" adored by the *cofrades* (members of the *cofradia*) is often a Mayan god (for example, the god of a hill or cave) who now has a Catholic name. Moreover, some Cristo-pagan *cofrades* worship the wooden image itself more than the person/god it represents; for them it is a divinely inhabited idol rather than a merely symbolic icon. They take elaborate care of the image itself, dressing it, cleaning it, offering it food and other sacrifices, and taking pains not to drop it when transporting it.

Cristo-pagans also believe that certain places—such as particular mountains—are sacred, and they visit those places regularly to offer sacrifices of candles, incense, or chickens. They plant crosses in sacred, dangerous spots where humans have come to some tragedy because of the malevolent action of a god. They have a tenuous relationship with nature, believing that most objects (trees, rocks, soil) have a spirit-owner, or *dueño*, whose permission must be sought before using or touching these things. The "earth god," *dios del mundo*, or "god of the Sacred World," is a particularly volatile member of the Mayan cosmology (as indicated by Ignacio's remarks in the opening quotations to this introduction about the earth god causing the massive 1976 earthquake in Guatemala).

Cristo-pagans also worship the spirits of their dead. In funeral rituals, they include cups of coffee and handkerchiefs filled with tortillas in the deceased's coffin (to supply him or her on the journey to the spirit-world). They say prayers over graves, lighting candles and pouring libations of liquor to cheer the dead. They fear inciting the wrath of the deceased by neglect of such *costumbres* (rituals or ceremonies). For Cristo-pagans, the supernatural is all around them, and life's events, whether large or small, are interpreted in spiritual terms. Illness and tragedy are the result of sin, neglect of rituals, or the evil, capricious acts of the spirits. Good fortune is the consequence of having a good fate or luck granted to one at birth; no one controls the fate he or she receives, and no one can change it.

Many villagers who call themselves Catholic, however, are neither devout followers of these ancient Mayan ways nor of Rome's. These sorts of Catholics attend mass sporadically and baptize their children in the Catholic Church. On special occasions (before deciding on a marriage partner, for example), they may consult a Mayan diviner, called a daykeeper, for advice. When ill, they may go either to the local health post or to a *curandero*. On the whole, though, unlike the Cristo-pagans, these Catholics are not as deeply influenced by animist beliefs and do not perform the numerous rituals expected by the spirits of their dead ancestors, by the *dueños* of rocks, trees, animals, and birds, or by the powerful earth god. But neither are these Catholics overwhelmingly influenced by Catholic doctrine. They do not attend catechism classes or Bible studies; they may not even bother to get formally married in the

Catholic Church. Rather, they and their spouses live together under an informal, common-law arrangement known as being *unidos*.

A few other Catholics, definitely the minority, are orthodox and devout. Some of them belong to Catholic Action, a lay Catholic movement begun in the 1950s (with the blessing of Rome) to purge the syncretistic elements from the Mayans' Catholic faith. These *Accionístas* teach the Roman Catholic catechism, criticize the drunken fiestas and saint processions of the cofradias, and deny the existence of dueños, el dios del mundo, and naguales. They sponsor Bible studies, promote church-sanctioned marriages, and condemn worship of the mountain spirits in the high places of the altiplano.

Other orthodox Catholics are called *Renovacionístas*; they belong to so-called Catholic renovation fellowships that, like the *Accionístas*, stress Bible study and faithful attendance at mass. In addition, though, the *Renovacionístas* are charismatics, emphasizing the gifts of the Holy Spirit. Much like the Pentecostals, the *Renovacionístas* sing and pray in tongues; dance "in the spirit"; enjoy loud, enthusiastic guitar-led worship; and believe in miraculous physical and psychological healing. Still other Catholics, members of neither the Catholic Action nor the Catholic Renovation movements, have disregarded traditional Mayan customs and embraced Christian orthodoxy and a Protestant ascetic ethic. As explained later, these Catholics are like hidden converts to Evangelical faith, imitating many of the beliefs, attitudes, and behaviors of orthodox Evangelicals without publicly converting to Protestant faith.[12]

Just as there are different kinds of Catholics in Guatemala, so there are different kinds of Evangelicals. Some are very orthodox, adopting a strict monotheism, acknowledging the inspiration and final authority of the Bible, affirming the exclusivity of faith in Jesus Christ as the only path to salvation, and embracing a new set of ethical standards. These people claim they have rejected completely animistic beliefs and have opted out of traditional social institutions such as the cofradias and the "fiesta system."

As explained in greater detail in chapter 3, the fiesta system embodies beliefs about both the religious construction of the world and the proper ordering of community life. Important annual celebrations are organized by the cofradias to honor local saints. These fiestas include religious processions, dancing, music by marimba (xylophone) bands, games of sport, prayers, special sacrifices, the shooting off of fireworks, and, most predominantly, drinking of locally brewed *aguaro* or *aguardiente* (sugarcane liquor, corn liquor) or store-bought beer. Typically, an individual family is asked to sponsor the expensive, three- to-five-day fiesta. While it is a great honor to be asked to be a host, it is also a substantial economic burden. Usually better-off members of the community are requested to play this role, and their acceptance of this *cargo* (office or burden) reduces their economic surplus and brings their own domestic wealth more into balance with that of the rest of the villagers.

Other Evangelicals have made less of a break from Mayan traditions. These nominal or "weak" Protestants may rely in secret on the counsel of shamans, disobey the Protestant prohibition against drinking alcohol, and—just to play it safe—make sacrifices to the earth god and the spirits of the dead. They are like the Catholics who are neither Cristo-pagans nor orthodox Christians. These "weak" Evangelicals live with one foot in the old religious ways and one foot in the new, Protestant ways.[13]

Because the nominal labels of *Catholic* and *Evangelical* can mean so many different things in Guatemala, comparisons of the two groups—when the groups are distinguished exclusively by nominal affiliation—can be misleading. In order to analyze accurately the socioeconomic and political effects of the Evangelical explosion in Guatemala, researchers must go beyond nominal categories. Sometimes few empirically substantiated differences between Evangelicals and Catholics are evident when only nominal affiliation is used to distinguish the two groups. Since most studies do simply compare Protestants with Catholics, without identifying *what kind* of Protestants or Catholics the respondents are, the causal significance of religious life is downplayed. As noted earlier, many social scientists suggest that religion has little explanatory value in assessing different people's behaviors and attitudes. Nominal-level comparisons of Catholics and Protestants, since they often show few differences between the two groups, reinforce the idea that religion does not matter. In contrast, a central theme of this book is that religion *does* matter and that important differences among adherents to different religious worldviews can be measured when the appropriate categories for comparing these groups are constructed.

This argument can be made clearer at this juncture by reference to sociologist James Davison Hunter's important book, *Culture Wars*.[14] Hunter notes that in America much comparative study has been made of members of different religious traditions—Jews, Protestants, and Catholics. For a long while, significant differences between these groups were discernible. More recently, however, such differences have diminished, and greater religious toleration exists. Hunter asserts, however, that cultural conflict in America along religious lines has not ended; rather, such conflict has adopted a different shape along new dividing lines: "The divisions of political consequence today are not theological and ecclesiastical in character but the result of differing worldviews. . . . [T]hey revolve around . . . our most fundamental and cherished assumptions about how to order our lives—our own lives and our lives together in this society."[15]

The new dividing lines, Hunter explains, are between the "orthodox" and "progressives" in America, rather than between Catholics, Protestants, and Jews. New alliances have formed across these nominal religious boundaries: orthodox Catholics collaborate with orthodox Jews and orthodox Protestants to defend their idea of transcendent moral authority against the progressivists within the three religious communities who embrace the "spirit of the modern age, a spirit of rationalism and subjectivism."[16]

Similarly, in my attempts to understand the current and potential influence of Evangelical conversion in Guatemala, I discovered that nominal affiliation was usually an unhelpful category for analysis. I found in Guatemala that conversion has positive effects (or, to phrase it more conservatively, is correlated with certain positive indicators of development) *if conversion is genuine and profound*. Obvious, important socioeconomic differences are evident between Cristo-pagans and orthodox Evangelicals in Guatemala. The former, much more than the latter, adhere to certain development-hindering attitudes and actions (described in chapters 3 and 4). To the extent that converts to Protestantism adopt a truly orthodox and serious faith, apply its moral demands in their daily life, and shun old, Cristo-pagan patterns of thinking and acting, their economic prospects appear to improve. "Weak" Evangelicals, in contrast, show few significant differences from Cristo-pagans and "half-hearted" Catholics; their conversions have not been profound and life-changing.

I also found that liberation from a focus on nominal affiliation paved the way for recognizing the socioeconomic importance of orthodoxy itself, whether it is embraced by Evangelicals *or Catholics*. My investigations indicated that the minority of Catholics in Guatemala who can be called orthodox tend to do just as well, or better, economically, than do orthodox Evangelicals. They also hold similarly modern attitudes on important variables related to development (such as views toward merit, equality, fate, innovation, and education.) This finding not only reinforces the claim that the use of nominal categories, when comparing the socioeconomic life of members of different religious groups, is insufficient. It also may indicate that, in some communities, an imitation effect is playing out, whereby Catholics adopt biblical orthodoxy and the rigorous moral life of Protestant asceticism without formally joining Evangelical churches.

## Methodology of the Study

In order to probe beneath nominal categories, and to uncover those dividing lines among worldview groups that reveal the influence of worldview on development prospects, I employed a combination of qualitative and quantitative research methods. This proved to be a valuable and well-suited methodological plan, partly because I needed to distinguish between varying types of Catholics and varying types of Evangelicals, and partly because some of the socioeconomic effects of conversion were elusive and difficult to calculate. Quantitative methods helped me address the first concern, and qualitative methods, the second.

As discussed in chapter 4, many of the arguments advanced in these pages emerge from my "Worldview and Development Survey," a formal study of 1,000 Guatemalans from five different villages. The lengthy survey instrument included a battery of questions designed to separate orthodox Catholics and Evangelicals from Catholic Cristo-pagans and weak Evangelicals. Since the time I had for field research in each community I studied was limited (I spent a total of about six months in Guatemala), it would have been impossible for me to determine accurately, solely on the basis of informal interviewing, the world-views of a large number of individuals. The survey thus proved an efficient way of grouping large numbers of respondents into worldview categories (orthodox Evangelical, nominal Catholic, Cristo-pagan, weak Evangelical, and so forth) that more accurately captured the nature of their religious convictions than did the simple labels of Catholic and Evangelical.

The Worldview and Development Survey also provided me with some hard data on the correlations between indicators of development and respondents' worldviews—such as information on income, education, occupation, literacy, and the physical conditions of the respondents' homes. This information is particularly valuable since most commentary about the effects of conversion has been exclusively ethnographic and anecdotal. Many observers have suggested on the basis of fieldwork that conversion to Evangelical faith, or to a more orthodox Catholicism, has encouraged positive economic changes. But empirical data reinforces and lends greater credibility to such claims.

Some of the socioeconomic effects of religious worldview are not easily measurable, however, and for this reason my field research and extensive interviewing helped to identify those consequences of conversion not detected by the survey.[17] Information about the subjective, emotional changes that converts experience following their conversion —such as feeling healthier, less fearful, more content in their marriage, more hopeful about the future, more confident about their prospects for economic advancement—was best gathered through informal interactions with respondents over time.

During such interactions, I found that the consequences of conversion first mentioned by informants typically were domestic in nature: they related to the beneficial effects of male sobriety. In numerous instances, conversion meant that male heads of households quit drinking alcohol and began to treat their wives and children more responsibly. Converts spoke frequently of enjoying domestic tranquility and of having a more optimistic attitude toward life. They also reported that decreased alcohol consumption freed up money for investment in better clothing, housing improvements, more nutritious food, and children's educations. Typically, though, it was only after enunciating the less tangible, subjective benefits of conversion that converts spoke of these more objective economic benefits.

Most of my interviews were with Evangelical pastors, but I had numerous conversations with Evangelical and Catholic lay people and with outside observers (professionals at local health posts, local government staff, leaders of nonprofit organizations, missionaries, etc.) as well. I interviewed in total more than 100 Guatemalans. These interviews and my numerous site visits (six visits of about one month each) allowed me to "put a human face" on the hard data generated by the Worldview and Development Survey. In chapter 5, I attempt to portray the human stories behind the numbers in a descriptive excursus styled along the lines of a *National Geographic* feature.

## Overview of the Book

Many of the scholars who have been reluctant to acknowledge the potential influence of religious conviction on economic and political behavior have been, predictably, unenthusiastic about or critical of the so-called culture-and-development school. This school of thought asserts that cultural factors affect a society's prospects for development. Some analysts sympathetic to this school concentrate specifically on religion, since, as Hunter has put it, "faith and culture are inextricably linked."[18] Others have a wider scope of investigation and consider aspects of culture in addition to religion in their assessments of culture's effects. All of these researchers share in common a rejection of cultural relativism because they all are willing to make critical judgments about the cultures they study. In what nowadays is very politically *in*correct, these authors assert that some cultural practices facilitate economic development and enhance human welfare more than others.

In chapter 1, I show how the arguments of this book are located in the culture-and-development school of thought, and I summarize the contributions of some of the most important scholars in this field. I do this by way of a loosely chronological bibliographic essay reviewing the key literature, beginning with the school's founding father, Max Weber, and concluding with a discussion of one of the better-known neo-Weberian scholars of our time, Lawrence Harrison. In chapter 2, I narrow my focus to a subset of this general culture-and-development literature and summarize the findings from a variety of studies concerned specifically with Protestantism and development in Latin America (particularly those studies of Guatemala). These two literature review chapters, which compose part I of the book, help set the context for the discussion of my own fieldwork and empirical research on worldview and development in Guatemala.

Before delving into the findings of my research, however, I conclude part I with a description and analysis of Cristo-paganism. This is the worldview from which many poor Guatemalan Mayans have converted, and chapter 3 provides a sort of "before conversion" snapshot that serves as the backdrop against which the effects of conversion can be assessed. In the latter half of the chapter, I evaluate the socioeconomic implications of the Cristo-pagan worldview and suggest that, in several ways, it hinders its adherents' prospects for socioeconomic betterment. As I describe in chapter 3 and others, I discovered that anthropologist George Foster's thesis—namely, that the prevalence of a "zero-sum" mentality among peasants hinders their prospects for development—was confirmed in the Guatemalan context. The zero-sum mentality pervades the Cristo-pagan worldview. It is reflected in the worldview's prohibitions against individual initiative, in its etiological assumptions, and in the equality-enforcing fiesta system it undergirds and reinforces.

In part II, Orthodoxy and Transformation, I argue that religious worldview is, in fact, correlated with development prospects and with improved economic performance. The evidence I have gathered in Guatemala suggests that conversion to orthodox Evangelicalism *or* orthodox Catholicism has set in motion a pattern of attitudinal and behavioral changes conducive to enhanced well-being. The two chapters of this section—chapter 4, which explains the evidence from the Worldview and Development Survey, and chapter 5, which tries to help the reader experience that evidence—are the heart of the book. In chapter 4 and subsequent chapters, I broach the intriguing question of the relative importance of behavioral versus attitudinal changes for affecting development prospects. Put simply, some of the culture-and-development scholars discussed in part I of the book, particularly Max Weber, emphasize the importance of *behavioral* changes and the so-called Protestant Ethic. Others, such as Foster, and to some extent Lawrence Harrison, emphasize the importance of *attitudinal* changes resulting from conversion. The diversity of the Guatemalan communities I studied allowed me to draw some tentative conclusions about the relationship between behavioral and attitudinal changes and their relative importance for micro- and macrolevel economic development. I describe these determinations in the book's conclusion.

In part III, I review the evidence with an eye toward the implications of the growth of Christian orthodoxy for the nurturing of democratic capitalism. The third wave of Protestant revival is occurring more or less simultaneously with a trend of democratic-capitalist reform in much of Latin America. The most serious proponents of democratic capitalism recognize that if institutions of political and economic freedom are to be consolidated in Latin America, they must be grounded in a supportive, nurturing moral-cultural soil. Consequently, I was interested in exploring whether the current Evangelical explosion is conducive to the cultivation and fertilization of that moral-cultural soil.

Some of the data gathered by the Worldview and Development Survey reported on in chapters 6 and 7 is sobering for enthusiasts of democratic capitalism. It shows that roughly half of the respondents were reluctant to embrace the free market as the best economic system or to affirm competitive elections as the best method for selecting political leaders. If it is to be made fertile for the consolidation of democratic capitalism, the moral-cultural soil in Guatemala needs a lot of tilling and weeding. The insights I gained from fieldwork, as well as the results of the Worldview and Development Survey, indicate that poor Mayans lack confidence or interest in Guatemala's national political institutions. Also, a significant number of poor Mayans are unsympathetic to the notion of a merit-based economy and unenthusiastic about the free market. I suspect that this is explained, in part, by a general, cultural misunderstanding of capitalism. Many Guatemalans, I think, confuse interventionism or statism with capitalism and blame the market for what really are the economic failings of interventionist policies. But some of the lack of enthusiasm stems as well from the underlying presuppositions of the Cristo-pagan worldview, which are hostile to the ideas of profit-making, individual initiative, competition, and possibility for "positive sum" economic relations.

The work that democratic-capitalist enthusiasts in Guatemala must do to educate the population and persuade their fellow citizens of the benefits of political and economic liberty is considerable indeed. It is against this backdrop that some findings in the Worldview and Development Survey take on special importance. In brief, the survey results suggest that orthodox respondents are more likely than nonorthodox respondents to hold attitudes supportive of competitive elections, the free market, and political participation. Moreover, as described in chapter 7, the Evangelicals have created an "alternative community" that challenges the definitions of socioeconomic justice offered by both Marxists and Cristo-pagan traditionalists. Animating the Evangelicals' community are ideas and practices that resonate more fully with the norms of democratic-capitalist society than do either the Marxist or Cristo-pagan philosophies of public life. The Evangelical growth in Guatemala, it seems, may help make the work of democratic-capitalist enthusiasts a little easier.

Of course, the recent demise of Evangelical President Jorge Serrano in Guatemala has some observers wondering whether Guatemala's Protestant revival bodes ill for democratic prospects in the country. Many in the elite media and in academia believe that Evangelicals are naturally inclined toward authoritarianism and unable to make the compromises that are necessary for democratic life. In evaluating these claims, I argue that in fact Evangelicals can contribute to the strengthening of democracy. I interviewed several prominent Evangelical politicians, including former President Efrain Rios Montt, during my time in Guatemala, and report on those interviews in chapter 6.

## Significance of the Study

It is intriguing and gratifying to write about foreign places. Many people like to travel, and even those who do not often enjoy reading about exotic peoples and ideas, about events and practices very different from their own. Good travelogs are marketable. The problem, at least for the scholarly writer, is that conclusions drawn from remote locales may seem to have little relevance or application to our own situation. A good analytical travelog may leave us fascinated or entertained, but also wondering what the larger significance of the story is.

The larger significance of the story I tell in this book is twofold. First, it provides empirical legitimation for the claim that cultural attitudes and values, and not just objective, material factors, are correlated with development prospects. Specifically, the data gathered by the Worldview and Development Survey demonstrated that openness to innovation; desire for personal achievement; acceptance of merit-based inequalities; belief in the possibilities for overcoming "fate" or "destiny"; disparagement of laziness; and rejection of animistic beliefs about nature and the supernatural were all correlated with objective measures of socioeconomic advancement. The insight that poverty is not rooted exclusively in material factors is relevant and significant for debates about both domestic and international development.

A few years ago, economist Glenn Loury spoke bluntly of the moral-cultural roots underlying the crisis of the urban underclass in the United States. In an address entitled, "Ghetto Poverty and the Power of Faith," Loury argued that "the fundamental assumption behind our public language about ghetto poverty is a materialist viewpoint: Economic factors are supposed ultimately to underlie behavioral problems." Such a view, Loury continued, failed "to engage questions of personal morality, . . . [of] character and values." Positive changes in the moral-cultural climate are needed, Loury asserted, for "it is clear that the behavioral problems of the ghetto . . . are spiritual in part."[19]

For many years, arguments like this were considered largely out-of-bounds in the public square, and even now Loury's ideas are in the minority. Perhaps because the disaster of the ghetto is so horrifying, though, there has been in the last few years a slightly greater willingness to listen to the sorts of contentions raised by Loury (and Thomas Sowell, and Charles Murray, and other commentators on the underclass). Consequently, empirical research demonstrating the connection between particular cultural values and practices and persistent poverty—even research based on study outside the United States—is helpful for buttressing the argument that our discourse about poverty cannot exclude attention to moral-cultural matters.

This newfound (admittedly limited) openness to discussions of the moral-cultural nature of domestic poverty is paralleled today by a greater openness for discussing the possible cultural factors contributing to Third World poverty. Throughout the 1960s, 1970s, and into the 1980s, the prevailing assumption among development practitioners was that structural inequities rooted in the international economy kept the less developed countries (LDCs) poor. The dominant theories then emphasized factors external to the LDCs as the root sources of stagnation. With the fall of communism, the rise of the newly industrializing countries, and the abysmal failures of statist regimes in Africa, neoliberal ideas are now beginning to displace such theories. The neoliberal school of thought asserts that the most important reasons that poor countries are poor are to be found inside the LDCs rather than in the nature of international economic relations. Today, it is common to hear arguments about how factors internal to LDCs—such as misguided fiscal, monetary, and trade policies and unfair, discriminatory legal structures—contribute to economic stagnation. And with the focus on internal factors has come a greater appreciation for the culture-and-development connection. Research that provides evidence of the influence of cultural factors on development prospects is valuable for reinforcing the emerging shift towards neoliberalism in development thinking.

In addition to showing that culture matters, this book also demonstrates that religious worldviews matter. Put simply, some religious worldviews are more likely to facilitate development than others. In Guatemala, I found that orthodox Christianity correlated with certain development-enhancing attitudes and practices while the syncretistic blending of traditional Mayan animism and "folk Catholicism" was correlated with values and behaviors that hindered socioeconomic advancement.

It is important to note at this juncture that this is not the same thing as saying that *only* orthodox Christianity is conducive to socioeconomic development. Such a claim cannot be made on the evidence of this study; moreover, such a claim should not be made in light of the phenomenal economic success of the newly industrializing countries of East Asia. The economic boom in these countries suggests that the Confucianist worldview provides similar impetus to development.

In the United States and elsewhere, the "habits of the heart and mind" of orthodox Christianity stimulated, accompanied, and reinforced the growth of the free market. The market, embedded in a moral-cultural context characterized by the virtues of hard work, frugality, honesty, cooperativeness, rationality, self-discipline, and personal responsibility and initiative, was the engine of development. Today, across the globe less developed countries and the nations of the former Soviet empire are looking to the market to be their engine of development.

The newfound interest in the free market is welcome, and it is certainly far more desirable than an outdated fascination with state-centered development schemes that have brought so much human misery. It is instructive, however, to remember that the free market functions best and is most widely legitimized when it is embedded in a supportive moral-cultural order that encourages both personal initiative and creativity *and* self-restraint. The market is unlikely to be just or successful apart from this sort of moral-cultural order. Market institutions are not magical pills that will automatically encourage development in impoverished societies. Consequently, the growth of some religious communities in LDCs—such as orthodox Protestant communities —may improve the prospects for market success by providing appropriate moral-cultural underpinnings for development.

# PART I

# SETTING
# THE
# CONTEXT

## ONE

# Locating the
# Argument

Exaltation of the primitive was perhaps best captured in Jean-Jacques Rousseau's famous phrase about the noble savage. Pre-industrial, pre-civilized man, Rousseau asserted, lived an idyllic existence in harmony with nature. In our times, Hollywood glamorizes traditional, indigenous cultures—a well-known example being *Dances With Wolves*—while politically correct anthropologists blame colonialism for destroying the morally superior and ecologically conscious folk societies it conquered. Multiculturalism is perhaps the latest banner under which many cultural relativists march, lauding the contributions of all diverse cultures (except, often, their own Western heritage).

To a certain extent, the current fascination with the primitive is an expression of the *anomie* felt by many moderns in the cold universe their secularism has created. God may be "dead" in much of the postmodern, postindustrial West, but the search for the spiritual and magical lives on. Small-scale, traditional societies are thus romanticized, and, with the growing influence of the environmentalist movement, upheld as exemplary stewards of Mother Earth. Primitive communities, it is argued, enjoy placid and cooperative social relations, have developed ingenious and environmentally conscious medicinal remedies and appropriate technologies, and live free of the stress and frenzy of the Western capitalist world.

Even those who do not paint such a rosy picture often refuse to make judgments against such societies. Cultural relativism asserts that no objective standards exist for comparing the cultural practices of different groups; rather, each's patterns of belief and habits can only be understood and evaluated from *within* their own context. What others do may appear to us to be bizarre, pointless, inefficient, cruel, or harmful but these actions must be accepted as different from our own, and most likely appropriate and positive for others. Adaptivists argue that the longevity of such practices is proof positive of their value to the community: to have survived so long they must be fulfilling some important or necessary function.

In his important recent book, *Sick Societies*, anthropologist Robert Edgerton presented a politically incorrect rebuttal of this prevailing wisdom.[1] While quick to affirm the adaptive and impressive achievements of many small-scale societies, Edgerton forcefully disabused his readers of the romanticized claims of the adaptivists. "Traditional beliefs and practices may be useful, may even serve as important adaptive mechanisms," he wrote, "but they may also be inefficient, harmful, and even deadly."[2] *Sick Societies* called for "a moratorium on the uncritical assumption that the traditional beliefs and practices of folk populations are adaptive while those of modern societies are not," and for a "commitment to examining the relative adaptiveness of the beliefs and practices of *all* societies."[3]

Surveying hundreds of studies, Edgerton reported on countless maladaptive practices that limited the physical well-being of various communities' members, caused stress and dissatisfaction, and, in some extreme cases, led to groups' extinction. According to Edgerton, although ethnographers were often reluctant to criticize native practices in communities they studied, they did report the judgments that came from community members themselves. Critical judgments also came from neighboring societies, who, facing similar geographic, climatic, and economic constraints, managed to respond more favorably to the ecology. In short, though cultural relativist anthropologists have searched tenaciously for reasonable explanations for cultural practices that appeared bizarre, harmful, and irrational, some tribals themselves have labeled those practices for what they are: pointless and maladaptive. Some societies, as Edgerton put it, are "sicker" than others: they are unaware of or unwilling to change cultural practices that inhibit human development. If anything is to be done about alleviating the suffering that results from maladaptive practices, the idol of cultural relativism must be torn down.

## The Culture-and-Development School

Cultural relativism is a somewhat modern phenomenon. Social scientists have not always been so hesitant to compare and critique different cultures. Those who have made such critiques always run the risk of being seen as ethnocentric or racist, and it should be admitted that some commentators have indeed been those things. But other sociologists, economists, political scientists, and anthropologists have conducted their investigations of the varying performances of different cultural groups with detachment. Some of these researchers sought to understand cultural differences in order to identify patterns that appear to hinder the prospects for economic development. As I studied individuals with different worldviews and cultural practices in Guatemala, this was my motivation.

Much has already been learned about the cultural values that seem to promote (or at least be correlated with) socioeconomic advancement. This book is part of that wider body of literature that concerns itself with the relationship between culture and development. In the following pages, I hope to advance some of the arguments made by earlier scholars and to offer some additional insights based on my research that may woo culture-and-development scholars to take some fresh directions. This chapter summarizes some of the most important contributions in the culture-and-development field in order to "locate" my arguments in this wider body of investigation and analysis. Themes raised by some authors are resurrected in my study; in other instances, the evidence I have gathered suggests that, at least for Guatemala, some of the lessons learned from this school of literature need to be modified or amplified. The summary begins with Max Weber, who is possibly the father of this literature, and ends with Lawrence Harrison, perhaps the best-known neo-Weberian scholar of our time. In chapter 2, I pick up this discussion with a description of David Martin's 1990 book, *Tongues of Fire: The Explosion of Protestantism in Latin America.* The latter part of his book has much to say about the culture-and-development equation in connection with the rise of Protestantism in Latin America, and his discussion was the springboard for my own investigations.

## Max Weber

Among those interested in the intersection of culture and development, Max Weber is best known for *The Protestant Ethic and the Spirit of Capitalism.*[4] Weber was intrigued by the rise of capitalism in Europe and sought to explain the connections between religious developments in the period after the Protestant Reformation and what he called "the spirit of capitalism." His book concentrated especially on the complex of virtues—frugality, hard work, devotion to duty, self-control, shunning of indulgence and luxury—that Protestant faith spawned. These virtues, in turn, helped Protestants to advance economically. In his study, as a contemporary commentator notes, Weber uncovered a paradox:

> Weber emphasized the autonomy of religious reformers from economic motivation while at the same time attributing to their dogmas certain inexorable (if unintended) consequences for the accumulation of wealth and the division of labor . . . [Weber] showed how believers, in their restless search for religious justification, committed themselves to a "this-worldly" asceticism that made them rich and acquisitive almost in spite of themselves.[5]

The root sources of what Weber called "inner-worldly asceticism" were Protestant theology's conception of God and this world, its rationality, and its understanding of salvation. These concepts are probed in greater detail in Weber's essays on the sociology of religion (e.g., "The Protestant Sects and the Spirit of Capitalism" and "Religious Rejections of the World and their Directions").[6]

"Inner-worldly asceticism"—a habitual, careful self-discipline that exalts duty, thrift, temperance—assumed, according to Weber, that this world was evil and full of temptations. The world and its goods and pleasures were not to be sought by the believer; rather, one's focus should be on the Kingdom of God. However, *Protestant faith did not lead to a rejection of or flight from this world*. The contemplative lifestyle was not upheld as the moral ideal. Protestantism did not encourage men to see themselves as *vessels* of God's presence, seeking to be filled with divinity. This was the way of the mystical, Eastern religions, where divinity was seen as impersonal and immanent and where the objective of religious devotion was union with, or possession of, the divine.

The Protestants posited a supramundane, holy, and personal God. Protestants viewed themselves as *instruments or tools* of God and of God's work in this world.[7] Whereas the Eastern religions encouraged men toward a sort of "religious incognito existence," proving themselves "*against* the world," Protestant faith encouraged men to prove themselves *in* this world through action: "To the inner-worldly asceticist the conduct of the mystic is an indolent enjoyment of the self; to the mystic the conduct of the inner-worldly asceticist is an entanglement in the godless ways of the world combined with complacent self-righteousness."[8] With this view, Protestants, despite themselves, created wealth in this world even though the intent of their industriousness was to be found faithful to the commandments of a rigorous and holy God and to fulfill their sense of worldly calling, rather than to accumulate the world's goods.

The Protestant experience emphasized obedience to a set of divine commandments, and these commandments helped to rationalize the lives of the faithful. Protestant faith was rational in that it posited a rational God and a rational universe, an immutable code of ethics, absolute standards of right and wrong, and a consistent conception of justice in which good was rewarded and evil punished. While there was no embarrassment over belief in the *supernatural*—the understanding of the possibilities for action in this world by a supramundane, rational, omnipotent, and omniscient God—there was no place for the *magical*—the activities of capricious, irrational, often humanlike deities. Hence, the Protestant answer to the problem of suffering and the need for salvation differed from those offered by, for example, animist and Eastern religions. In Protestantism, sin is the root cause of suffering, and sin is understood as not merely "magical offense"—the failure to perform religious ritual—but as an ethical shortcoming—breaking the commandments. This "rational theocidy of misfortune" led to the development of the concept of a redeemer, and in this concept, Weber believed, was found the germ of "the rational conception of the world."[9]

These beliefs spurred the faithful to a rational systematizing of life and an exaltation of duty. This lifestyle was further ingrained by the Calvinist idea of predestination as a subset of the Protestant conception of salvation. Predestination asserted that God would show favor to certain individuals—the "elect"—and grant them access to eternal life through the redeeming work of Jesus Christ, whereas others were outside of the elect and could not benefit from his covenant. As Weber explained, religious folk could not be entirely certain whether they were or were not members of the elect. But the faithful began to think that certain external characteristics could make one appear more or less likely to be in the fortunate company. Over time, worldly success or prosperity began to be seen as one such "external mark" of the elect, which spurred Protestants on toward ever greater feats of business prowess and provided a hospitable climate for entrepreneurial initiative.[10]

The rationalism, ethical rigor, and inner-worldly asceticism—in short, the "world and life view" of Protestantism—was conducive to the rise of a spirit of capitalism. But beyond the behavioral outworkings of Protestant theology, Weber saw the importance, economically, of certain *social dynamics* arising within Protestantism. These he examined in his essay, "The Protestant Sects and the Spirit of Capitalism." In this essay, Weber underscored the importance of the creditworthiness provided by a person's membership in a Protestant community. Sect membership, Weber argued, meant a "certification of moral qualification and especially of business morals for the individual."[11] This stemmed from the fact that membership in a sect was voluntary (rather than compulsory) and that full membership (for example, permission to be baptized or to partake of the Lord's Supper) was extended by the faith community only after a period of inspection and probation.

Additionally, Protestant membership brought tangible benefits in terms of aid from fellow congregants in times of economic distress. Fellow Christians were also more likely to patronize one another's businesses, and nonbelievers also favored these establishments because they were known for integrity and fixed prices.[12]

The key themes Weber raised—calling, work, asceticism, and the breaking of traditions and escape from "magical" religions—resurfaced in much of the literature that followed his foundational works.

### Gunnar Myrdal

The Swedish economist Gunnar Myrdal agreed with Weber's contention that the traditional religions of Asia encouraged irrationality and were a source of inertia. Since the faithful assumed that life was lived in a capricious universe, they had little incentive for planning. Rather, *fatalism*—the belief that one has no control over one's destiny, that life is something that happens to one—reigns. Outsiders tended to interpret these religious systems as producing the stereotypical serene, contemplative, "detached" Asian who exalted spiritual life over the material. Myrdal considered these worldviews in a less positive light, asserting that they reinforced a rigid social stratification, and perhaps more important, contributed to an antiwork mentality. As one interpreter summarized:

> Myrdal [saw] changes in attitude toward work at the heart of the problem of poverty and development. He note[d] that in poor countries many people do not work, and that it is their preference to be unemployed. *They do not work because it is prestigious not to do so.* Educated people dislike manual work especially, and when they do work they are not interested in the kinds of jobs that help the economy; for them degrees are passports to sitting in government offices, which is much more prestigious than commercial and agricultural activities.[13]

*Familism*, in Myrdal's view, was a further hindrance to development in the Asian context, limiting the sense of community identity and encouraging nepotism and corruption. In his classic work, *Asian Drama*, Myrdal wondered about the presence of a "general asociality that leads people to think that anybody in a position of power is likely to exploit it in the interest of himself, his family, or other social groups to which he has a feeling of loyalty."[14] This lack of affiliation and identification with others, Myrdal believed, combined with disdain for work and an irrational, other-worldly religious system, kept South Asia in the grip of underdevelopment. In his view, extensive government intervention in education, in the social system, and in the economy was necessary to break that grip.

## Schumpeter and His Followers

While Myrdal's analysis of the cultural problems underlying underdevelopment led him to put the state in the center of the development equation, the Austrian economist Joseph Schumpeter's brand of economic sociology encouraged him to focus on the central and irreducible role of the individual entrepreneur. Schumpeter's greatest contribution to the culture-and-development literature was his extensive exploration of the factors undergirding entrepreneurial behavior. For him, the entrepreneur was an innovator, and Schumpeter carefully distinguished between innovation and invention. Entrepreneurs thought up new ways of doing things, processing things, combining technologies, or penetrating markets—this was innovation—while inventors invented new products.

In Schumpeter's analysis, entrepreneurial innovation was rooted in key psychological factors. Entrepreneurs tended to be people with strong leadership skills and a strong volition. Since innovation was about doing things in new ways, courageous leadership was indispensable for the entrepreneur, who had to be able to persuade others to try the new ways. Entrepreneurs, as nonconformists, typically faced resistance from society, and sometimes from political authorities; as a result, they had to be strong-willed and able to absorb the smarts that came from criticism, ridicule, or hostility to their ideas. They had to persist in the face of opposition, and they had to see that their ideas were actually implemented. They had to be people of action, as Schumpeter wrote: "[Entrepreneurs] reform or revolutionize the pattern of production by exploiting an invention . . . opening up a new source of supply of raw materials or a new outlet for products, by reorganizing industry . . . [their function] consists in getting things done."[15]

Contemporary scholars, picking up on points Schumpeter made several decades ago, have continued to emphasize the role of the entrepreneur and of society's legitimation of entrepreneurship. Amitai Etzioni has measured different societies' legitimation of innovation by examining the degree of public investment made in the education and training of future entrepreneurs and the presence or absence of various incentives (such as tax policies) undertaken to encourage entrepreneurial activity.[16] Schumpeter had hinted at the importance of legitimation when he considered the economic factors contributing to the environment in which entrepreneurship could flourish. Societies that permitted private property and encouraged the availability of credit, he argued, were more favorable to entrepreneurial behavior.

### McClelland and Fillol

In the 1960s, increasing attention began to be paid to psychological factors influencing societies' levels of development. Perhaps the best-known work in this school was David McClelland's much-discussed book, *The Achieving Society*. In this book, McClelland examined the role of motivation and the societal "weight" put on achievement, by which he meant the desire to complete tasks more efficiently and in less time.[17] McClelland argued that the forces spurring economic development rested largely within man, and he concentrated on exploring the varying levels of emphasis that different societies gave to inculcating a need for achievement. In *The Achieving Society*, McClelland analyzed children's literature in 30 countries and then asked whether countries with evidence of a high need for achievement displayed economic progress (as measured by such indicators of development as growth in electricity produced). He found that such a correlation existed but admitted in a later edition of the book that other psychological variables in addition to the need for achievement (for example, "other-centeredness") were also probably important. Nevertheless, the "need for achievement" variable has been used in subsequent studies and was found to be consistently related to economic progress and typically independent from other key variables, such as education. In reviewing the evidence generated by other analysts, McClelland concluded in the preface to the 1976 edition of his book that growth in the need for achievement "seems to have been quite generally important in different times and places, under varied circumstances."[18]

Other books, not nearly as well-known as McClelland's, also addressed the issue of the psychological factors conducive to development. Argentine scholar Tomas Roberto Fillol's book *Social Factors in Economic Development* explored how a society's answers to basic questions about human nature, the relationship of people to nature, and society's time orientation affected its prospects for socioeconomic advancement.[19]

In Fillol's view, one hindrance to economic development in his native land was the Argentine propensity to believe that human character was shaped by external influences and that individuals had little hope of improving themselves through, for example, "work, enterprise, or material achievement."[20] Argentines viewed human nature as basically "fixed," Fillol explained, and therefore had little motivation for self-improvement efforts. A second hindrance to development that Fillol noted was the Argentine belief that humans are subject to nature rather than nature to humans. He argued that "Argentines simply accept the inevitable as the inevitable" and tend to be passive, to wait and hope, feeling impotent in the face of nature.[21] Fillol also suggested that the

Argentine focus on the present time hindered progress, for, as he claimed, Argentines "do not live or work for the future." Finally, Fillol was concerned about the way in which social status is ascribed in Argentina. In his analysis, the Argentine focus on "being"—on what one now is rather than "becoming"—made Argentines reluctant to ascribe social status to people on the basis of their accomplishments or wealth. Rather, Fillol explained, in Argentina social standing derives from lineage and class. In his view, this inhibited economic progress by reducing entrepreneurial activity (because few social rewards are posed for such activity).

### The 1970s and the Decline of Culture-and-Development Analysis

In the 1970s, economists, political scientists, and sociologists interested in development shifted away from investigations of the culture-and-development connection. Rather, the most popular subject was neo-colonialism and "world systems analysis." Scholars in this line of thinking focused greater attention on the workings of the international economic system and began to blame inequities in that system for producing or exacerbating Third World poverty. Dependency theorists such as Andre Gunder Frank went so far as to argue that global capitalist development actually produced Third World underdevelopment; for example, he asserted that the very process by which the rich North achieved economic prosperity ground the poor South into ever-worsening poverty.[22] Economists began to look more closely at trading relationships, worrying that the South's dependence on raw materials exports and manufactured goods imports set them up for chronic balance-of-payments problems. Meanwhile, political analysts considered the economic consequences of inequitably distributed political power: since the Western industrialized countries controlled the international financial institutions (the IMF and World Bank) and the "rules" of global trade (GATT), it was no wonder that the system operated to benefit the wealthy North at the expense of the politically impotent South.

All these investigations spurred enthusiasm for a New International Economic Order, in which the South would receive a greater voice in international economic decisions. It also stimulated inward-looking development strategies that encouraged Third World states to reduce their dependence on the international market. The key thread holding the various arguments together was the assumption that the causes underlying Third World poverty were largely to be found in factors *external* to those countries (and hence, external to their cultural patterns). Attention to cultural issues waned.

### The 1980s and the Resurgence of Cultural Analysis

By the 1980s, the neocolonialist school of thought was under attack from neoliberals who pointed to the dramatic success of the East Asian newly industrializing countries (Hong Kong, Singapore, Taiwan, South Korea) as a conclusive invalidation of dependency theory. Dependency scholars predicted that increased integration by Third World states into the global economy would bring increased impoverishment. But these countries had pursued an aggressively outward-looking trade policy and had prospered rather than declined. Meanwhile, evidence mounted that even massive transfers of international capital (through foreign aid) were not spurring economic growth in the recipient countries. Instead, having used received capital (both loans and grants) in economically nonproductive ways, Third World countries found themselves not only no richer, but also strapped by a burden of debt.

With the election of free-market enthusiasts Margaret Thatcher in England and Ronald Reagan in the United States, the classical liberal ideas of Adam Smith gained a new ascendancy and neoliberal scholars such as Anne Krueger and Bela Balassa began publishing persuasive studies pointing to the overriding importance of *internal* economic policies.[23] Of course, the classical liberal P. T. Bauer had been dissenting from the prevailing development doctrines throughout the 1960s and 1970s, but until the 1980s his had been a voice crying in the wilderness.[24] Influential publications throughout the 1980s—such as the World Bank's annual development reports[25] and the U.S. AID's "Alan Woods" report[26]—were dominated by neoliberal rather than neocolonial assumptions. The time for looking again at the *internal* factors contributing to persistent poverty in the underdeveloped countries was ripe. Hence, it was no surprise when cultural arguments again came to the forefront.

### Thomas Sowell

In 1983, African-American economist Thomas Sowell published a provocative and original work, *The Economics and Politics of Race*.[27] One of its purposes was simply "to recognize that economic performance differences [among cultures] are quite real and quite large."[28] While other scholars were assiduously trying to avoid cross-cultural comparisons that were effectively off-limits in the academy's prevailing atmosphere of cultural relativism, Sowell carefully documented the different economic performances of the overseas Chinese, European immigrants, and blacks:

> [T]o ignore the large role that performance differences have played in human history is to ignore or misdiagnose important causal factors at

work in that history. Cultures are ultimately ways of accomplishing things, and the differing efficiencies with which they accomplish different things determine the outcomes of very serious economic, political, and military endeavors.[29]

As to the overseas Chinese, Sowell reported that despite considerable persecution and ostracism in most of the countries where they took up residence, Chinese immigrants prospered. Throughout Southeast Asia, "the Chinese have represented a modern, urban, commercial element in traditional, rural, peasant societies."[30] The Chinese "brought new economic vitality to the tradition-bound peasant folk cultures" by working harder and saving more than the locals.[31] Through industriousness and business acumen, they soon dominated wholesale and retail trade. In the United States, the Chinese suffered considerable discrimination and most often were employed in low-wage manual labor. Nonetheless, through hard work and frugal living, Chinese immigrants provided their children educational opportunities. The younger generation "carried into the schools the same sense of purpose and perseverance that characterized the Chinese."[32] They were well-behaved, studious, and tended to specialize in the most demanding—and lucrative—fields (engineering, mathematics, medicine, and natural sciences). Over time, the percentage of Chinese employed in professional occupations jumped dramatically, with income gains following apace. By 1959, the income of Chinese Americans passed the U.S. national average.[33]

As to European emigrants, Sowell found that economic performances varied by ethnic group. Germans and Jews tended to prosper in whatever setting they found themselves. Germans were reputed to be hardworking and careful farmers and skilled and quality craftsmen. German emigrants established a flourishing civic culture within their ethnic enclaves, bringing with them German customs of wholesome recreation—parades, picnics, folk dancing, sports, literary societies—as well as their churches and German-language periodicals.[34] They were innovators in their fields and moved quickly into the ranks of the middle classes.

Jews, despite enormous and continuous persecution and discrimination, worked hard, saved, and emphasized educational attainment. Denied access to various economic pursuits, they became middlemen— "petty peddlers, junk dealers, pawn brokers, and a fortunate few became substantial merchants and bankers. . . . Their skills, work capacity, and frugality made Jews valuable additions to many economies, and the money they lent made them welcome by rulers and the nobility, who were often in need of loans to sustain their wars or other extravagances."[35]

The Irish, in contrast, indulged in cultural practices that hindered their economic advancement. According to Sowell, they had a reputation for fighting, alcoholism, uncleanliness, and unreliability. While some of their misfortunes can be blamed on the oppressions they suffered (principally at the hands of the British), Sowell argued that these historic injustices were not entirely to blame:

> [They] cannot automatically be assumed to be the reason for Irish poverty. . . . Ireland was poor and fragmented before the British arrived, and long after achieving independence has remained one of the poorer nations of western Europe. Moreover, the Irish as a people have languished in poverty for generations after immigrating to other countries, even when (as in the U.S.) they ultimately advanced to prosperity.[36]

Italian emigrants manifested some cultural traits that were conducive to economic advancement and some that served as a drag on progress. Sowell distinguished between northern and southern Italians, noting that northerners tended to be small businessmen, who worked hard and saved for reinvestment. Southern Italians tended to be unskilled laborers, who saved income mainly for return passage to Italy and the hopes of an easier life there. Both groups were hardworking and drank less than the Irish and thus, found it easier to gain employment. But they lacked the initiative and creativity of other immigrant groups. Even more important, Italians were "familistic" and did not create a vibrant associational life. Their sense of identification with or trust of others was limited to relatives; this lack of community spirit contrasted sharply with that, for example, of the Germans. Southern Italians, in particular, still had a further strike against them: their resistance to education. Educational achievement had had little economic payoff in Italy and was not encouraged in the emigrants' new homelands.[37]

### Lawrence Harrison

Although Sowell's case studies were like a breath of fresh air in the early 1980s, the most significant contribution of the decade in the culture-and-development field was Lawrence Harrison's book, *Underdevelopment Is a State of Mind*. Examining a variety of Latin American and Caribbean countries, Harrison suggested in this work that different worldviews were more or less likely to facilitate economic advancement. In his opinion, three elements were particularly crucial: "(1) the world view's time focus—past, present, or future; (2) the extent to which the world view encourages rationality; and (3) the concepts of equality and authority it propagates."[38]

Harrison argued that a forward-looking mentality encouraged development by helping people to focus on the possibilities for change and progress. Societies that were always glancing over their shoulders at a glorious past, or were preoccupied with the many problems of today, would not emphasize investment, savings, and planning—tasks that are critical to economic advancement.

Rationality, too, was a key in Harrison's analysis (as it had been in Weber's before him). As Harrison wrote:

> If the society's world view encourages the belief that humans have the capacity to know and understand the world around them, that the universe operates according to a largely decipherable pattern of laws, and that the scientific method can unlock many secrets of the unknown, it is clearly imparting a set of attitudes tightly linked to the ideas of progress and change. If the world view explains worldly phenomena by supernatural forces, often in the form of numerous capricious gods and goddesses who demand obeisance from humans, there is little room for reason, education, planning, or progress.[39]

In his later work *Who Prospers?* Harrison continued his argument, identifying four cultural factors that further hinder or encourage development in a society: a society's "radius of trust" (or "sense of community"); the rigor of its ethical system; the way authority is exercised in it; and its attitudes about innovation, work, saving, and profit.[40]

The level of trust within a society, Harrison explained, determines in large measure its prospects for cooperativeness, for democratic politics, and private enterprise. "Where trust and identification are scarce," Harrison asserted, "political polarization, confrontation, and autocratic government are likely to emerge."[41] In the absence of a sense of social empathy or "identification," commercial enterprise and public administration become more centralized, weighed down by "a variety of checking mechanisms and procedures designed, ostensibly, to assure conformity and to control dishonesty."[42] Where the radius of trust is limited to family and kin ties, outsiders are looked upon with suspicion or even hostility, and there is little incentive for community organization for "common purposes and causes."[43]

A strict ethical code, Harrison added, can encourage development progress and increase the radius of trust. Societies where religious communities make strict demands upon their adherents for honesty and self-control promote a respect for law and a trustworthiness that facilitates market exchanges and credit and undergirds the fairness of the judicial system.[44]

Harrison also argued that authoritarianism can hinder development, as it "implies a hierarchical view of the world, one that nurtures paternalism, patron–client relationships, and social rigidity, conditions commonly found in the Third World."[45] He added that authoritarianism can stifle initiative, innovation, and risk-taking, and often leads to corruption and the diversion of a society's resources away from economically productive investments.

Attitudes toward work, innovation, saving, and profit are also critical in Harrison's judgment. Clearly, respect for hard work, rather than
an exaltation of leisure or disdain for manual labor, can contribute to
economic progress. Similarly, societies that encourage, legitimate, and
reward innovation and entrepreneurial behavior are more likely to succeed than those that discourage risk-taking or delegitimate nonconformist initiative. An emphasis on saving, rather than on instant gratification and consumption, Harrison wrote, is important for building up the
capital necessary for future investments. And a legitimation of profit
(and one might add, income inequalities resulting from differential economic performance) is also important: societies that place negative
sanctions on getting ahead suppress the initiative, originality, and energy that could spur innovations and the creation of new wealth.

Harrison distilled these key cultural variables that influence development prospects by comparing countries with differing levels of prosperity. As mentioned, his first book concentrated on case studies from
various Latin American and Caribbean countries: Costa Rica, Nicaragua, Haiti, the Dominican Republic, Argentina, and Barbados. This
selection proved particularly fruitful because these countries shared
similar climatic and geographic circumstances, historical experiences,
and opportunities in the global marketplace. Despite the similarities,
however, Costa Rica, for example, outperformed Nicaragua, and the
Dominican Republic economically bested Haiti. Such variety in economic performance, Harrison argued, resulted from the differences between Costa Ricans, Nicaraguans, and Dominicans.[46] The key, he asserted, was how thoroughly these peoples retained their Hispanic
traditions and beliefs. Hispanic culture had a more attenuated influence
in Costa Rica, and this helped explain the country's superior socioeconomic and political development. What the other case studies revealed, Harrison argued, was that Hispanic culture tended to put a
brake on development. The Hispanic worldview is, in his phrase, "anti-
democratic, anti-social, anti-progress, anti-entrepreneurial, and, at least
among the elite, anti-work."[47]

In *Who Prospers?* Harrison carried his empirical investigations outside Latin America. Given the remarkable economic success of the East
Asian newly industrializing countries, it is not surprising that he next
explored the factors contributing to the Korean and Taiwanese boom.
But Harrison's analysis gave more weight to cultural factors than have
many other studies of these countries (which have focused more exclusively on economic factors). "Some long-range economic policies emphasizing the world market have had a lot to do with the success of
Taiwan and Korea," Harrison acknowledged. "[But] those policies
would not have gone far had it not been for the blossoming of a robust
entrepreneurial drive in both countries. That entrepreneurial drive is, I

believe, rooted in some of the key tenets of Confucianism, as indeed are the effective economic policies of these two countries."[48]

According to Harrison's interpretation, the Confucian emphasis on the five "right relationships" (between ruler and ruled, father and son, elder and younger brothers, employee and employer, and friend to friend) fostered a more extensive radius of trust. So did Confucius' Golden Rule: "Do not do unto others what you would not have them do unto you." In addition, Confucius emphasized education—and the merit-based examination system he devised for selecting political leaders permitted social mobility. Confucian ethics were also strict, enjoining everyone to be honest and upright and proscribing immoderation, corruption, and selfishness. Such values are still prevalent in Taiwanese and Korean society, Harrison reported, though they may be somewhat subdued and considered old fashioned.[49]

Harrison admitted that some Confucian values, such as authoritarianism and hierarchy, can work against economic progress. Indeed, these values are also found in the economically inferior Iberian cultures Harrison had examined in *Underdevelopment*. Nonetheless, he believes that Confucianism's overall contribution has been positive. This is largely because the influence of authoritarianism and hierarchy has been tempered by other elements of the worldview. For example, the fifth key relationship in Confucist thought, the friend-to-friend relationship, extends the radius of trust and mutual obligation outside of the family. This has manifested itself, Harrison argued, in concrete differences between East Asian and Ibero-American societies: the "broader identifications [of Confucianism] are substantially stronger than those of traditional Iberian culture, which is reflected in the income distribution patterns of Taiwan and Korea, which are so much more equitable than the typical Latin American pattern (and than Spain's until recent decades)."[50] Similarly, while authoritarianism is found in both cultures' worldviews, in the East Asian context it is tempered by an equally important emphasis on the values of education, work, discipline, merit, and frugality, which "are powerful engines of economic growth and economic pluralism."[51]

## Putting It All Together

The richly diverse culture-and-development literature surveyed in this chapter identifies a considerable number of key variables that influence a society's prospects for development. Although the studies examine different cultures at different times, several common themes emerge. To simplify, the various variables affecting socioeconomic life can be categorized under four principal headings: philosophical aspects, social/psychological aspects, behavioral aspects, and institutional aspects.

Some of the variables, of course, do not fit neatly into one category. Entrepreneurship, for example, could be considered a "behavioral" variable (the actual activities of an entrepreneur such as risk-taking, innovation, invention) or a "social/psychological" variable (the mind-set of the entrepreneur that encourages him or her to buck tradition, assume risk, and persevere in the face of criticism or skepticism). Nonetheless, these categories help us comprehend the large number of factors that have been identified by different analysts in the culture-and-development field as being important for encouraging development.

Most fundamental are the variables included in the "philosophical" category. These are a society's answers to questions about the nature of the universe, the nature of humankind, humans' relationship to creation, and about history and its direction and purpose (or lack thereof). Different religious worldviews offer different answers to these questions and thus inculcate varying values through socialization mechanisms, such as child-rearing patterns and school. For example, if the universe is viewed as irrational and inhabited by unpredictable and powerful deities, then a fatalistic attitude about the ability of humans to influence their circumstances or future is ingrained. If human nature is believed to be essentially and irretrievably evil, the radius of trust in society may be limited. If history is viewed as progressing forward with a purpose and the universe is believed to be decipherable (and hence in some measure, natural forces are viewed as controllable), then values of progress and achievement will be taught.

What people believe about reality on an abstract, philosophical level and what they are taught in the socialization process affects how they behave. When people believe they have stewardship over nature and society inculcates the value of initiative and achievement, behaviors such as working hard, taking risks, accepting new challenges, changing traditions, pursuing education, and planning for the future emerge in the society. Such behaviors (e.g., saving, innovation) are legitimized at the social level because they are "appropriate"; that is, they correspond with or "fit" with what is known about reality and the ways things work.

Finally, societies develop certain policies and institutions that are concrete manifestations of this legitimation or approval. If entrepreneurship is desired and legitimated, then incentive structures will be arranged to reward entrepreneurial behavior. Private property will be recognized and guaranteed by the state, a patent system will be put in place, legal structures for addressing breach of contract will be established, and credit will be made available.

Of course, there is not always a one-to-one correspondence between what people believe and how they behave. There is not always a direct relationship between the values societies inculcate in their members and the institutions those societies create for the ordering of political and economic life. Oddballs and nonconformists exist in all cultures, and certain individuals may prosper even while their society stagnates. Similarly, in prosperous societies not every individual will absorb the general culture or worldview, and not everyone will advance economically. In short, it is difficult to capture accurately the complexity of the connections (or lack of expected connections) between worldview and practice and between practice and economic outcome. Nonetheless, as the evidence surveyed in this chapter suggests, certain, somewhat predictable patterns of beliefs, values, behaviors, and institutions are evident in underdeveloped societies, and these are very different from the patterns characteristic of developed societies. Moreover, within a particular society, some groups seem to prosper more than others—and these are often characterized by similar, "development-enhancing" cultural values.

## Conclusion

The 1990s have been a strange decade thus far from the perspective of the culture-and-development scholar. On the one hand, multiculturalism and cultural relativism seem at an all time high. On the other, the collapse of communism, coupled with the success of the many newly industrializing countries, indicates the superiority of Max Weber's explanations for economic prosperity over Karl Marx's. The deterioration of Haiti and Somalia (countries rich in what Harrison or Edgerton might call "maladaptive" behaviors) are just a few recent examples of the inadequacy of *material* explanations for underdevelopment and the necessity of *cultural* (i.e., nonmaterial) explanations. Ironically, at just the time that historical evidence for the importance of cultural explanations for development success is overwhelming, evaluative discourse about different cultures and worldviews is anathematized. But if multiculturalism is really about respect and care for others (as its defenders maintain), then discourse about maladaptation and the cultural causes of human suffering and poverty should be welcomed.

T W O

# Latin American Protestantism and Economic Development

While the previous chapter summarized the most influential studies in the *general* culture-and-development field to provide readers an introduction to some of the presuppositions animating this book, this chapter looks exclusively at that segment of the culture-and-development literature concerned with the dynamics between religious worldview change and socioeconomic life. In many of the studies referred to in chapter 1, religion was one of several variables under consideration. Religion is only one part of culture, but it is an exceedingly important one. Consequently, a number of scholars have concentrated specifically on the relationship between Protestantism and economic development.

In a latter chapter of his landmark 1990 book, *Tongues of Fire: The Explosion of Protestantism in Latin America*, David Martin writes:

> There is a general, indeed notorious, supposition in sociological and anthropological studies that Protestantism is associated with economic success. This supposition derives in a loose way from Max Weber and the endless debate about how the Protestant Ethic influenced, and was influenced by, the Spirit of Capitalism. But that debate has been mainly focused on the first wave of Calvinist Protestantism in the sixteenth, the seventeenth and (marginally) the eighteenth century. The debate has been less concerned with the second wave of Methodist Protestantism; and so far as the third and Pentecostal wave is concerned, the evidence we have is recent and rather fragmentary.[1]

The "fragmentary" evidence to which Martin makes reference is admittedly anecdotal, meandering, and less than conclusive. The field is still ripe for further explorations of the impact of the presently unfolding, global third wave of Protestant revival. Over the past few decades, though, several studies of the relationship between religion and economic development in Latin America have argued that Protestant conversion and socioeconomic change are linked. Of course, the exact nature and direction of that link is in dispute.

Studies of the kind Martin refers to are more or less concerned with exploring two questions. The first is the "why" question: "Why have so many Latin Americans (or, specifically, Guatemalans) converted to Protestant Christianity?" Though this question has been the one most commonly addressed by students of Latin America who are examining the Evangelical explosion, it is not the most important question examined in this book. For my purposes, the importance of this question rests in its relation to the intersection between religious conversion and economic development. Some analysts posit that it is economic forces that create the conditions for conversion. In this instance, religious change serves as a *dependent* variable—as something that has to be explained.

The second question is the "so what" question, concerning the consequences of conversion. The bulk of the book addresses this question, which can be worded: "In what ways do converts differ from their neighbors?" or, "What changes (familial, social, cultural, economic, political) occur in the lives of converts?" In their attempts to answer this question, some scholars treat religion as an independent variable while others treat it as a dependent one. In some accounts, religious conversion is believed to set in motion various processes of change that manifest themselves in socioeconomic advancement. In others, conversion is seen as a response to economic advancement that legitimizes economic success and income inequalities (a legitimation that traditional folk Catholicism does not provide). The varied answers that have been offered for both the "why" and the "so what" questions are briefly surveyed here. A number of issues related to the "so what" question are taken up in chapter 3 as well.

## The "Why" Question

*The experience was so complete that my whole life turned around . . . I am almost completely at peace with myself right now. We had a [service] Saturday, everyone sat in a circle. The spirit . . . had been hitting me . . . touching me, making me aware that I was not living the way He wanted me to. The spirit of God was so real that in that building you could reach it—touch it almost. It was like heaven.*[2]

—Testimony of a young, male
Puerto Rican Evangelical

In a 1978 essay in *American Ethnologist*, anthropologist James D. Sexton suggested that the variables contributing to the large number of Evangelical conversions in Guatemala could be categorized under two headings, which he called "internal" and "external."[3] Internal variables include such things as the inner spiritual experiences of converts (such as that described in the previous quote) or the fulfillment of intrinsic needs they believe conversion will provide. External variables are those social and political conditions that facilitate conversion.

### Internal Reasons for Conversion

Sexton asked converts in San Juan la Laguna, one of the towns around Guatemala's Lake Atitlan, why they had converted, and some replied: "God spoke to me," or "God himself told me to believe is to be saved."[4] This is an example of an internal factor contributing to conversion. In my conversations with Guatemalan Protestants, the most immediately articulated reasons for conversion were internal; that is, converts found in Evangelical faith some answer to the questions, trials, or longings of their own lives. For them, conversion was first a supernatural experience, an "encounter" with God or God's word that convicted them of sin and showed them a new and better way of living or one that comforted them with the experience of God's presence in the midst of their trials. Moreover, several Evangelicals I spoke with had experienced supernatural physical or psychological healing in Evangelical congregations, which prompted their conversion. David Martin's research (discussed at length later in this chapter) uncovered similar testimonies.[5]

A second internal reason for conversion that scholars have identified is the desire to escape the disarray and suffering caused by alcoholism (the convert's own or a relative's). According to June Nash, who conducted fieldwork in the 1950s among the Maya-Quiche people of Guatemala, for many believers, joining the Protestant church was like joining Alcoholics Anonymous.[6] Nash (and others) found that more women convert to Protestantism than men, in part because of the hardships many women experience while living with drunken, unfaithful husbands. Their hope is that they will be able to draw their husbands (and other male family members) into the Evangelical fellowship, for male conversion is usually conducive to positive changes in family life. This erosion of "machismo" behavior (drinking, gambling, sexual promiscuity) brought about by Evangelical conversion was the theme of Elizabeth Brusco's research on Protestantism in Colombia.[7] Additionally, Liliana Goldin, who has conducted substantial fieldwork among the highland Maya, found alcoholism at the center of discourse in her conversations with Protestants in Guatemala:

Women's accounts of religious conversion often appear in the context of discussing their husband's, father's, or brother's drinking. The fact that within the Evangelical church men do not drink was particularly attractive to women subject to abuse from their male relatives when they are drunk. This important incentive prompts many women to try to convince their spouse or other relative to convert while the women and their children have already begun to attend the new church.

There are slight differences between men and women but almost without exception, male heads of households talk about religion in the context of their youth and how their parents were very poor, had little or no land, and also drank too much. Often the informant himself would refer to his own drinking but proudly emphasize his life change as he converted to Protestantism.[8]

Dissatisfaction with the Catholic church is a third internal reason cited by Evangelicals for their conversion. Prior to conversion, many Evangelicals began to believe that the Catholic church was practicing idolatry through its veneration of saints, and they wished to disassociate themselves from this practice. Some felt ignored or neglected because their parish enjoyed no resident priest. Others thought the Catholic church was full of "vices"—such as drinking, smoking, and toleration of sorcery and divination—and sought a "holier" lifestyle. And still others found in the Protestant churches a more stimulating intellectual atmosphere; they experienced more and better teaching there than they had in the Catholic church.[9]

### External Reasons for Conversion

Although internal reasons for conversion are the ones most frequently mentioned by converts themselves, a number of scholars studying the phenomenon have offered external (or "materialist" or "structural") reasons. These analysts stress the explanatory value of economic and social forces for the growth of Latin American Evangelicalism. For some of these researchers, religion has little independent power to affect personal or social change. Rather, in their view, religion is a response to objective social or economic forces. One gets the sense in reading their material that, without the influence of these structural forces, few Guatemalans would change their religion. The spiritual or supernatural motivations for conversion, and the benefits from conversion, are downplayed. Other analysts, though, have a deeper appreciation for the independent value of religion and the possibility for supernatural explanations for the growth of Protestantism. These scholars posit a more dynamic relationship between the internal and external forces contributing to worldview change. They suggest that certain social or economic circumstances may predispose an individual to convert. Or, individual spiritual experiences independent of personal socioeconomic status may motivate conversion, which in turn lead to attitudinal and behavioral changes that influence the convert's objective socioeconomic circumstances. The new religious worldview then also justifies or reinforces those objective changes.

*Escaping the Fiesta System*    The first and most frequently mentioned explanation for conversion offered by scholars focusing on external variables is that conversion allows people to escape the economic implications—at the personal and societal levels—of the folk Catholic fiesta system. This issue is fundamental to both the "why" and the "so what" questions. Indeed, it is at the center of the worldview-and-development intersection explored in this book. Understanding the potential economic consequences of rejecting the folk Catholic system requires an understanding of the origins and meaning of that system itself—and the religious presuppositions that underlie it. Consequently, I will delay discussion of this critical issue until the following chapter, where I describe the folk Catholic or Cristo-pagan worldview.

*Improving One's Social Status*    A second external reason analysts posit for conversion relates to converts' desires to gain a new social status by changing their religion. According to this theory, marginalized members of society convert to Evangelical faith in order to gain a new identity. Benson Saler argues:

> Religious conversion may sometimes constitute a therapeutic act of self-aggrandizement. Where an individual with a strong drive to affirm himself existentially cannot achieve adequate gratification of that drive utilizing traditional socio-cultural means, conversion to a new religion in the face of strong social disapproval may be instrumental in achieving the greatest gratification.[10]

In traditional Guatemalan society, Saler explains, social prestige could be gained through service in religious brotherhoods called *cofradias*. These organizations guard village saints, perform religious rituals, offer prayers for the community, organize community events, and provide leadership. Service in the brotherhoods requires economic resources. People desiring to attain the highest-ranked positions in the cofradias have to give years of patient service to the brotherhood and expend considerable resources. Those without the time or economic means to hold a position in the cofradia have limited ways to achieve the prestige they desire from the community.[11] For them, membership in a Protestant group is an alternative to the *esprit de corps*, prestige, and sense of belonging that cofradia membership offers.

Additionally, conversion can also offer a new identity to community members dissatisfied with their social standing. In one example, Saler discusses a woman who had suffered ridicule for alleged sexual improprieties; after conversion, she attained a new status as a paragon of virtue in her congregation. In another instance, a man teased for effeminate mannerisms converted to Evangelicalism and gained respect as a good preacher and evangelist.[12]

While Saler focuses on cases of Mayans wishing to attain a higher status within the context of their own ethnic identity, other analysts posit that Indians wishing to attain status in the Ladino culture sometimes see conversion as a relatively inexpensive means to that end. In the bi-ethnic Mexican–Maya town of Ticul, which anthropologist Richard Thompson studied, some Indians wished to "Ladinoize" and identify with the dominant ethnic group.[13] Thompson explains that the Indians could achieve this goal by securing decent paying jobs, becoming more prosperous, buying and wearing European-style clothing, learning to speak excellent Spanish, or perhaps even changing their surnames. But these were difficult routes; conversion was, by comparison, a cheaper alternative. Protestant converts, Thompson says, "disavow identification with Maya–Meztizo culture"; adopt the requisite changes in dress and speech (often with help from Spanish language classes taught in the Protestant churches); and distance themselves from the practices of Mayan folk Catholicism, embracing a rigid moral code. This wins them a "Ladino" status, especially within the ethnically mixed Protestant churches.[14]

*Improving One's Opportunities* A third external reason researchers offer for conversion is that converts view conversion as a means toward social betterment. The emphasis here is not only negative—that converts avoid the economic costs of the folk Catholic system—but also positive—that converts enjoy a range of new opportunities for social advancement. For example, some Protestant churches have established high-quality private schools. Congregants may enjoy greater access to such schools or tuition assistance from their church. Converts can also take advantage of the literacy and Spanish language classes that some Evangelical churches offer. Perhaps even more important, membership in a Protestant church may expose congregants to the world outside their local village. Some Protestants have the opportunity to travel to other communities for conferences and revival meetings. Many seek to attend religious boarding schools in other towns. Activities like these allow converts to develop relationships with fellow Evangelicals from other areas of the country.[15] Such long-distance contacts can then increase their awareness of business, job, and educational opportunities.

Moreover, the emphasis on lay initiative and responsibility in the Protestant churches provides converts with opportunities to develop their self-confidence by assuming leadership roles. And, as Martin notes in *Tongues of Fire*, this participation enables believers to develop practical social skills—including literacy, public speaking, organizational and leadership talents—that are transferable to the workplace.

In urban settings, converts gain additional benefits from their membership in Protestant churches. For urban migrants, Evangelical congregations offer what Martin calls "fraternal networks" of support. As he explains, newcomers, removed from their traditional ties to village and family, discover in the Evangelical churches a network of protection; an alternative "family"; an egalitarianism often hard to find in stratified Latin America; and a place to get practical needs met—such as an education, health and child care, credit, and job referrals.[16]

The motivations behind Protestant conversion are varied. For some individuals, predominantly spiritual and emotional forces stimulate them to consider Protestant religion. For others, the perceived economic and social benefits of conversion are attractive. For most, it is some combination of internal and external factors that leads them to embrace a new religion. It is probably accurate to surmise that for all converts, the testimony and example of Protestants has been important in attracting newcomers to the faith. As one of Sexton's informants commented, "When I visited other towns, I saw that Protestants were getting ahead, and I wanted to improve myself also."[17]

## The "So What" Question

"Getting ahead," "living better," "having peace in my home"—these were the common phrases I heard expressed when talking with Mayan Protestants about their lives following conversion. While most of the converts I met were poor by American standards, few suggested that conversion left them worse off economically. In fact, many enthusiastically reported positive postconversion economic changes. Even those who did not see any personal financial improvement were quick to identify other beneficial changes—better health, less anxiety, stronger marriages, a new self-confidence in work, new insights as parents, or greater peace with neighbors. In nearly every instance, converts— even those who had paid dearly for converting by incurring the anger of their families or the rejection of friends—never expressed regret for their decision. Whatever the *objective* evidence for the consequences of conversion, converts *subjectively* interpret their decision in a positive light and believe their lives have improved in important ways because of their new faith.

Many researchers (myself included) have wanted to try to gather objective, empirical evidence regarding the consequences of Protestant conversion. This has proven to be a daunting task because of the enormous challenges of conducting quantitative research in less developed countries. As a result of such challenges, most studies of the connection between conversion and development have relied predominantly on qualitative data gathered in informal interviews. A few combined both qualitative and quantitative methods. These studies have sought to identify those attitudinal and behavioral changes encouraged by religious conversion that affected converts' socioeconomic prospects.

David Martin's revisitation of the Weberian hypothesis on Protestantism and the spirit of capitalism in *Tongues of Fire* summarizes perhaps the widest body of literature on Protestantism and development in Latin America. Drawing from a rich database of anthropological and sociological studies,[18] Martin cautiously concludes that any relationship between Evangelical revival and the prospects for capitalist development is contingent—not necessary. Nonetheless, he does argue that "Evangelical religion and economic advancement do *often* go together, and when they do so, appear mutually to support and *reinforce* one another."[19] My research findings, and those of several other scholars reported in this chapter, support this contention. Indeed, taken together, these studies probably permit an even more assertive claim for the connection between Evangelicalism and development.

The studies Martin reviews provide considerable anecdotal evidence that Protestant converts' attitudinal and behavioral changes are conducive to economic advancement. Converts' attitudinal changes are inextricably bound to their rejection of the Cristo-pagan worldview. Converts escape not only the financial obligations, social arrangements, and mores of the folk Catholic system, but also the mentality of that system. The consequences, along these lines, of Evangelical conversion cannot be grasped fully apart from an understanding of the ideas, rules, and values of the folk Catholic system. Since these are described in chapter 3, I include my discussion of the *attitudinal* changes resulting from conversion there.

## Behavioral Changes Resulting from Conversion

The rejection of the folk Catholic system also encourages *behavioral* changes. Specifically, converts are freed from the obligation to serve in cofradias and to make sacrifices to the pantheon of gods worshipped by Cristo-pagans. These sorts of changes, too, can be best understood against a background of knowledge about Cristo-pagan belief and so, are also examined in chapter 3. In terms of other behavioral changes, researchers have uncovered eight areas of difference distinguishing converts' pre- and post-conversion lifestyles.

*Adopting the Protestant Ethic*　Not surprising to those familiar with Max Weber's work, the first set of changes relates to the adoption of the so-called Protestant ethic. Hard work, sobriety, thrift, and personal responsibility are encouraged from Evangelical pulpits and put into practice by many converts.

*Integrating into the Fraternal Network or Alternative Community*   Second, Evangelicals sometimes create a vibrant associational life that reinforces positive behavioral changes and keeps believers accountable to one another. The "fraternal network" also helps converts meet their physical needs and can provide critical support when the convert has been cut off from family and friends as a result of leaving the Catholic faith. The Protestant ethic, combined with the Protestants' alternative community, have been key factors in a variety of Evangelical success stories.[20]

*Curtailing Alcohol Consumption*   Active church involvement, the close relationships among converts, and firm Biblical teaching reinforce what is probably the most important behavioral change: curtailing alcohol consumption. In their study of ten towns around Lake Atitlan, Sexton and Woods found that "sobriety correlate[d] highest with [Protestant conversion.]"[21] As mentioned previously, Elizabeth Brusco, in her study of Colombian Evangelicals, found that Protestant conversion among males had a dramatic effect in reducing alcohol consumption.

*Investing in Family Well-Being*   The reduction in alcohol expenditures gives Protestant families more money to invest in household goods such as children's clothes and schooling, better nutrition, and physical improvements to their homes. Brusco found that the savings enjoyed by Evangelical households as a result of the male's curtailment of "macho" pursuits such as drinking, gambling, and sexual promiscuity meant that 20 to 40 percent of the household income could be redirected to the family's well-being, thus raising the standard of living for women and children.[22] Other researchers have also seen that some Protestants have more money available for investment in cash crops or land purchases.[23]

*Strengthening Marital Bonds*   Moreover, researchers have discovered that male conversion to Protestantism often contributes to a general strengthening of marital bonds. These scholars report that there are fewer instances of infidelity and wife abuse among Protestant households than in non-Protestant ones. Changes such as these in the home, in conjunction with the opportunities for female leadership and participation in Pentecostal churches, led Brusco to conclude that "Colombian Evangelicalism serves to reform gender roles in a way that enhances female status."[24]

*Pursuing Literacy and Education*   Several studies also reveal that Protestants were more likely than traditional Catholics to be literate and to have attained more years of formal schooling. In a study conducted in Panajachel, Guatemala in the 1960s, anthropologists Sol Tax and Robert Hinshaw found that "Protestants constitute roughly one-sixth of the population and all but six of the thirty-two Indians who have gone beyond the fourth grade."[25] In an earlier study, of Santiago Atitlan in the department of Solola, researcher John Early reported that according to the 1964 census, approximately 6 percent of male Indians and 1 percent of female Indians attended school. "The only Indian group in Atitlan that makes a point of sending its children to school," Early wrote, "is the Central American Evangelical Church, which comprises about ten percent of the town's population."[26] Anthropologist David Clawson concluded from research in 1984 in a rural Mexican village that Protestants did better economically than their non-Protestant neighbors in part because Protestant emphasis on individual Bible reading motivated new believers to become literate. Protestants were also more likely than non-Protestants to encourage higher education: 82 percent of the village students in postsecondary schools were Evangelicals.[27]

One important difference is that the educational consequences of Protestant conversion have not been limited to men. In fact, Sexton found that "Protestant wives in Panajachel are more educated than Catholic wives, but there is no difference between Protestant and Catholic men. Also, Protestant families are getting more of their daughters and sons through the sixth grade."[28] Similarly, economic anthropologist Sheldon Annis found in his study of San Antonio de las Aguas Calientes that Protestant children were more likely to be attending school than Catholic children.[29]

*Pursuing Nonagricultural Employment*   Sexton also discovered that Protestants had higher occupational aspirations than did Catholics. Annis found actual occupational differences between the two groups. Protestants, he explained, created livelihood strategies that were not necessarily dependent on land. (This stemmed in part from the fact that many of the converts were from the community's lower classes and had little access to land.) Protestants showed a propensity for developing nonfarm sources of income. Wage labor among Protestants was likely to be in higher-paid, upwardly mobile occupations (e.g., tailors and transporters). In addition, Annis reported a greater Protestant tendency toward business activity.[30] Similarly, some studies Martin reviews point to a connection between the Evangelicals' new-found self-confidence and initiative and their propensity to begin their own small businesses.

*Increasing Exposure to Outsiders*   By breaking with traditional beliefs and organizations, Protestants set themselves up for the possibility of contact with new groups and ideas. Their frequent relationships with Western missionaries opens up their previously cloistered world. For example, as Clawson reported from Mexico, because of their initial bonds with North American missionaries and then their contact with fellow Evangelicals outside their area, Evangelicals tended to be more open in general toward outsiders. This sometimes led to an economic payoff, since such openness increased the Protestants' circle of contacts, enabling them to hear of educational, job, or marketing opportunities.[31]

Nash's findings from Quiche were similar. The Protestant groups, she reported, "drew their younger and more alert members into a network of social relations which was national in scope. Visiting other communities for conferences and attending boarding schools outside of town, young members of the sects were mentally stimulated, and the possibility of realizing their ambitions increased."[32]

Indian converts' rejection of folk Catholic traditions has also sometimes led them to greater interaction with and acceptance of Ladinos. Several researchers have noted "Ladino-izing" tendencies among Protestants. In his research in Ticul, Mexico, Richard Thompson found that "one of the principal features of the town's Protestants . . . is their total disavowal of all identification with Maya–Meztizo culture. By design, European-style clothing is worn, the Indian language is not spoken, and formal classes are given to encourage members to improve their use and understanding of Spanish."[33] Sexton found a similar pattern in the highlands villages he studied: "Protestantism appears to be reinforcing the adoption of Ladinoized culture, such as wearing more Europeanized clothing, living in modern-style houses with more modern possessions, and speaking more Spanish."[34]

For many Mayan Protestants, bi-ethnic interaction takes place both inside and outside the church. Some congregations are ethnically mixed, providing opportunities for informal interaction between Mayas and Ladinos. Moreover, relationships inside the churches are often more egalitarian in nature than otherwise experienced in bi-ethnic intercourse. In Panajachel, Tax and Hinshaw found that only Protestant Mayans participated in voluntary associations that included a mixture of Indians and Ladinos; folk Catholic Mayans avoided them. "As a result of these new bases of association, patterned upon Ladino norms," the researchers wrote, "Protestant Indians rapidly assimilate attitudes and beliefs which have not yet diffused to any measurable extent among the Catholic majority, whose norms of social interaction have changed little over the past three decades."[35]

In addition to contacts with Westerners, with Indians from other areas, and with neighboring Ladinos, Sexton and Woods found that Evangelicals had greater contact with media (radio, television, movies, newspapers, magazines, and books) than did Catholics. In their survey of more than 700 Mayans, Protestant faith was statistically correlated with the variable they called "exposure"—frequency of contacts with outsiders and frequency and distance of travel. Evangelicals also demonstrated superior political knowledge in comparison with their traditional Catholic neighbors (e.g., they were likely to be able to identify by name the governor and mayor of their local area, as well as the president of the United States and other world leaders).[36]

## Community Level Studies

Most of the changes described in the studies reviewed in this chapter are at the "micro" level: they are changes affecting individuals and families rather than larger social units. In a few instances, whole communities have appeared to benefit economically from the conversion of a critical mass of their residents. Of the studies described in this chapter, only Sexton and Woods attempted to assess the community-level impact of conversion.

These researchers found that a town's level of development (as measured by the presence or absence of 47 traits, including piped water, electricity, television sets in homes, resident doctors, bus service, and others) did correlate with "new religion," a variable measuring Protestant conversions and conversions of traditional Catholics to the more orthodox worldview of Catholic Action. Development also correlated with Ladino-ization, which, as already mentioned, is a process encouraged by, or, at minimum, accepted by, Protestant converts. Exposure and development were related, and, as mentioned previously, conversion increased exposure. The statistical correlation between new religion and development was significant, though weaker than the correlations between development and Ladino-ization and exposure. Of the ten towns in Sexton and Wood's study, Panajachel was the most developed, most Ladino-ized, most exposed, and most Protestant. It was also the town where Protestants had had the longest historical presence. Some of the lesser developed towns had significant percentages of Evangelicals, but those communities had not been Protestant for very long.[37]

## Digging Deeper

Taken together, the various studies reviewed in this chapter form a formidable case for the argument that Protestantism and development are linked. But they also leave some areas unexplored. Most are studies of individual towns, or small clusters of towns; none are national in scope. The Worldview and Development Survey of 1,000 households distributed across five towns in four regions of the country represents one small step toward a national study.

Moreover, these studies do not, generally, examine the particular aspects of Protestantism that explain the noted differences—on socioeconomic indicators—between Protestants and non-Protestants. The Worldview and Development Survey attempts to dig deeper in this regard, in an effort to identify just what it is about being Protestant that stimulates the changes noted by researchers. The survey is discussed in part II of the book. Before delving into it, though, it is useful to gain a picture of the worldview that characterized many Protestants *before* their conversion. The next chapter examines the nature and values of the Cristo-pagan worldview and suggests some socioeconomic implications of this religion.

# THREE

# Cristo-Paganism Described and Analyzed

*Hypersensitive to the fact that his life is in the hands of supernatural powers, the Indian takes no chances. He worships the litany of pagan gods left him by his forefathers. He pays homage to the all-powerful Christian God imposed on him by the friars of Spain. As a result, in the most sacred of pagan rituals or Christian services, he plays it safe by including some devotions for the deity whose presence at that particular time is not admitted.*

Vera Kelsey and Lily de Jongh Osborne[1]

The world of Cristo-pagan Mayan Indians is a crowded place. Walking down dirt trails to their *milpa*,[2] they may pass all sorts of supernatural beings—the *dueños* (spirit owners) of the trees, birds, rocks, and animals, and the spirits of the sacred hills. Entering the local Catholic church, they confront images of Christ, Mary, and the most important saints of that area. Passing the cemetery, they are reminded of their dead ancestors and the responsibility to care for their souls through prayer and the sacrifice of candles, food, and drink—lest they punish them with illness or a bad harvest. Considering a business deal, they must take into account what day it is, since the "gods" of certain days can be more or less favorable to commercial activity. Even in slumber they may not find solitude, for sleep can bring dreams and, through dreams, unsettling encounters and conversations with *dios el mundo*, the "god of the earth."

Not only is it crowded, the Mayans' world is essentially malevolent. The supernatural beings they worship typically are capricious, quick to rebuke, and capable of inflicting accidents, physical infirmity, natural catastrophe, and the death of one's loved ones. Daily activity, if one is devout, includes careful devotions and sacrifices—some seeking permission from the gods to use "their" possessions, some trying to appease gods made angry by sin or neglect. The "Father of the Skies"—the Christian God figure in the Cristo-pagan cosmology—can be kind but is also distant, having become, on the whole, bored with his creation.

Only his son, *Kub'aal Q'ii*, the Sun God or Christ figure, really cares for mankind by providing humans light and warmth.[3] Nonetheless, the Cristo-pagan devotee's prayers are dominated by fear, penitence, and pleas for mercy; the goal is to avoid confrontation with others and with the gods.

Like any worldview, the belief system of Cristo-paganism seeks to answer certain fundamental questions about the origins of life, human purpose in the world, and humans' relation to nature and to the supernatural. It also asks and attempts to answer questions about the future, about right behavior, about community organization and authority, about suffering. It explains to believers who they are and what is expected of them, why things are the way they are, and why things happen. It teaches them where they have come from and where they might be going. The kinds of explanations the Cristo-pagan belief system provides to these questions differ from those offered by the Evangelical worldview. Consequently, attitudes and behavior patterns based on Cristo-pagan presuppositions differ from those based on Evangelicalism.

To understand how converts' Evangelical beliefs and habits differ from those they held formerly as Cristo-pagan traditionalists, a picture of the "before" is necessary. The first half of this chapter describes the traditionalist worldview that many converts subscribed to before their conversion. This section summarizes the Cristo-pagan answers to a variety of questions about the origin and meaning of life, an individual's place in creation and relationship to the supernatural, and the proper ordering of individual and community life.

The latter half of this chapter assesses the socioeconomic implications of the Cristo-pagan belief system. This section describes the economically burdensome responsibilities, and the economically constraining logic, of the folk Catholic fiesta system referred to in chapter 2. It also highlights some studies of the economic experiences of Evangelical converts following their departure from the folk Catholic system. This discussion concentrates especially on the *attitudinal* changes resulting from rejection of the Cristo-pagan worldview.

## The Cristo-Pagan Worldview Described

### How Did Life Begin?

According to anthropologist Kay Warren, who conducted extensive fieldwork in the Guatemalan highlands, no one single Indian myth regarding the creation of the world exists; rather, there is a whole oral tradition.[4] In conversations with various Indian traditionalists, one will catch slightly differing accounts of creation. Warren reported that the

Cakquikel describe creation unfolding in three separate epochs—that of *Eterno Padre* (the Cakquikel's Christian "Father God" figure), that of JesuCristo, and that of the saints. During the first epoch, humans and animals were undifferentiated—both could talk and neither was particularly intelligent. The Eterno Padre visited his creation to monitor activities there but did not pass judgment. Indeed, he became bored with his creation and separated himself into a completely spiritual and distant existence. In the epoch of JesuCristo, Christ took dominion over the earth and separated the land from the waters and humankind from animals. Eventually humans divided into different races and scattered. During this time, an apostle rebelled against Christ, trying to imitate Christ's creative powers and to usurp his authority. Christ punished the fallen apostle with a scourging; at each strike of the lash the apostle grew horns and eventually turned into *Sátanas* (the Cakquikel's devil figure). Christ then banished him to the underworld. In the last creation epoch, Christ gave dominion over certain places to the different Christian saints.[5]

This Cakquikel account of the origin of things differs in a variety of respects from those of other Mayan groups, though essential elements are shared. Benjamin and Lore Colby discuss the Ixil creation account in their lengthy ethnographic study, *The Daykeeper*.[6] Like the Cakquikel, the Ixil also have creation unfolding in a series of events, including the creation of a "first people" who styled themselves as equal to their creator, *Kub'aal* (the Father God figure), thus engendering his wrath. Kub'aal attempted to destroy these people through a series of natural disasters, including a major flood. But the first people proved resourceful and resistant, eventually impressing Kub'aal. He called these people into his presence and said he would no longer try to destroy them. These first people then became the angel-like figures with magical powers the Ixil call *aanhel*. After this, the Christ figure (Kub'aal Q'ii) created humans. Christ's "older brothers" in heaven were unable to create humans; their powers seemed to be limited to the creation of animals and plantlife. They were jealous of Christ's skills and plotted to kill him during the years of Christ's visitation on earth.

Despite the differences in these creation narratives, similar themes emerge. Christ is active in creation and engaged with the lives of humans, whereas the Father God figure is more distant. Good and evil exist from the beginning. Geographic place is important, for different gods and saints inhabit and own specific physical areas.

## How Should Humans Relate to Nature?

Since the Father God and Christ figures created the earth, all of nature belongs to them. However, the syncretism of Cristo-paganism also posits the existence of a multitude of lesser gods—called *aanhel* by the Ixil, or dueños, lords, or saints by other Mayan language groups. Many of these deities have dominion over particular places (such as a mountain-top or cave), particular things (such as a tree or rock), and particular activities (such as sewing or bus driving). As commentator Eugene Nida explains, "Almost every significant object of nature has a spirit owner which must be properly propitiated if his 'property' is to be exploited by man . . . before the corn is planted, the 'dueño' of the hillside must be prayed to, or in anger he will ruin the crop, bring sickness to the farmer, or withhold the rain."[7]

In addition, the dios el mundo or "earth god" is a tremendously important figure in the Cristo-pagan cosmology. It is difficult to discern whether this figure is associated in the Cristo-pagan's mind with the devil (as Warren reported from her study) or with the Father God image (as reported in ethnographies from among the Kekchi).[8] In any event, the relationship of humans to the creation is not one of dominion or even stewardship, as that term is defined by orthodox Christians. For example, Evangelical theology teaches, on the basis of the so-called Cultural Mandate in the first chapter of the book of Genesis, that humans have dominion over nature. Since, as Psalm 24 says, "The earth is the Lord's and the fullness thereof," humans are not allowed to rape and pillage the creation. But orthodox Christianity teaches that they are permitted to harness the forces of nature and exert their minds and strength to shape the raw creation to serve the interests of human welfare. In the Cristo-pagan worldview, in contrast, an individual is at the mercy of nature and "nature's owners," and can easily provoke the wrath of the dueños through thoughtless actions.

The Colbys report that their principal informant, an elderly Ixil day-keeper named Sha's, was always careful to maintain a proper relationship to nature. In Sha's' mind, cultivation was a sort of necessary evil. In a prayer recorded by the Colbys, Sha's explains that people must farm to satisfy their stomachs but that this hurts the creation: "We seek pardon before Kub'aal: the Holy Land, the Holy Earth—We use machetes, we wield machetes, we cut [the brush]. But what was their fault? It's our offense. It's our fault alone. It's ours for fault of our stomach. It's ours for fault of our food."[9]

Sha's wonders whether the trees he cuts to clear his fields are the "resting place" for the aanhel, their "place of frolic." He is saddened that he cuts the trees, which are full of "the desire to grow." He begs pardon of the gods for "the urgings of my insides for food, for drink," imploring them to forgive "because there is no other place to get [food] from."[10] In another passage, Sha's laments to the Colbys after clearing a *cuerda* (unit) of land:

Well, those are many souls; it's a cuerda of souls that I've killed because I cut the trees. Perhaps there was a small animal. Perhaps there was a little bird. Lord, have mercy, perhaps it was his roosting place. Perhaps it was his nest, and I moved it. I cut the trunk, the tree disappeared, the bird disappeared because it fled, it stayed no longer in the tree. All for the offense of my stomach.[11]

Linguist Paul Townsend uncovered a similar sentiment in another Ixil town. He recorded an Ixil prayer from Cotzal in which the shaman asks forgiveness of the earth god for the farmers' "cutting, bumping, and bruising of the earth's face."[12] Linguists Ruth Carlson and Francis Eachus, long-term residents among the Kekchi Indians, report that the Kekchis must perform "counter-acting" rituals whenever "anything pertaining to nature is disturbed without having first obtained special permission. Ideally, permission is asked of Cu:l Taq'a [the earth god] before moving a large stone, cutting a tree, clearing a planting site, harvesting, or hunting. These rituals must be performed at certain crosses or in mountain caves as well as at the site of the activity for which permission is being sought."[13] The Cakquikel of the Western highlands relate to nature in a similar fashion. Warren discovered, for example, that they consider gathering firewood a form of "trespassing."[14]

### How Should Humans Relate to the Supernatural?

*Rituals*  Mayan Indians live in the presence of multiple deities while they perform the many necessary duties of life. Because their duties require them to interact with nature, and nature's gods, much of the Indians' time is consumed in religious ritual. As one scholar has asserted, Indian religion seeks to "maintain harmony with an unpredictable and essentially malignant universe." Much of this is accomplished through "bargaining"—making vows and offering sacrifices, gifts, and penance.[15] The point is to interact with the supernatural in a such way as to avoid trouble, to correct trouble, or to cause trouble for an enemy. All these sorts of activities are known generally by the phrase "making *costumbre*." Specific rituals differ such that one type may be performed in certain places on certain days and another type on other days and in other locales. The content of ritual, though, remains essentially the same. The chief elements are humble prayer and the offering of candles, incense, and, occasionally, food, drink, and blood. Costumbres are performed before clearing land, to ask the earth god's permission for cutting down trees and clearing brush. Rituals are also done before planting and harvesting.

Some costumbres can be done by an individual petitioner, but often the services of professional diviners, shamans, and prayersayers are sought. Diviners (also called "daykeepers"), are employed by individuals facing major decisions—such as those about marriage or business deals—or experiencing illness or depression. Barbara Tedlock conducted an extensive study of the lives and thought of diviners, having apprenticed herself to one in the late 1970s in the Quiche town of Momostenango. She suggests that daykeepers perform both prophetic divining and priestly services; some may not only offer advice and insight but also perform healings and intercede for or represent their clients before the gods.[16]

*Supernatural Communication*  Communication between the diviners and the gods occurs through the media of "counting the days," "casting the mixes," and "reading the blood." The 260-day Mayan calendrical system, with its 20 different "day" deities, is at the center of the divination process. Each day has a name and a specific character. Usually this character has a mixture of good and evil qualities. The day imparts its essence to people born on it, so that a person's fate is influenced substantially by his birthdate. In the "casting of mixes," the shaman creates a pattern of seeds and small stones on a special divination table, arranging them in small groups in a sort of chart based on the calendar. When the pieces are arranged and rearranged several times, they reveal certain days and numbers that provide the shaman insight into the gods' message to his client.[17]

Suppose, for example, a client wishes to know whether or not he should proceed with a particularly important business deal. If, through the process of casting the mixes, the day *Tz'i'* appears, the client will be advised against the deal. Tz'i' is associated with uncertainty and weakness—thus the risk and inadvisability of the proposed venture. If the number revealed with the day Tz'i' is high, this is an emphatic sign that the deal is no good. In contrast, should the procedure reveal a high-numbered *Batz* day—the high number indicating strength and Batz being a lucky or successful day—success in the business venture is foretold. Should the day *Imox* be revealed, the business deal will not be implemented, for Imox is associated with being crazy or possessed. Following through with the plan might cause the client to become stressed and "crazy" with its complications, worries, and responsibilities.[18]

Signals and messages from the gods are also transmitted through "lightening" movements in the blood of a diviner who has a special kind of soul that can receive such communications. The person with this skill prays over the client's needs, asking specific questions of the gods; certain twitches then indicate supernatural responses.[19]

*Dreams*   Communication between humans and deities also occurs through dreams. Sha's, the Ixil daykeeper interviewed by the Colbys, took dreams very seriously, basing major decisions on them. There are other examples for the importance of dreaming as well. Recruitment for key positions in the religious system—including daykeepers, shamans, and healers—often takes place through dreams in which the individual receives a "call." For example, a potential daykeeper might start dreaming the names of the days of the Mayan calendar or experience flying dreams. Messages from upset ancestors can also be communicated in dreams. Since dreaming is often an unpleasant experience of disturbing communications, the Ixils' common morning greeting is "Are you well? Did you have any dreams?" with the response (hopefully), "No, I didn't dream anything, I am fine."[20]

## How Should Humans Act?

The Cristo-pagan worldview provides guidance to the Mayan faithful in relating not only to the natural and supernatural but also to their fellows. The Mayans' understanding of appropriate individual and corporate behavior—and their traditional social structures—are deeply influenced by their Cristo-pagan worldview.

*The Fiesta System and the Civil-Religious Hierarchy*   Perhaps the most prominent institution of the Cristo-pagan or folk Catholic religion practiced by traditional Mayans is the *cofradia* or "religious brotherhood." This group is composed typically of eight to ten individuals or couples, each with a carefully delineated rank. Villages may have a variety of different cofradias, and some may be more prestigious than others. Rank within the cofradia is based on age and seniority.

The principal functions of the cofradia are two. First, the cofradia must protect and take care of the image of an important town saint. The saint's image itself is believed to possess supernatural powers and is prayed to and treated with meticulous care. In the Cristo-pagan's mind, the image is not an icon that *represents* a deity; rather, it is an idol that is itself divine. The highest ranked member of the cofradia (often called a *mayordomo*) usually keeps the "saint" in his own home; in other instances, the image may reside in the Catholic church.

Second, the cofradia oversees the organization of the village's annual saint's day fiesta—a three-to-five-day period of celebration, feasting, drinking, dancing, and musical plays. This is the social highlight of the year, a time of tremendous entertainment, drinking, and religious ritual (e.g., special prayers and offerings, processions). Often a high-ranking cofradia member serves as the fiesta sponsor, which requires funding the many expenses involved: food, drink, marimba bands, professional dancers, firecrackers, candles, and other supplies. The fiesta requires (relative to local standards) an enormous financial outlay and consumes substantial capital that might otherwise be used for investment.

The cofradias, in addition to caring for the saints and organizing fiestas, make petitionary rituals for good weather, good harvests, health for the community, protection from enemies, and so forth. Before the cofradia system began to erode in the last quarter of this century, members of the cofradias (especially the highest ranked ones) were the most authoritative figures in the local community. From the nineteenth to the early-to-mid-twentieth century, offices in the religious brotherhood paralleled civil offices (mayor, assistant mayor, etc.) The *principales* (or oldest, highest ranking members of the cofradias, or alumni of these positions) offered the slate of candidates for *cargos* (offices) in both the civil and religious authority structures. This unity of the civil-religious brotherhood was challenged under the political reforms of the Ubico regime in 1935, and a slow erosion of the power of the principales continued with the rise of political parties and competitive elections in the 1940s.[21] The system further declined in influence under the pressures of Protestant growth, the increased activity of more orthodox Catholic groups such as Catholic Action,[22] and economic changes brought about by the modernization process.

Anthropologists have offered different explanations for the origins of the fiesta system. Some suggest that the system was created and imposed by outsiders (principally Ladinos) for the purpose of keeping the Indians economically weak.[23] This is probably an exaggerated claim; it is more accurate to argue that the Indians created the system but that Ladinos have exploited it. For example, Ladino shop owners earn much by selling the goods necessary for Mayan rituals (e.g., candles, firecrackers). Additionally, in the past (but to a lesser extent nowadays) recruiters for migrant labor on Ladino plantations would often visit the Indian towns prior to major fiestas, just when Indians were most in need of cash to purchase dance costumes, liquor, or ritual offerings. Recruiters advanced these Indians pay in return for promised future labor, at terms highly unfavorable to the Maya. Other times, recruiters would visit toward the end of the fiesta, when many men would have been drinking for days. Having run out of money, these Indians would agree to harsh contract terms in return for an advance paycheck with which they could purchase more alcohol or pay off the bar tab they had already accumulated.

Other interpreters suggest that the cofradias and fiesta system protect Indian identity in the midst of pressures and discrimination from the dominant, Spanish-speaking Ladinos. By creating their own social customs, rituals, and authority and decision-making structures, these scholars argue, the Mayans reinforce their separate ethnic identity. Doing so helps them cope with their subordinated status in bi-ethnic Guatemalan society. In part, this strategy requires defending a value system that counters the Ladino one. Since the Ladino system is seen as valuing wealth, the Indian system exalts the purity of poverty and places social prestige above material wealth.[24]

This is evident most clearly in the arrangements for fiesta sponsorship. Members of the community who have done particularly well economically are enjoined to shoulder the financial burden of fiesta sponsorship. As I explain in greater detail later, this custom acts as an economic leveling mechanism, reducing the sponsor's wealth to the average level of other villagers, which maintains economic equality in the village. Though he loses economically, the sponsor gains a higher social status in the community.

*Responding to Suffering and Illness*   The egalitarianism characterizing the fiesta system is also reflected in the way the highland Maya of Guatemala interpret illness and disease. The Maya strongly emphasize balance, harmony, and equal division of burdens and resources. Accumulation of wealth and income inequalities are seen as sinful, for they break with this idea of balance. Illness is viewed as a symptom of imbalance; the victim is in "disjunction with the social world and cosmos," as researcher Linda Greenberg put it.[25]

In her study of Mam Indians in the Guatemalan village of Cajola, Greenberg found that "accumulation, whether it be of material or symbolic 'goods', creates tension in Cajola's predominantly egalitarian society."[26] As in most other Indian villages, Cajola's fiesta system acted to level wealth and bring the wealthy sponsor back into balance. The idea of balancing "hot" and "cold" experiences or elements, which is pervasive in Indian etiology,[27] was also brought to bear in explaining the rationale behind the fiesta system. Wealthy sponsors, by their excessive (and perhaps sinful) accumulation, were thought to be too "hot"; the ritual expenditures required of them as sponsors served as "cooling" actions helping to bring them back into balance.

Greenberg found that the Maya typically interpreted diseases in terms of a lack of balance between hot and cold elements (food or experiences). Some diseases were categorized as hot and required a counterbalancing cold remedy, and vice versa. Greenberg also discovered that the Mayas' scorn of overconsumption and inequality carried over into their interpretation of regurgitation. In their view, nausea resulted from mixing food in a greedy or indulgent way: "Regurgitation undoes the over-consumption or retention of the world in one's being (at the expense of others) caused by overindulgence, and reverses the normal process of digestion, returning the food back to the world."[28]

The imbalance referred to in Indian etiology can be either accidental or deliberate. In the latter case, accumulation or overconsumption is a transgression leading to disease. The connection between illness and sin is a common one among Guatemalan folk Catholic Mayans. In answer to a series of questions related to suffering and disease, the Ixil day-keeper Sha's told the Colbys that the most common cause of illness is sin (note that the disease itself is personified in Sha's' style of speaking):

> Certainly we have done lots of things. That is why we have sickness. For example, there are people into which sickness has already entered. If one committed a transgression, already the sickness will enter. If his [the sufferer's] time has come, already he [the sickness] goes. But if he [the sickness] stays, the only remedy left is incense. If they have a healing ceremony he [the patient] will get better if he has luck; if he does not have luck—even though lots of incense is consumed—time hunts him down. But sometimes one gets better because of the incense, and candles. So it is done.[29]

On the basis of long-term work in the Ixil Triangle, linguist Paul Townsend confirms the connection between the Mayan animist world-view and etiology: "For the traditionalist, the majority of illnesses, from spider bites to broken bones, are attributable to spirit world phenomena such as the patient's sin, an angered spirit of a deceased relative, or chastisement by the [earth] spirit for poor treatment shown him."[30]

Sometimes illness may be the result of malicious persecution by someone who has put a curse on the sufferer. Townsend recorded a healing prayer in Coztal, where the shaman was dealing with a patient with a broken leg. In the prayer, the shaman asks the bone "Who has made you cry? Who has called for you?" in an attempt to discern who has cast the malevolent spell against his unfortunate client.[31] Sorcery is condemned in the Mayan cultures, yet some Indians practice covert witchcraft against others, even employing the assistance of evil shamans. The Indians believe that a person can inflict harm on an enemy by casting an evil spirit on him; beseeching some aanhel to torment him; or burying a piece of his clothing, fingernails, or hair.[32] When sickness is traced to such actions by another, the patient must solicit a shaman to perform counteracting rituals to rid him of the curse because medical science alone will be unable to cure the problem.

*Respect for Ancestors and Traditions and Rejection of Change*
The Mayan folk Catholic worldview exalts the community elders. These are the men who serve in the top ranks of the cofradias. They make decisions and intercede for the community before the pantheon of gods who must be appeased. Frequently, older men (and sometimes women) serve as the daykeepers and shamans who perform rituals in order to cure physical ailments and counteract witchcraft.

Another crucial role of the elders is to nurture the memory of ancestors and to encourage devotion to traditional costumbres. Among the
Cakquikel Indians, costumbres such as praying at caves, planting
crosses at strategic places, burning offerings of incense and candles, and
repeating sacred prayers over the graves of loved ones are believed to
have originated with the very first Cakquikel men and women. These
were a holy, obedient people who enjoyed peace, tranquility in their
relationships, and good harvests. Their descendants believe they should
imitate their ancestors to earn rewards from God. This includes more
recent ancestors as well; as one informant told Warren: "We should act
like our grandparents acted, behaving well, believing in [the father
God], adoring him."[33] Because of this exaltation of ancestors and traditional ways (and the vested interest the village principales have in per-
petuating those old customs), the Cakquikel view change suspiciously.

Warren, due to her emphasis on Indian–Ladino relations, interprets
the Mayan reluctance to innovate as another example of their rejection
of Ladino values. In the Cakquikel worldview, she asserts, change is
associated with the powers of Sátanas—to change one's behavior is to
act Ladino, and "one becomes like the Devil . . . if one assumes the
characteristics of the class of people whom the Devil represents."[34]
Other researchers have found other Mayan groups equally unwilling to
change. Barbara Tedlock, for example, reported that the Quiche were
reluctant to change (though she acknowledged that some innovations
could be accepted if they were seen as additions to, rather than replace-
ments of, old ways).[35]

*Ethics*   Folk Catholic religious beliefs also influence Mayan concep-
tions of appropriate moral behavior. Not surprisingly, given the information presented before, the failure to perform necessary costumbres,
the mistreatment of nature, the accumulation of too much wealth, and
the refusal to participate in the cofradia system when requested are
considered major sins. Other serious sins include murder, adultery,
gossip, and theft. Ostentatious living—such as making improvements
to one's home—is condemned as prideful; the offender is accused of
attempting to "shame his neighbors." Minor sins include fornication,
lying, failure to repay one's debts, and inadequate provision for one's
family. Interestingly, drunkenness, polygamy, and improvidence are not
regarded as sins.[36] Individuals enjoy a fairly broad scope for personal
indulgence provided their actions do not bring harm to the community.
In terms of virtues, hospitality, respect for elders, and selfless community service are highly ranked in Mayan culture. Respect is also ac-
corded those who sponsor fiestas, especially if the sponsor goes beyond
the call of duty by serving in the cofradia several times.

In Warren's interpretation, Indian ethics are also influenced by the

Mayas' objective social status as a subordinate ethnic group. She asserts that the Mayans attempt to separate themselves as much as possible from Ladino society and influence and reject Ladino ways as being associated with the "law of the devil." According to this interpretation, *moral* behavior is *Indian* behavior—performing costumbres, seeking harmony and peace, and participating generously in community activities.[37]

## Implications for Development

If Warren's interpretation is accurate, clearly Mayan Indians exhibit a pride in their own culture and values while shunning the attitudes and behaviors of Ladinos. The Mayans make conscious judgments about the Mayan and Ladino cultures and assert the superiority of their own. In this they differ little from other societies; most people tend to believe their own ways are best. This book does not attempt to compare and critique the Mayan and Ladino cultures. It does, however, evaluate different cultural patterns and beliefs as to their impact on a society's prospects for economic development. As I argued in chapter 1, development scholars cannot pay homage to the idol of cultural relativism if it is indeed true that some worldviews, and the practices deriving therefrom, contribute to socioeconomic and familial well-being more than others. In the case of the Cristo-pagan worldview described in this chapter, the socioeconomic costs are substantial.

### The Burdens of the Fiesta System

First, as noted earlier, any Indian who assumes a *cargo* or office in the civil–religious hierarchy wins increased social prestige but at enormous personal expense. Cofradia members incur expenses for entertaining guests and caring for the saint's image. Fiesta sponsors bear even heavier burdens. Waldemar Smith, whose book, *The Fiesta System and Economic Change*, is one of the fullest treatments of the economic dynamics of the folk Catholic system, comments:

> An outstanding feature of the fiesta system is the extraordinary costs that families bear during their year in office. Fiesta sponsors are expected to hire ritual specialists, perform considerable ceremonial labor, and host a fiesta complete with food, drink, and musical entertainment for other members of the community. Host families generally employ household supplies as far as possible to meet festive budgets, but some items such as sky rockets and the services of priests and musicians must be purchased with cash.[38]

Smith goes on to report that such expenditures can cost the sponsor the equivalent of one year's local wages.[39] (Other studies suggest the costs range from 25 percent to 50 percent of an Indian's annual income.)[40]

In addition to the financial obligations of cofradia service and fiesta sponsorship, Cristo-pagans also expend substantial funds on the required costumbres (e.g., offering candles, incense, and food to various gods.) They also incur expenses in paying curanderos (witch doctors or shamans), diviners, and professional prayer-sayers. Anthropologist Paul Deiner relates a tragic story about the financial burdens of Cristo-pagan religion from eastern Guatemala during his fieldwork there in 1973. A family in Esquipulas he visited was grieving over the ill health of their eight-year-old son. Deiner could tell that the boy was suffering from advanced protein-calorie malnutrition. The parents recognized the boy's need for protein, yet had fed him only one egg, three days prior to Deiner's visit. They told the anthropologist they had no money to purchase additional food. Meanwhile, Deiner noticed that their house altar held several candles burning as gifts for the "saints." He reported:

> When I inquired about these ritual expenditures, the head of the household responded, "What can be done? If we do not pray, we will all fall ill and die, there will be no harvest, we will lose our land. Only the saints can help us. Praying to the saints is a great burden, but one must pray." The child died three days later.[41]

The folk Catholic system has negative socioeconomic consequences not only for individuals but also for the community as a whole. As noted previously, the fiesta system acts as a leveler of economic wealth. Whenever a family begins to outdo others, they are recruited as fiesta sponsors. The subsequent expenditures they incur decrease their wealth (and may even put them into debt). The fiesta system appears economically irrational from an outsider's perspective, for it channels extra earned income into economically nonproductive consumption, which leads to stagnation rather than development. Capital accumulation and investment are curtailed, thus reducing job creation and economic productivity generally. Analyst Sheldon Annis refers to the economic outworkings of the folk Catholic system as "*milpa* logic." Like James Sexton before him, Annis conducted his research in the villages around Guatemala's Lake Atitlan. Annis concluded that Protestant conversion occurred most often among members of the highest and lowest strata of the community because both had a vested interest in escaping the folk Catholic system. The system, Annis explained, reflects the economic realities of small-scale, subsistence milpa agriculture. This form of production is characterized by farmers' dependence on the traditional crops of corn and beans and by their low tolerance of risk. Their methods, Annis wrote, "optimiz[ed] input rather than maximizing output." For example, milpa production could absorb noncash inputs such as children's after-school work hours and grandparents' knowledge of plants. Farmers shunned cash cropping because it was a riskier venture requiring start-up capital. The milpa-based economy created a certain

egalitarianism in the village (commensurate with the egalitarian emphasis of the Cristo-pagan worldview). As Annis noted, "*milpa* production,
for the most part, is consumed by the family or traded within the
village. [N]o one can get rich or make someone else rich by farming a
*milpa*. Since it works against capital accumulation, it is antithetical to
entrepreneurship."[42]

Marginalized community members lacking land, Annis found, could
not participate fully in the milpa economy nor enjoy its social benefits.
(They were so poor they had no hope of being able to serve in a
cofradia.) The most prosperous segment of the society, Annis discovered, was held back in its economic activity by the wealth-leveling
mechanisms of the fiesta system—which both expressed and reinforced
milpa logic. Consequently, both groups—the poorest and the richest in
the community—had an incentive to escape the folk Catholic order.
Indeed, in one of the boldest statements of the external explanations for
the rise of Protestantism, Annis asserted: "Religious behavior is rooted
in economic production [and] production is both an idea and expression of social circumstance. . . . The rise of Protestantism is an expression of the anti-*milpa* forces taking gradual hold upon village life."[43]

## The Folk Catholic System and the Image of Limited Good

While researchers like Annis feel the reasons for Protestant conversion
are obviously economic in nature, the reasons for the perpetuation of
the folk Catholic system—given its negative economic effects—are far
less obvious. Researchers interested in development have wondered
why the folk Catholic system continues. In a brilliant essay written
some 25 years ago, anthropologist George Foster offered perhaps the
most incisive and persuasive interpretation for the apparently irrational
economic behavior common in peasant societies. His analysis also sheds
light on the kind of worldview change most likely to increase peasants'
prospects for economic development:

> [Peasants] view their social, economic, and natural universe—their total
> environment—as one in which all of the desired things in life such as
> land, wealth, health, friendship and love, manliness and honor, respect
> and status, power and influence, security and safety, *exist in finite quan-
> tity and are always in short supply* as far as the peasant is concerned. Not
> only do these and all other "good things" exist in finite and limited
> quantities, but in addition *there is no way directly within peasant power
> to increase the available quantities.*[44]

Once this presupposition of a zero-sum or finite universe is recognized,
peasant economic behavior becomes more comprehensible than at first
glance. Since resources are finite, a member of the community can
advance economically only at someone else's expense; consequently,

getting ahead is scorned. When the individual's gain is the community's loss, the community must prohibit individual initiative and entrepreneurship. Peasants try to hide any economic gain they may accumulate, rather than engage in socially disapproved consumption (such as spending money on school tuition or home improvements).

Moreover, the Image of Limited Good leads a peasant to see "little or no relationship between work and production techniques on the one hand, and the acquisition of wealth on the other. Rather, wealth is seen by villagers in the same light as land: present, circumscribed by absolute limits, and having no relationship to work. One works to eat, but not to create wealth."[45] In the zero-sum view, wealth can be divided up and redistributed, but not created.

This perceived scarcity of resources leads peasants to gossip about or curse community members who are seen as getting more than their fair share of wealth. In order to avoid discrimination and ill treatment, community members who do outperform their fellows seek to expend their resources in a socially acceptable way. Hence the development of the fiesta system, which provides a legitimate and face-saving way for the successful peasant to exchange his wealth (which is envied rather than respected) for prestige (earned through cofradia service and fiesta sponsorship). As one observer puts it, "the system takes from those who have, in order to make all men have-nots. By liquidating the surpluses, it makes all men rich in sacred experience but poor in earthly goods."[46]

The dynamics of the fiesta system are stronger the more isolated the peasant community, for the isolation reinforces the sense of a fixed universe of resources. When outside contact is possible, and opportunities for making money in other locales exist, the accumulation of wealth resulting from such endeavors is more socially acceptable. In this context, the individual's gain is not seen as coming at the community's expense. However, success in cultivating and exploiting such outside economic activities is perceived to be largely a matter of luck or fate. The predominance of treasure-finding themes in peasant folklore reflects this idea: luck or destiny, rather than hard work, energy, innovation, or thrift, allows some individuals to prosper.[47]

Consequently, according to Foster, in traditional peasant societies "hard work and thrift are moral qualities of only the slightest functional value."[48] This is a provocative insight for neo-Weberian scholars, for it suggests that the development of qualities associated with the Protestant ethic (asceticism, hard work, frugality) are not the ones most related to economic advancement in peasant societies. Foster argues:

> The Anglo-Saxon virtue of hard work and thrift seen as leading to economic success are meaningless in peasant society. Horatio Alger not only is not praiseworthy, but he emerges as a positive fool, a clod who not

knowing the score labors blindly against hopeless conditions. The gambler, instead, is more properly laudable, worthy of emulation and adulation. If fate is the only way in which success can be obtained, the prudent and thoughtful man is the one who seeks ways in which to maximize his luck-position. He looks for the places in which good fortune is most apt to strike, and tries to be there. This, I think, explains the interest in lotteries in underdeveloped countries. The man who goes without lunch, and fails to buy shoes for his children in order to buy the weekly ticket, is not a ne'er-do-well; he is the Horatio Alger of his society who is doing what he feels most likely to advance his position . . . The odds are against him, but it is the *only* way he knows in which to work toward success.[49]

Indeed, in the peasant conception, the gambler exhibits what David McClelland calls a high "need for achievement."[50] Since other avenues for expressing that need to achieve (e.g., entrepreneurial behavior, investment in innovation, aggressive profit-seeking) are foreclosed in peasant society, gambling is a likely (and socially acceptable) display of initiative.[51]

This implies that development, rather than being associated first and foremost with Weber's Protestant ethic, will be correlated with escape from a fatalistic worldview; assent to the idea of an open, rather than closed universe; and acceptance of innovation, individual initiative, and income inequalities. In Foster's opinion, the principal task of developers is to help change the peasant's "view of his social and economic universe, away from an Image of Limited Good toward that of expanding opportunity in an open system, so that he can feel safe in displaying initiative."[52]

### Escaping the Folk Catholic Mentality

To the degree that Protestant conversion leads to the adoption of the new attitudes and behaviors Foster identifies as crucial, it is likely to improve peasants' socioeconomic prospects. Several studies of Protestants in Guatemala have concluded that conversion is correlated with rejection of traditional Cristo-pagan beliefs. (My research, discussed in the following chapters, also affirms this.) Moreover, in some instances, conversion not only signifies a rejection of the old beliefs but also an embrace of new attitudes conducive to economic advancement. The findings of a variety of studies (some already referred to in the previous two chapters) are discussed below.

*Rejection of Traditional Beliefs*    While conversion to Protestantism does not lead every convert to reject previously held traditional beliefs, studies show that converts' acceptance of old dogmas does erode over time. In particular, common beliefs about the calendrical system, the inhabitation of inanimate objects by spiritual forces, and the necessity of performing "permission" rituals before harvesting and planting are renounced.

In a comprehensive and fascinating study of Indian worldviews in Panajachel, Guatemala, Tax and Hinshaw concluded that Protestant-ism had a marked influence upon belief patterns.[53] Tax had studied Indian beliefs in the 1930s and 1940s, concluding that the Mayan worldview was animistic and that the religion's basic beliefs (about sorcery, the strength of blood, the ability of animals to talk, about unlucky days, and so forth) were widely shared by young and old alike. Tax and Hinshaw revisited Panajachel a generation later and discov-ered that many traditional beliefs remained strong—except among vil-lagers who had completed a certain level of education or who had converted to Evangelical faith.[54] Traditional beliefs, they reported, had measurably eroded among Protestants:

> Protestants are questioning the interpretation of dreams as the wander-ings of the spirit . . . [they] do not conceive of the spirit as permeating one's possessions and body as pervasively as do traditionals. . . . Protes-tants are less concerned over the danger of imitating the dead, and, in part because Protestants question the concept of strong days and hours, they are less worried about the vulnerability of the living to molestation by spirits at such times. . . . The concept of a predestined length of life is questioned by almost half the Protestants interviewed but is universally accepted by the traditionals.[55]

Similarly, in their ambitious study of worldview and development in ten Guatemalan towns, James Sexton and Clyde Woods found that Protestantism was negatively correlated with acceptance of traditional beliefs.[56] In addition, Protestants' rejection of animism was paralleled by their rejection of the fatalism common in folk Catholic circles: the same study showed a negative correlation between Protestantism and fatalism. Specifically, Protestants rejected the idea that a person born with good luck will have success in life and that a person born with bad luck can do nothing to change it.[57] In another study focusing on just two towns, Sexton found similar results.[58]

*Acceptance of Change and Innovation*   With the erosion of tradi-tional beliefs has come the emergence of more favorable attitudes toward change and innovation. The folk Catholic system exalted tradi-tion. And, in terms of community social structure, the cofradia system ensured that village elders held the positions of greatest influence and authority. This reinforced traditional customs and cast suspicion on innovation. The growth of Protestantism (among other variables) has contributed to the decline of the traditional cofradia system.[59] As an-thropologist Benjamin Paul explains, this change has slowly reduced deference to age and traditional authority, "thus increasing receptivity to innovation."[60]

*Acceptance of Inequalities, Profit, and Personal Initiative and Ambition*   In the study on Panajachel, Tax and Hinshaw noted that with the rise of Protestantism came a greater acceptance of wealth accumulation and less emphasis on (nonmaterial) social prestige earned through service in the civil-religious hierarchy and fiesta sponsorship.

> Formerly, when cofradia service was obligatory and [was] the primary basis of allocating status and authority in the community, the naming of the wealthier men to the offices involving major expenses prevented accumulation of wealth sufficient to expand the economic base of the community. With the expanded economic opportunities [that had come to Panajachel by the late 1960s] the hierarchy of values slowly has altered, acquisitive and entrepreneurial values basic to the culture gradually gaining ascendancy over traditional norms of conspicuous consumption in fiesta ritual and cofradia service.[61]

Tax and Hinshaw went on to say that the cofradias had not been eliminated totally by the 1970s. The town elders, however, were no longer able to expect service from more than a "small and diminishing minority" of citizens because of the inroads made by Protestantism and Catholic Action—groups that provided a religious exemption from cofradia participation.[62]

The Protestant creed also exempts individuals from the use of personal income on community ritual expenses; indeed, it condemns these expenses as wasteful. According to Annis, while Mayan Catholics morally reject the "accumulation of wealth . . . in favor of reinvestment in a kind of social currency negotiable only at the village level," Protestants encourage a "personal rather than collective use of wealth."[63] He continues: "Ideological rationalization of personal gain is not the only—and probably not the most important—incentive to conversion; yet, by and large, Protestants do seem better geared for and more motivated than Catholics to pursue lifestyles that will either lift them out of poverty or protect hard-won financial gain."[64]

Sexton's research reinforces this idea, for he found "support for McClelland's (1961) postulate that Protestants in Latin America feel a greater need to achieve because they see themselves as a disadvantaged but superior minority."[65] In his research with Woods, Sexton discovered that Protestants, for example, had higher occupational aspirations than Catholics.[66]

## Recapitulation

It is clear that several elements of the Cristo-pagan worldview inhibit socioeconomic progress. The crowded Mayan cosmology of capricious and often malevolent deities is not conducive to viewing the universe as rational and decipherable. This fact inhibits the possibilities for planning, scientific inquiry, and the development of technology. Traditional Mayan animism leaves humans at the mercy of nature, unable to harness nature's forces for human benefit. Rather, fatalism and fear prevail: individuals do not believe they can influence their own destiny and must busy themselves with a plethora of appeasement rituals designed to protect them from the harm inflicted by supernatural powers. Mayans who sense the possibilities for change and progress find themselves trapped in an intellectual and institutional structure that prohibits innovation. Bucking traditional customs is viewed as immoral. Showing too much individual initiative is viewed as a threat to the egalitarian community whose resources are perceived as fixed. Similarly, the overt and covert sanctions against economic inequalities (such as the fiesta system and witchcraft, respectively) mean that entrepreneurship and profit-seeking are discouraged rather than legitimated.

Obviously, the reasons for underdevelopment among Guatemalan Mayans are many and complicated, and I do not wish to imply that the explanation for such stagnation derives exclusively from the traditional Cristo-pagan worldview. Misguided economic policies at the national level, corruption and mismanagement, persecution of and discrimination against the Maya, skewed patterns of land distribution, lack of infrastructure, and the absence of a strong educational system are all important and contributory factors. Moreover, not all Mayans accept the traditional worldview, and even those who do may not apply all the logical behavioral and attitudinal outworkings of their beliefs in their day-to-day behavior. Throughout Guatemala, individual Mayans who accept the tenets of belief described in this chapter may nevertheless pursue modern medicine, try agricultural innovations, or refuse to serve in the cofradias. In short, there is not always a one-to-one correspondence between belief and action.

Nonetheless, at a general level, Cristo-pagan beliefs are more likely to act as inhibitors of economic progress than as facilitators. As the studies surveyed in this and the previous two chapters demonstrate, culture does matter. While there is much that is rich, beautiful, and laudable in traditional Mayan culture, it also includes beliefs, values, and habits that hinder human development. To the extent that Evangelical conversion leads to a rejection of the Cristo-pagan worldview and the attitudes and behaviors it engenders, prospects for socio-economic progress improve.

# PART II

# ORTHODOXY
# AND
# ECONOMIC
# TRANSFORMATION

FOUR

# Worldview and Socioeconomic Development

## The Evidence Explained

*Pentecostal communities have become havens and way stations in the journey up the socioeconomic ladder. They teach empowerment, a sense of worth, new meaning for life, new disciplines for work, new models for family, [and] new skills for articulate communication and group organization. . . .The cultural impact of the new [E]vangelicalism is unquestionable.*

Jorge E. Maldonado[1]

As the studies described in the previous chapters attest, anecdotal accounts of the positive consequences of conversion to Evangelicalism are fairly easy to find. Such reports are often colorful and express the multifaceted experiences of converts. Conversion is decidedly personal and impassioned; each convert has his or her own story to tell. While each is unique, nonetheless, many stories are similar. Chapter 5 describes some of the common themes emerging from conversations with converts throughout rural Guatemala. I include this material to put a human face on the quantitative data presented in this chapter.

While the reports from the field are colorful, they can also be scattershot. A powerful sentiment exists in academia that anecdotal accounts may be rich with description but they lack generalizability. Formal empirical study involving statistical analysis is extolled as a more sophisticated way of understanding social phenomena. This emphasis may be somewhat overstated since qualitative and quantitative methods each have their place.

To complement the anecdotal evidence gathered through field research, I developed a formal public opinion poll of 1,000 rural Guatemalans. This chapter summarizes the results from my Worldview and Development Survey (henceforth W&D Survey). The W&D Survey findings provide considerable evidence for the correlation of orthodox Christianity with various indicators of economic development and reinforce the anecdotal testimonies described in chapter 5. Since the W&D Survey was cross-sectional, not longitudinal, strictly speaking, it provides evidence only of the *association* of religious worldview and various development-related variables. The data cannot prove cause-and-effect relationships between conversion to orthodox Christianity and various indicators of improved socioeconomic well-being. In light of the consistent weight of evidence uncovered through my fieldwork, however, and various ethnographic studies (such as some of those profiled in chapter 3), I have chosen to employ causal language in this chapter.

It is possible that all the orthodox Christian respondents in the survey held various development-enhancing attitudes before their conversion or had already attained higher standards of living before changing their religious worldview—possible, but not likely. For one thing, the testimonies related to me by informants in each of the surveyed communities suggest that conversion came first and was then followed by improved socioeconomic well-being. For another, studies of the growth of Protestantism emphasize that most converts come from the poorest, most marginalized sectors of society. The results of the W&D Survey indicate that orthodox Evangelicals consistently outperform adherents of other religious worldviews in various objective measurements of development. They are also more likely than other people to embrace certain development-enhancing attitudes (e.g., openness to change, rejection of fatalism, etc.). Frequently, the statistically significant differences among worldview groups remain when the relationship between worldview and a particular aspect of development (e.g., attitude toward modern medicine) is controlled for the influence of possible intervening variables—such as ethnicity, income, occupation, and years of schooling.

Guatemalans of similar socioeconomic status but different religious convictions express different opinions on questions in the survey related to fate, change, modern medicine, initiative, merit and equality, and profit. They also show different levels of economic performance as measured by the physical conditions of their homes, their ability to read and write and to speak Spanish, and, in some instances, by their income. What all this suggests is that the combined evidence of my qualitative and quantitative research permits some assertions about the independent causal influence of conversion to orthodox Christianity on economic life.

This chapter is divided into seven sections that describe the purpose of the W&D Survey, the survey instrument, the sampled population, and the principal findings. Here I concentrate on the survey's conclusions regarding the relationship between religious worldview and socioeconomic development. In chapters 6 and 7, I review the survey results with an eye toward the connection between religious worldview and the nurturing of democratic-capitalism.

## Purpose and Scope of the Survey

The W&D Survey explores the attitudinal and behavioral differences among persons of varying worldviews. The study included 1,000 Guatemalans residing in five villages. It examined four principal questions: (1) What variables are related to objective measurements of economic development? (2) What aspects of religious life, if any, are correlated with those key variables (e.g., nominal affiliation, level of integration, religious activism, doctrinal orthodoxy)? (3) Do adherents to different religious worldviews vary in their attitudes toward democracy and in their personal levels of civic participation? (4) Do adherents to different religious worldviews differ in their attitudes toward the free-market system, and does one group legitimate the norms animating this system more than the others? The first two of these four questions are addressed in this chapter; the latter two are discussed in chapters 6 and 7, respectively.

## The Survey Instrument

The W&D Survey included nearly a hundred variables and was divided into eight sections.[2] The survey instrument used during the interview, while including all the questions described in this chapter, did not ask them in the order presented here (see Appendix A for a complete copy of the questionnaire showing the order in which questions were asked). One section gathered demographic information—age, gender, ethnicity, residence, civil status, and household size. A second collected information regarding the respondent's educational profile. This section included questions on the number of formal years of schooling the respondent had attained, the kind of school (if any) the respondent's children attended, whether the respondent could read and write, and the respondent's and spouse's level of Spanish-speaking proficiency. A third section explored the respondent's work life. People were asked about their occupation and whether they grew any crops. Those who did farm were asked what sorts of crops they grew, whether they used fertilizer, and if so, what kind. Respondents were also asked what their father's principal occupation had been.

The fourth section gathered data on the independent variable—religious life—and was lengthy and somewhat complicated. Several questions were asked of each of the respondents. Each respondent was asked his or her religious affiliation: Catholic, Catholic Action, Evangelical, "Other" (including Jehovah's Witnesses, Mormons, and other non-Christian religions), or "None." Respondents were also asked for their opinion on eternal life. The exact wording of the question follows:[3]

> *People hold different opinions about different religious matters like what happens after we die. I'm going to read you some statements that people sometimes make, and I'd like you to tell me which one of the statements best reflects your own opinion. First I have four statements we sometimes hear about life after death. Which one best reflects your own opinion?*
>
>     *1. There is no life after death.*
>     *2. There is life after death—but what we do in this life has no bearing on it.*
>     *3. Heaven is the reward for those who earn it by their good life.*
>     *4. Jesus Christ is the only way to eternal life.*

Every respondent was asked his or her opinion on the purpose of religion:

> *Now here are three statements that have to do with what people sometimes think about religion. Which one most closely reflects your own opinion about religion?*
>
>     *1. Religion is a guide to help people get to heaven.*
>     *2. Religion is a guide for transforming society.*
>     *3. Religion not only helps people get to heaven, it also helps them change and improve their way of living here on earth.*

Finally, all respondents were asked to agree or disagree with a series of statements expressing common, traditional folk Catholic or Cristo-pagan beliefs. These included, among other things, items such as whether or not the respondent believed it necessary to make costumbres before planting or harvesting a field; whether or not the respondent sought the aid of curanderos (shamans/witch doctors) when ill; whether or not he or she believed that the spirits of dead ancestors or the "earth god" could inflict harm on the living; and whether praying to saints was wrong.

In addition to these questions, respondents who gave their affiliation as Catholic, Catholic Action, or Evangelical were each asked a series of specialized follow-up questions designed specifically for their particular group. Catholics, for example, were asked whether they had ever served in a cofradia, whether and how often they made costumbre, whether they attended mass on specially prescribed days, and whether they tried hard to follow all the teachings of the Roman Catholic church. *Accionístas* were asked whether they had ever been catechists, whether they were members of a Bible study or prayer group, and how faithfully they obeyed the teaching of the Roman Catholic church. Evangelicals were asked what their denominational affiliation was, whether they belonged to a prayer or Bible study group, when they had converted to Protestantism, and whether they tithed. Members of all three groups were asked how often they attended religious services and what their parents' religious affiliation had been. (For the exact wording of all these items, see Appendix A.)

A fifth section of the W&D Survey briefly probed respondents' attitudes toward democracy and gathered information on their personal participation in civil society. The sixth section explored respondents' attitudes toward the free-market economic system. (For an extended discussion of these issues, see chapters 6 and 7.)

The seventh section of the survey included a series of questions probing attitudes on several development-enhancing variables posited by various scholars (such as those profiled in chapters 1 and 2). These included attitudes toward work, achievement, fate, education, and innovation. Respondents were asked, for example, whether laziness was a sin, whether a person could overcome his fate, whether change was desirable, and whether children should be sent to school or kept at home to help with domestic and farm chores.

Finally, the eighth section gathered some information relating to the respondents' objective level of socioeconomic development. Each respondent was asked to choose the range most representative of his or her estimated annual income (e.g., under 3,000 quetzales, 3,001–6,000 quetzales (Q), etc.). Additionally, interviewers were asked to answer several exit questions after concluding each interview (and leaving the interview site) in order to shed more light on the respondent's standard of living. Interviewers noted the type of roof and floor that the respondent's dwelling had and whether or not the home had electricity and a latrine.

## Methodology and Sample

The interviewing for the W&D Survey was conducted in June 1993 by a private Guatemalan research firm, which was responsible for hiring, training, and supervising the interviewers, all of whom were bilingual (i.e., fluent in Spanish and in the indigenous language spoken in the region where they were gathering data). Most of the interviewers had a college-level education and had worked for this firm previously. Each interviewer had a regional supervisor, and each supervisor reported to the national project director, who served as the "on-site" manager and worked closely with me. A pretest was conducted in early June that revealed few significant problems with the survey instrument; following it, formal interviewing of individuals began in the Guatemalan communities selected for study: La Tinta (a hamlet in the Polochic Valley in the department of Alta Verapaz); Uspantan (a medium-sized village in north-central Quiche); Almolonga and Zunil (two small neighboring communities outside Quetzaltenango in the western highlands); and Chimaltenango (a mid-sized town approximately one hour by bus from Guatemala City). Two hundred interviews were conducted in each community.[4]

## Demographic Overview

The sample divided fairly evenly between male and female respondents (55.8 percent and 44.2 percent, respectively). The median age of the respondents was 34. Slightly over 60 percent were married; 18.5 percent lived with a companion in an informal arrangement known as being *unidos*. Families had about three children on average living in the home. More than half of the respondents had an annual income of under Q3,000 (roughly $572). Table 4-1 summarizes the principal demographic characteristics of the sample.

TABLE 4-1 Demographic Characteristics of the Sample (*N* = 1,000)

| Characteristic | No. of Respondents (%) |
|---|---|
| Gender | |
| Male | 55.8 |
| Female | 44.2 |
| Marital status | |
| Presently married | 62.6 |
| Living together *unidos* | 18.5 |
| Widowed | 3.7 |
| Divorced/separated | 1.8 |
| Single/never married | 13.4 |
| Income | |
| Q3,000 and less | 49.1 |
| Q3,001–Q6,000 | 27.7 |
| Q6,001–Q12,000 | 17.5 |
| Q12,001–Q24,000 | 4.3 |
| Q24,001–Q36,000 | .9 |
| More than Q36,001 | .5 |
| Ethnicity | |
| Indigenous | 70.3 |
| Ladino | 29.2 |
| Religious affiliation | |
| Catholic | 49.9 |
| Evangelical | 43.8 |
| Catholic Action | 1.9 |
| Other | 1.5 |
| No religion | 2.9 |
| Literacy | 70.4 |
| Spanish-speaking ability | 86.7 |
| Education | |
| None | 25.3 |
| Early elementary | 26.4 |
| Late elementary | 24.6 |
| Junior high school | 11.4 |
| High school and above | 12.3 |

SOURCE: W&D Survey, Guatemala, June 1993.

While the sample was somewhat representative of the Guatemalan population as a whole, there were at least two important exceptions that resulted from the deliberate design of the interviewing strategy. First, the sample overrepresented indigenous respondents. Most of the sampled communities were in the *altiplano*, which is dominated by *indígenas*. Second, the sample overrepresented Evangelicals. While estimates of the size of Guatemala's Evangelical community nationally range from 20 to 35 percent of the population, fully 44 percent of the W&D Survey respondents were Evangelicals.[5]

## Literacy and Spanish-speaking Ability

The high literacy and bilingualism rates among the sample population were surprising. Of those sampled, 70.3 percent claimed the ability to read and write, but there was no procedure in the survey itself for evaluating this claim.[6] The rates of bilingualism were also higher than expected. Nearly 85 percent of the respondents said they spoke and understood Spanish well enough to understand a Spanish language radio broadcast. I elected not to test the accuracy of the respondents' claims by asking them to perform any sort of Spanish-speaking or reading test. It is unlikely, though, that the 85 percent figure is grossly exaggerated. Interviewers were asked to get a sense of the respondents' Spanish proficiency and could conduct the interview wholly in Spanish, partly in Spanish and partly in the indigenous language, or wholly in the indigenous language. Eighty-five percent of the interviews were conducted principally in Spanish. Moreover, the interviewers were asked, after they had left the home site, to evaluate and note each respondent's proficiency in Spanish. They judged that 82 percent of the respondents who spoke with them were "very" or "somewhat" proficient in Spanish.

## Socioeconomic Status

In terms of socioeconomic status, many of the respondents in the sample were poor by almost any definition of that term. Just under half earned an annual income of under 3,000 quetzales (or roughly $572 a year). Many lived in small, two-room cottages with earthen floors, and about 16 percent did not have electricity. Eighty percent of the respondents said that they grew some crops; for many, farming was an activity undertaken in addition to their regular work. In terms of occupation, 10.3 percent of the sample were *commerciántes* (traders/businessmen); nearly 10 percent were artisans; 33.5 percent were housewives; and 22 percent were full-time farmers. Many other occupations were also represented: carpenters, taxi drivers, agricultural day laborers, merchants, clerks, government employees, construction workers, and some professionals (accountants, teachers, lawyers). In terms of education, 25.3 percent of the respondents had never attended school; 51.7 percent had three or fewer years of education; and only 25 percent had six or more years of formal education.

## Beginning the Analysis

### *Which Variables Were Related to Socioeconomic Development?*

The survey employed two general, objective measurements of economic development: income and status of dwelling. As previously mentioned, respondents' income was calculated in ranges.

One of the principal findings of the survey was that rejection of traditional beliefs was clearly related to improved economic well-being as measured by income and status of dwelling. A score for each respondent was calculated on a seven-point Traditional Beliefs Index (TBI) to measure each respondent's level of acceptance of common animistic beliefs and customs. The seven items in the TBI included such questions as whether respondents visited the curandero when ill; whether they believed the earth god or angered ancestral spirits could harm them; whether they thought praying to the saints was wrong; whether they believed certain places (such as particular caves or hills) were sacred; and whether they believed it was necessary to make costumbre before cutting down a tree or planting a field. Respondents were given one point for each answer that suggested a retainment of the traditional belief or practice. They were then divided into three categories according to their scores—low, medium, and high—each category representing the extent to which respondents maintained traditional beliefs.

Respondents who scored low on the TBI (i.e., those who tended to reject traditional beliefs) had a higher average income than those who scored medium or high. Moreover, those who rejected traditional beliefs had a higher standard of living as measured by the physical status of their homes. For example, about 77 percent of the respondents who scored low on the TBI had a cement, rather than dirt, floor in their home. This compares with 64 percent of those who scored medium and 52 percent who scored high.

Ten other variables besides rejection of the traditional worldview were also correlated with economic development as measured by income and the physical status of the respondent's dwelling: (1) literacy; (2) the Spanish-speaking ability of the respondent; (3) the Spanish-speaking ability of the respondent's spouse; (4) "fate" (whether an individual can overcome what lies in his fate or luck); (5) "lazy" (whether laziness is a sin or the lazy person is born that way and cannot

TABLE 4-2 Variables Associated with
Economic Development as Measured by
Income and Physical Status of Dwelling

Rejection of traditional beliefs
Literacy
Spanish-speaking ability
Rejection of fatalism
Affirmation of personal achievement
Legitimation of a merit-based economy
Acceptance of innovation
Ethnicity (Ladino)
Years of education

SOURCE: W&D Survey, Guatemala, June 1993.

change); (6) "achieve" (whether people should try to do better economically than their parents); (7) "just economy" (whether a just economic
system is one in which everyone earns the same amount or one in which
people with higher skills earn more); (8) "change" (whether innovation
is desirable or it is better to do things the way they have always been
done); (9) "ethnicity" (indigenous or Ladino); and (10) years of education. These ten represent a mixture of "objective" items (e.g., ethnicity,
years of schooling, literacy) and "subjective" items (e.g., attitudes
toward change, fate, initiative). Table 4-2 lists the variables in the W&D
Survey found to be associated with economic development.

The survey results suggest that literacy and Spanish-speaking ability
facilitate an individual's participation in the formal economy and improve his or her economic prospects. Spanish-speaking respondents
were more likely to live in better homes than non-Spanish-speaking
ones. Not surprisingly, a respondent's ethnicity and years of formal
education were also correlated with income and status of dwelling.

But the data show that cultural attitudes, too, are important as pre-
dictors of improved socioeconomic well-being. In the survey, attitudes
regarding "fate" or "destiny," for example, were important. Respondents who said people could overcome their fate or luck and influence
their own future scored, on average, 2.48 on a 3-point "Standard of
Living Index," compared with a 2.25 mean score for those who said
people could not rise above their fate. (A score of 3 on the Standard of
Living Index indicated that a respondent lived in a home with electricity, which had a cement floor and a latrine.) Answers to this question
were also correlated with income. Similarly, opinions about laziness
were related to development. Those who rejected the idea that lazy
people could not change their fate had higher average incomes than
those who accepted this notion. Attitudes toward achievement were
also significant. Those who thought it best to try to improve on the

previous generation's accomplishments scored higher on the Standard of Living Index and had higher incomes. Respondents who believed that a just economy is one that is merit based, as opposed to one that assures everyone an equal income, also scored higher on these measures.

In a few instances, attitudinal variables were correlated with income but not with status of dwelling, or vice versa. Whether respondents believed that they should send their children to school or keep them at home to work in the fields, for example, was correlated with income (those who affirmed children's education had higher average incomes), but not with status of dwelling. What respondents thought about the legitimacy of profit was related to the Standard of Living Index but not to income. Those who said that an economically successful man must have robbed or cheated his neighbors in some way lived in meaner conditions than those who rejected this statement.

## What Role Does Religion Play?

Having determined which variables were critical in shedding light on differential economic progress, I then sought to determine which, if any, aspects of religious life were associated with these key items. Few statistically significant differences between Protestants and Catholics emerged when only nominal affiliation was used to distinguish between these two groups. The only dramatic difference between Catholics and Evangelicals (when only nominal affiliation was considered) was that Evangelicals were more likely to reject traditional religious beliefs. This is graphically displayed in Table 4-3.

TABLE 4-3 Acceptance/Rejection of Traditional Beliefs by Religious Affiliation ($N = 937$)

| Belief | Evangelical (%) | Catholic (%) |
|---|---|---|
| Agree that certain places are sacred | 16.2 | 40.5 |
| Think praying to saints is wrong | 55.7 | 34.7 |
| Reject idea that costumbre is necessary before planting | 68.5 | 51.5 |
| Reject idea that ancestors' souls can punish the living | 75.8 | 64.3 |
| Reject idea that "earth god" when angered can punish the living | 72.1 | 58.5 |
| Reject practice of seeking aid from curandero when ill | 79.0 | 57.0 |

SOURCE: W&D Survey, Guatemala, June 1993.

All differences are significant at $p = .05$.

For example, 79 percent of Evangelicals said that they did not use the services of curanderos when they needed medical attention, compared with only 57 percent of Catholics. Among Evangelicals, 72.1 percent, versus 58.5 percent of Catholics, rejected the idea that the "earth god" could punish people. Similarly, while 75.8 percent of Evangelicals rejected the notion that ancestors' souls could punish their living relatives, only 64.3 percent of Catholics did. Evangelicals were also more likely to reject the idea that making costumbre is necessary before planting: 68.5 percent of them, compared with 51.5 percent of Catholics, thought this unnecessary. The survey also showed that 55.7 percent of Evangelicals thought that praying to the saints is wrong, compared with only 34.7 percent of Catholics. And while 40.5 percent of Catholics believed that certain places (such as particular caves or hills) are sacred, only 16.2 percent of Evangelicals affirmed this.[7] Since scores on the TBI were closely correlated with objective measures of development, Protestant conversion, by influencing some converts to reject some or all of their previous traditional beliefs and customs, indirectly encourages converts' socioeconomic betterment.

Beyond this difference in TBI scores, no statistically significant differences between Catholics and Evangelicals emerged on such key variables as literacy; Spanish-speaking ability; years of education; or attitudes toward fate, change, justice, equality, and the legitimacy of profit and initiative. Clearly, finer distinctions among Catholics and Protestants were necessary to shed light on the possible connections between religion and socioeconomic development.

The W&D Survey provided a way of getting at those distinctions by including some 20 items that pertained to religious life. These included such things as religious affiliation (including, for Protestants, denominational affiliation); religious intensity (respondents were asked to rank the personal importance of their religious faith); beliefs about life after death; religious activism and integration (whether respondents were members of a prayer or Bible study group, and how often they attended religious services); charitable giving; a question about the purpose of religion; and a series of questions (those that composed the TBI) designed to measure the respondents' acceptance or incorporation of common, traditional Mayan religious beliefs and practices into their own belief system. These items allowed me to probe more deeply into the religious life of the respondents, separating the orthodox from the unorthodox, the serious from the nominal, the theologically sophisticated from the uneducated believers, and the congregants "embedded" in their faith community from the "Lone Ranger" types.

Using these various items in the questionnaire, I constructed a new composite variable called *cosmovision* (the Spanish term for "worldview") to categorize as many respondents as possible into different worldview groups. This variable then became my primary independent variable used in a lengthy series of statistical procedures.[8] The cosmovision variable grouped respondents into six general worldview categories: Orthodox Evangelicals, Moderate Evangelicals, Weak Evangelicals, Orthodox Catholics, Traditional Catholics, and Cristo-pagans. Orthodox Evangelicals were defined as those who scored low on the TBI (i.e., they rejected most animistic and pantheistic beliefs) and who gave the most traditional or exclusivist answer to the question in the survey about life after death ("Jesus Christ is the only way to eternal life"). Moderate Evangelicals were Protestants who scored medium on the TBI; Weak Evangelicals were those who scored high. Cristo-pagans (they could also be called "folk Catholics") were the least orthodox Catholics—they scored high on the TBI and failed to give the orthodox Christian answer to the question on eternal life. Orthodox Catholics were respondents who listed Catholic or Catholic Action as their religious affiliation, scored low on the TBI, and gave the exclusivist answer to the heaven question. (In other research, this group of morally strict Catholics has been labeled as Catholic hidden converts to Evangelicalism; see the discussion of Liliana Goldin's work in chapter 5.) Traditional Catholics were those who scored medium on the TBI and gave one of the two most traditional responses to the question on eternal life ("Jesus Christ is the only way" or "heaven is the reward for those who earn it by their good behavior in this life").

Employing this classification scheme, I was able to categorize two thirds of the respondents in the survey; 344 individuals could not be classified using these various criteria. This number of unclassified respondents included respondents who had no religious affiliation or who belonged to such groups as the Jehovah's Witnesses and the Mormons. It also included a number of so-called inconsistent responders. These included Catholics who scored high on the TBI and yet gave the most orthodox answer to the heaven question and Evangelicals who scored low on the TBI and yet gave highly unorthodox answers to the question on eternal life (such as "there is no life after death" or "what we do in this life has no bearing on life after death").

The essential criteria dividing respondents into the different worldview groups was religious doctrine. I did not use information about other aspects of respondents' religious lives (such as their charitable giving or attendance at religious services) as criteria in establishing the cosmovision categories. One reason for this was the problem of keeping a usable number of subjects in each category for the purposes of analysis. Each time additional criteria were used to make finer distinctions among respondents, the number of people who could be neatly grouped together in coherent categories decreased. But even more important, and as later analysis in this chapter reveals, several of these other aspects of religious life had few significant, *direct* effects on respondents' behaviors and opinions. Having a broad range of information about the respondents' religious lives was useful and shed light on a variety of matters (some of which will be discussed later). Still, orthodoxy of Christian conviction, more than nominal affiliation or religious activism or the social dynamics of religion, was the key issue in explaining socioeconomic differences among respondents.

## The Principal Findings

On the basis of studies conducted by others in Guatemala and on the culture-and-development relationships posited by authors such as Weber and Harrison, I began my empirical research with a fairly simple model, which hypothesized the connections between religious life and the prospects for economic development. My working theory ran something like this: conversion to Protestantism would be positively related to the rejection of certain traditional, animistic beliefs (such as those concerning nature and the supernatural). Conversion would also lead to the acceptance of certain development-enhancing attitudes previously posited by researchers, such as a positive view of hard work; an appreciation for change and innovation; a deemphasis on fate; a preference for modern forms of wealth over traditional forms; and a legitimation of initiative, profit, and accumulation of wealth. In turn, this rejection of traditional beliefs and acceptance of critical development-enhancing attitudes would be positively related to actual objective measures of socioeconomic progress, such as income and standard of living.

While this simple model proved to be relatively accurate, it did have to be refined somewhat in light of the findings from the W&D Survey. First, the survey results pointed to the importance (for one's prospects for development) of integration into the formal economy. Three variables representing this integration—the Spanish-speaking ability of the respondent and the respondent's spouse, and literacy—were consistently related to various measurements of economic progress.

Second, the research revealed that the cluster of development-enhancing variables that I had posited as related to development had to be modified. Some of the proposed variables were indeed significant, but not all.

Third, the data emphasize the critical importance of going beyond nominal categories when religion and socioeconomic development are considered. Knowing whether a particular Guatemalan is Catholic or Protestant is not nearly as important as knowing *what kind* of Catholic or Protestant he or she is—at least in terms of assessing socioeconomic prospects. "Catholic" and "Protestant" are insufficient categories for evaluating the distinctions between Guatemalans; new lines of differentiation that cut across nominal religious affiliation are required. For lack of better terms, the important distinction is between Christian orthodoxy and a syncretistic Christianity (i.e., one that incorporates traditional, Mayan, Cristo-pagan beliefs). The results of the W&D Survey clearly indicate that orthodox Catholics (i.e., those who adopt a biblical worldview and reject the traditional Cristo-pagan worldview) exhibit, on the whole, the same patterns hypothesized for Protestants. The findings also reveal that syncretistic or weak Protestants do not improve their prospects for development in the ways their orthodox co-congregants do.

Clearly, the W&D Survey results provide substantial support for the hypothesis that a person's prospects for development are influenced by his or her religious worldview. In most instances, for example, orthodox Evangelicals consistently outscored members of other religious worldviews on the attitudinal variables most associated with favorable development prospects. Adherents to Cristo-paganism, in contrast, consistently showed the least inclination toward the kinds of orientations related to development and consistently scored the lowest on the various objective measures of socioeconomic development. In this sense, it is fair to assert that conversion to Evangelical Christianity—when that conversion leads to a substantial rejection of old, animist ways—is correlated with the adoption of attitudes and practices conducive to development. However, when *Catholics* adopt a biblically informed worldview and turn from Cristo-pagan ways, they *too* adopt the development-enhancing orientations that bode well for future economic prospects. Moreover, in many instances, the objective, current development status of orthodox Evangelicals *and* orthodox Catholics is better than that of the Cristo-pagans and highly syncretized or unorthodox Evangelicals.

The relationships between religious worldview and various key dependent variables (literacy, Spanish-speaking ability, a positive attitude toward change and toward education, a rejection of fatalism, and so forth) were at times affected by intervening variables. The most important was ethnicity, but income and education were also factors in some cases. However, the influence of such intervening variables was not often such as to negate the independent influence of the variable cosmovision.[9] The accumulation of correlations between cosmovision and a host of key variables, at varying levels of statistical significance, suggests at a minimum that religious worldview had a serious and consistent influence.

### "Integration" into the Formal Economy

In terms of the important "integration" variables—literacy and Spanish proficiency—noteworthy differences between orthodox and syncretistic respondents were evident. As shown in Table 4-4, fully 84.7 percent of orthodox Evangelicals were literate, compared with only 58.6 percent

TABLE 4-4 Literacy Rates by Worldview Type (N = 632)[1]

| Literate | Orthodox Evangelical (%) | Moderate Evangelical (%) | Weak Evangelical (%) | Cristo-Pagan (%) | Orthodox Catholic (%) | Traditional Catholic (%) | Row Total (N) |
|---|---|---|---|---|---|---|---|
| Yes | 84.7 | 64.9 | 59.0 | 58.6 | 72.5 | 75.7 | 440 |
| No | 15.3 | 35.1 | 41.0 | 41.4 | 27.5 | 24.3 | 192 |
| Column total (N) | 144 | 111 | 100 | 116 | 91 | 70 | |

SOURCE: W&D Survey, Guatemala, June 1993.

[1]Significant at $p$ = .000

87

of Cristo-pagans. Orthodox Evangelicals were also more likely than Cristo-pagans to be proficient in Spanish, though only when indigenous respondents exclusively were considered. (Ethnicity is an important consideration in the integration variables, as should be expected. Among Ladinos, differences in worldview did not substantially affect Spanish-speaking ability, since Spanish was usually their first language anyway.) To summarize these data, I constructed an Integration Index composed of respondents' answers to the questions on literacy, Spanish proficiency, and the Spanish-speaking ability of the spouse. Among orthodox Evangelicals, 64.6 percent received the highest possible score on the index, compared to only 40.5 percent of Cristo-pagans.

### Occupation and Social Mobility

There were few dramatic differences in occupational status among the worldview groups. I categorized the 30-some occupations listed by respondents into five categories according to the hypothesized earning-capacity of the occupation. The categories were: very low, low, medium, medium-high, and high. The occupations listed by most respondents fell into the low or very low paying categories. The only notable difference among worldview groups related to the highest category. More orthodox Evangelicals and Catholics were found in this category than Cristo-pagans and weak Evangelicals.

Respondents were also asked to report their father's principal occupation during the time when they were growing up. I classified these occupations into the same five-part scheme according to earnings capacity. Using these data, I attempted to measure social mobility by comparing the mean score of each worldview group's parents' occupations with the mean score of their own occupations. The results, though, were not illuminating, except to show that each group had improved on their parents' generation (i.e., more of the respondents were working in higher-paying jobs than their parents had). No particular worldview group significantly outperformed the others in terms of economic progress as measured by occupational achievements over the previous generation.

### Fatalism

Orthodox respondents were, however, more likely than syncretistic ones to reject the importance of fate or luck. About 75 percent of orthodox Evangelicals and 71 percent of orthodox Catholics affirmed the idea that people can overcome that which "lies in their destiny," while about 68 percent of Cristo-pagans agreed with this. Another item in the survey also sought to probe attitudes toward fatalism, but from a different angle. Respondents were asked whether they believed that laziness was a sin or that lazy people had been "born that way" and couldn't do anything to change this fate. The results of analysis on this question were the purest in terms of the hypothesized pattern: only about 19 percent of orthodox Evangelicals, and 27 percent of orthodox Catholics, accepted the idea that laziness was part of a person's fate, while more unorthodox respondents were far more likely to affirm this notion (fully 49.5 percent of Cristo-pagans and 46 percent of weak Evangelicals did).

## Status of Women

Not surprising, given the conclusions of researchers such as Brusco and Goldin (see chapter 2), among indigenous respondents, conversion to a more orthodox worldview appears to be correlated with an enhanced status for women. The W&D Survey revealed, for example, that orthodox Evangelical and orthodox Catholic women were more likely to be able to read and write than nonorthodox women. It found that 77 percent of orthodox Evangelical women and 66 percent of orthodox Catholic women were literate, compared with 47 percent of Cristo-pagan women. Orthodox Evangelical and Orthodox Catholic women were also more likely than Cristo-pagan women to be able to speak Spanish (the percentages were, respectively, 89.3, 86.4, and 68.6). The findings of this analysis did not conform perfectly to the anticipated pattern, however, since women in the weak Evangelical group showed a surprisingly high rate of Spanish proficiency.

## Innovation and Education

Worldview also seemed to influence respondents' beliefs about change and education. With regard to innovation, the expected pattern was evident: orthodox Evangelicals were the most likely to affirm the value of change, orthodox Catholics ran closely behind, and Cristo-pagans were the least likely to embrace innovation. When controlled for ethnicity, these patterns remained. In the case of attitudes toward schooling, the expected differences generally emerged and were statistically significant at the 99 percent confidence level when controlled for ethnicity. A majority (82.4 percent) of orthodox Evangelicals affirmed the importance of sending children to school rather than keeping them at home to help with farm and domestic duties, and the percentage was virtually identical for orthodox Catholics; meanwhile, fewer Cristo-pagans (68.2 percent) agreed with this idea.

### Christian Orthodoxy versus the Image of Limited Good

The survey results suggest that some proposed development-enhancing attitudes are more influential in affecting the prospects for socio-economic improvement in the Guatemalan context than others. Specifically, openness to innovation, emphasis on personal initiative, legitimation of profit and of a merit-based economy, and rejection of fatalism were the most influential attitudinal variables. These findings reinforce anthropologist George Foster's interpretation of the culture-and-development connection.

As noted in chapter 3, Foster argues that in the context of peasant communities, the most important cultural or worldview inhibitor of development is the peasants' strong attachment to the so-called Image of Limited Good—the belief that only a fixed quantity of desirable resources exists. The mindset fostered by this presupposition manifests itself in suspicion of personal initiative, innovation, and attempts to better oneself, as well as hostility toward economic inequalities, profit, and wealth accumulation. Foster asserts that the central task of development practitioners should be to encourage the adoption by peasants of an open system view of the universe rather than their closed system, "limited good" model. This cultural transformation, Foster argues, would then legitimize personal initiative, entrepreneurship, and income or opportunity inequalities, freeing people to pursue their ambitions without fear of societal disapproval.

Two items in the W&D Survey get to the heart of Foster's contentions—the questions probing attitudes toward profit and the definition of a just economy. In both instances, a respondent's religious worldview had some influence on his or her answers. Most respondents in the survey were sympathetic to the notion of profit, but the Orthodox respondents showed even greater support for it. Roughly 91 percent of orthodox Evangelicals and orthodox Catholics affirmed the legitimacy of profit by rejecting the idea that "a man who advances economically probably was successful because he robbed, cheated, or otherwise hurt people." By comparison, 83 percent of syncretistic Catholics and Evangelicals rejected the statement.

Some may argue that the respondent's level of income would affect these findings and that poor people would be more likely to be suspicious of profit. The differences among worldview groups remained, however, even when data on the poorest respondents—those earning less than 3,000 quetzales annually—were extracted for analysis. The pattern also was evident when the test was controlled for ethnicity, though the statistical significance of the findings decreased.

The expected pattern of differences among the worldview groups, generally, also emerged when answers to the "just economy" question were considered. This question was designed to distinguish those respondents who affirmed a merit-based economy from those who believed in "justice as equality." As shown in Table 4-5, fully 70 percent of orthodox Evangelicals and orthodox Catholics believed that a just economy is a merit-based economy, as compared to only 50.5 percent of Cristo-pagans.[10]

To explore further the issues raised by Foster, I created a Foster Index, which gave each respondent a point for the "correct" answer on a series of six variables in the survey: the two crucial variables just discussed ("profit" and "just economy") as well as four others ("fate," "change," "school," and "achieve").[11] The relationship of the first two variables in this list to Foster's thesis is self-evident. I included the other variables because they are indirectly related to the notion of the "open system" worldview that Foster thinks should be encouraged by development practitioners. Overcoming fate, after all, refers to an individual's ability to look beyond one's visible resources or "station of life" to additional, as-yet-unseen possibilities. Similarly, a positive attitude toward innovation suggests the belief that one can create something new, something beyond the visible, finite goods one perceives in reality. A positive attitude toward school suggests a belief in the possibilities for bettering oneself and seeing this as a legitimate and desirable pursuit. And a respondent's affirmation of the idea that he or she should try to outdo the previous generation implies his or her belief in the possibility of doing so and the legitimacy of personal initiative and ambition.

The mean scores on the Foster Index of the various worldview groups were noticeably different. Orthodox Evangelicals had the highest mean score, and, in general, the more orthodox the respondents' views were, the higher they scored on the Foster Index. Of course, such differences are only of significant interest if the variables in the index in fact correlate with actual socioeconomic progress. They do. Analysis revealed that the Foster Index correlated well with various objective measures of development, including income and electrification of the home.

### Medical Care and Agricultural Practices

In addition to the differences among worldview groups on the various attitudinal variables described, some variations are evident in terms of health and agricultural practices. Orthodox Evangelicals and orthodox Catholics are extremely reluctant to seek help from traditional shamans or curanderos when they are ill. Fully 99.3 percent of orthodox Evangelicals and 93.4 percent of orthodox Catholics disagreed with the statement that they seek help from curanderos, whereas only 43.1 percent of Cristo-pagans and 54.3 percent of traditional Catholics dis-

TABLE 4-5 Definition of a Just Economy by Worldview Type (N = 576)

| A just economy is . . . | Orthodox Evangelical (%) | Moderate Evangelical (%) | Weak Evangelical (%) | Cristo- Pagan (%) | Orthodox Catholic (%) | Traditional Catholic (%) | Row Total (N) |
|---|---|---|---|---|---|---|---|
| Equality-based | 29.9 | 50.5 | 38.1 | 49.5 | 30.7 | 39.4 | 227 |
| Merit-based | 70.1 | 49.5 | 61.9 | 50.5 | 69.3 | 60.6 | 349 |
| Column total (N) | 139 | 101 | 84 | 103 | 88 | 60.6 | |

SOURCE: W&D Survey, Guatemala, June 1993.

Significant at $p = .003$.

agreed. There was no statistically significant difference among the worldview groups, though, in terms of their propensity to have their children vaccinated. Large majorities of each group reported that they had done this.

More differences emerged when agricultural practices were considered. Eighty percent of the respondents reported growing some crops. Considering only this group, the W&D Survey results show that orthodox Evangelicals, more than Cristo-pagans, use fertilizer (74.3 percent vs. 60.5 percent). Orthodox Evangelicals were also less apt than Cristo-pagans to limit the selling of their crops to the local market only (78.3 percent of Evangelicals said they sold at a local market compared to 96.1 percent of Cristo-pagans.) There were, however, no statistically significant differences between orthodox Evangelicals and Cristo-pagans in terms of their propensity for growing nontraditional crops.

## Summary

The survey results consistently demonstrate that orthodox Evangelicals and orthodox Catholics show a greater propensity than Cristo-pagans and other syncretistic Christians to adopt development-enhancing attitudes. This greater propensity contributes to the higher objective standards of living enjoyed by these groups. For example, 69 percent of orthodox Evangelicals, compared to only 47 percent of Cristo-pagans and 61 percent of traditional Catholics, were found in the highest category on the Standard of Living Index.

As noted earlier, the principal criterion used to distinguish among worldview categories was *religious doctrine*: whether respondents rejected syncretism and affirmed the core belief of Christian orthodoxy (the exclusivity of Christ as the means for eternal life). Analysis showed that other aspects of religious life—integration into the community of faith, religious activism, charitable giving, religious upbringing—were not as significant in affecting the adoption of development-enhancing attitudes or affecting the more objective variables of integration into the formal economy. If development is measured purely by income and status of dwelling, no significant differences exist between Evangelicals who are members of Bible study or prayer groups and those who are not; there are no differences between those who attend religious services often and those who go rarely; there are no differences among Evangelicals of varying denominational affiliation; there are no differences between those who tithe and those who do not.

One variable from the section probing respondents' religious lives that did have significant influence on development (in this case, on income) was their answers to the question concerning the purpose of religion. This survey item asked whether people held a "pietist" attitude (religion's role is to point the way toward other-worldly salvation); a "secular" attitude (religion's purpose is to transform the institutions of this world); or a "holistic" attitude (religion is to guide one toward eternal life but also to assist in this worldly life). The latter response most closely reflects the orthodox Christian position, and respondents who chose it had higher average annual incomes than those who selected the other responses.

## Factors Influencing Orthodoxy

Since the W&D Survey demonstrated that religious doctrine was a highly important influence on individuals' socioeconomic progress, I was interested in determining what factors influenced respondents' (both Catholic and Evangelical) levels of orthodoxy. Among the plausible influences are such things as believers' degree of integration into a faith community, their level of religious activity and church attendance, the length of time they have held their particular religious convictions, and their religious upbringing.

For Evangelicals, the W&D Survey indicated that membership in a Bible study or prayer group was not significantly related to believers' rejection of traditional, Cristo-pagan ideas. Membership in such associations did, however, influence Evangelicals' answers to the question about eternal life: members of Bible study or prayer groups were more likely to give the most orthodox answer. Sixty-four percent of Evangelicals belonging to such groups said that Jesus Christ was the only way to heaven, while only 57 percent of those who were not members of such groups gave this "exclusivist" answer. Attendance at Evangelical church services appeared to have some relation to the level of rejection of traditional beliefs. More than half of the Evangelicals who attended worship services more than once a week scored low in their retainment of traditional animistic beliefs. Only a third of those who attended such services only once a month or less scored low.

Somewhat surprisingly, the length of a convert's time as a Protestant was not significantly related to his or her propensity to reject traditional beliefs. Whether respondents had converted recently or had converted 10 to 40 years ago was considered; about 50 percent of each category consistently showed a strong rejection of traditional beliefs. Moreover, denominational affiliation also had little influence on orthodoxy. The Evangelical respondents were grouped into four denominational categories: Pentecostal, neo-Pentecostal, historic mission churches (such as Presbyterian, Nazarene, and Methodist), and unclassifiable. Statistical analysis revealed that none of these denominational groups were consistently more orthodox than the others.

One influential aspect of the Evangelicals' lives in facilitating their abandonment of traditional beliefs was their religious upbringing. While 56.3 percent of Evangelical respondents with Protestant parents scored low on the TBI, only 49.8 percent of Evangelicals with Catholic parents scored low. Evangelicals who grew up in Evangelical homes were also more likely than those who were nurtured in Catholic homes to give the most orthodox answer to the question on eternal life.

Similarly, among Catholic respondents, the religious faith of one's parents had a significant effect on one's orthodoxy of belief. Catholics raised in Evangelical homes were twice as likely to score low on the TBI as were Catholics raised by Catholic parents. In contrast, the level of integration into the Catholic community had an ambiguous influence. On the one hand, Catholic respondents who were, or had been, members of cofradias, were, predictably, less likely to reject traditional beliefs than Catholics who were not involved in such groups. About 31 percent of Catholics not involved in cofradias scored low on the TBI; only 11 percent of Catholics who were in cofradias scored low. This suggests that Catholics who avoided associations that reinforced the folk Catholic experience did better at rejecting animistic, pantheistic beliefs. On the other hand, Catholics who actively sought out other forms of fellowship did not necessarily find this to be helpful in reinforcing their orthodoxy. For Catholics, integration into the faith community as measured by attendance at mass seemed to have little effect on religious orthodoxy. Roughly 29 percent of Catholics who faithfully attended mass each week (or even more often) still scored high on the TBI, which was essentially the same as the 27 percent of Catholics who scored high and hardly ever attended mass. There was also no difference on the TBI between Catholics who affirmed that they tried hard to attend mass on special prescribed days and those who did not. The social dynamic of Catholic fellowship at religious services, in short, appeared to do little to strengthen Catholic orthodoxy.

The most important influence on a Catholic's rejection of traditional, Mayan beliefs was his or her familiarity with, and devotion to, the teachings of the Roman church. Catholics who said they tried hard to follow all the doctrines of the Catholic church were less likely to score high on the TBI than Catholics who were indifferent to such teaching (the figures were 46.7 percent and 61.1 percent, respectively). It is unclear where Catholics receive instruction in the essentials of Christian doctrine, since the survey results suggest that this does not happen during the mass itself. A large percentage of Catholics said they thought it was important to read the Bible everyday, so it is possible that they gain some understanding through their own study. Others may be members of catechism classes taught by the lay faithful, and they may learn doctrine there.

## Reinforcing an Open-System Lifestyle

This chapter's emphasis on religious orthodoxy does not imply that other aspects of religious life—integration, religious fervor, religious activism—are unimportant in affecting believers' prospects for socio-economic development. The information I gathered through field research suggests otherwise, as do the anecdotal reports of other scholars (such as Martin). As mentioned in chapter 2, some researchers have found that the Evangelicals' fraternal network provides believers with practical assistance, credit, and help finding employment. Other scholars have also noted the importance of conversion for opening up a convert's circle of acquaintances (e.g., by encouraging travel to attend regional religious conferences or to study at Bible schools or seminaries in cities distant from the convert's village). Finally, Protestants are, in many instances, more exposed to foreigners and to cross-cultural contact than are their non-Evangelical neighbors. All of these cross-cultural opportunities reinforce a convert's passage from a closed-system worldview—which is insulated and recognizes only the finite resources immediately evident—to an open-system worldview where new possibilities and opportunities, new contacts and relationships, and new ideas are nurtured.

In short, while conversion to Christian orthodoxy encourages a new set of beliefs about the way the world works and permits the convert to imagine a new and more advantageous interaction with his or her natural and social surroundings, the social network of the Protestant community can further reinforce and legitimize that thinking and the behaviors that flow from it. The Protestant community provides a safe place where a more ambitious and individualistic worldview can be nurtured, a place where initiative is encouraged rather than discouraged.

# FIVE

# Outback Journeys

## The Evidence Experienced

Standing on the dirt-packed airstrip just below Chajul—an adobe-and-tile town of some 4000 residents nestled in among the Altos Cuchumatanes mountains in west-central Guatemala—I welcomed a breath of fresh air after having spent days in stifling, smog-infested Guatemala City. Here in the country of the Ixil Indians, the blue sky seemed bluer, and the green mountains greener. I immediately fell in love with the Ixils' striking red *tipico traje* ("typical dress")—perhaps because they were the first I encountered in Guatemala, or perhaps because they really were the most beautiful. Nearly two years later, after seeing the traditional garb of ten other Mayan areas, I have yet to find their equal.

The red hems of the Ixil women's skirts—as well as the cuffs of my khakis—were spattered with brown mud clots more than once during my days in Chajul in January 1993. My assistant and I had missed several days of steady downpour, but the rains' effects on Chajul's dirt streets, combined with a road construction project under way, made for tenuous navigation up the winding paths to Gaspar Mendosa's crumbling cottage. I had come to Chajul to interview Mendosa because he was the town's oldest Mayan priest, or shaman. Several blocks below Mendosa lives a man by the name of Gaspar Laynez; I'd come to interview him because he was the pastor of Chajul's second-largest Evangelical church. (Since the patron saint of Chajul is San Gaspar, it is unsurprising that seemingly every third male one encounters among the town's residents bears that name.) During the course of my interviews, it became obvious that the two men epitimoze many of the religious and economic realities of Chajul and of rural Guatemala more generally.

## Interview with Gaspar Mendosa

Gaspar Mendosa is ancient—in his nineties. He preserves a variety of the old customs of Mayan animistic religion. He guards the secrets of the day gods of the traditional Mayan calendar. He makes special petitions of the spirit of the sacred mountain Andres. He carries out rituals asking permission of the dueños of trees before he cuts them down; he prays to the spirits of his dead ancestors, asking them to help him in this hard life; and he gets drunk at the fiestas sponsored by the cofradias. But he also praises JesuCristo and faithfully attends mass. He baptized his children in the Catholic church and appears there frequently, reverently praising God the Father. He adores the saints. He is, in short, the embodiment of Cristo-paganism in present-day Chajul—a syncretized belief system less pagan than I'd anticipated, but still far from orthodox Catholicism.

Gaspar Mendosa is also illiterate and very poor. He speaks little Spanish. He says he is thankful to God for giving him food to eat and water to drink. He doesn't know whether it is good or bad to be rich, he is simply grateful to have his milpa on which he grows his corn and beans. He says it is fate or luck that controls whether one is rich or poor and denies the possibility of overcoming what may lie in one's fate. "You can't change your luck; once the luck is over you, you can't change it . . . even if you light candles you can't change it."[1]

But Gaspar Mendosa is unconvinced of the merits of change anyway. I asked him to imagine a conversation in which two Ixil farmers, standing in a cornfield, were discussing how they might improve their harvest. One farmer suggests that they should try a new way of cultivating since this may increase their yield. The other says no, this is not a good idea because changing things from the way they've always been done could make the situation worse. I asked Mendosa with which farmer he agreed. He replied, "You shouldn't change things from the way they've always been done, because sometimes the new ways don't work. You can't change the way things have always been done."

Although Mendosa did not appear to me to be a person who was often afraid, he talked much about fear.

> [People] can get sick from bad spirits who frighten them," he said, and then they come to him to cure them of their *susto* (paralyzing fear). "The bad spirits come from the dead people's spirits in the fields; they come to inflict [suffering] on the living. Sometimes the dead get angry because a living family [member] isn't doing the signs, the crosses, and this is disobedience.

I asked him how often a person should pray and offer candles to the spirits of the dead, and he replied solemnly, "Everyday they should do it."

Like the ancient Mayan daykeepers, Mendosa knows the difference between certain days and the special powers of each. Although initially he denied that some days were more powerful, lucky, or better than others, his later comments contradicted this. I asked him how he came to have knowledge of the days: "No one taught me [the days]. I learned it from the wind. The wind came into my mind and stomach. Little by little I learned. An angel told the wind to teach me how to count the days." Mendosa noted that there are some special days when he always goes to Andres (the sacred mountain) to pray, rather than praying in the large, weatherbeaten local Catholic church. Some days are better for performing a ritual or attempting a cure than other days. "The *alcalde* days are the strongest," he reported.[2] When I asked Mendosa whether it is better to be born on one certain day than on another, he responded in the negative, but the next time we talked he implied something different. "If a person is born on a good day, like JesuCristo was," he explained, "then he'll do good things and never do wrong." Mendosa also affirmed the power of the "five days of taboo" or "five days of fear" that come at the close of the Mayan calendar year: "During those bad days you shouldn't go out to work. . . . It is a sin to work, to do laundry. It is a sin to wash on Holy Wednesday."

Unfortunately, we could not pursue this interesting conversation at any great length, for Gaspar had been drinking throughout the interview and had become progressively more inebriated. (We happened to be interviewing him around the time of Chajul's major annual fiesta.) Perhaps in his partially inebriated state, Mendosa was more generous in his comments about the town's Evangelical community than he might have been if completely sober. He adopted a "live and let live" stance on a variety of issues. When I asked him whether he thought it was a sin that some Evangelicals paid no heed to the rules governing appropriate conduct during the "five days of taboo," he answered:

> [Those people] aren't bad. If they have a different religion it is fine as long as they have faith and obey their faith's rules and do good. They have to follow the rules of their own faith just like I follow mine.

## Interview with Gaspar Laynez

This is the "anti-fatalism" philosophy of Gaspar Laynez, Evangelical pastor of Chajul's Elim Church (500 adult members):

> I preach against that belief, that idea that one can't change their luck. All days are blessed. I tell them that if they believe in these old ways they are thinking wrong. We are made by God and we can do all things. We can

improve our lives. We can make a better future for ourselves and our children. We have to erase those [old] patterns of thought. Some people have closed their minds, but it doesn't have to be this way—they can change.[3]

Gaspar Laynez is young—thirty-something—and has adopted a world-view fundamentally different from that of his elder, Gaspar Mendosa. He preaches on redemption through Christ alone as Savior, on the unity of the family, and on personal holiness. He considers alcohol anathema. He tells his congregants they must change their old ways and forsake their superstitions. While there is now less fear among the Evangelicals, he reports, it is still "a long process, a hard process, to change the old beliefs and ways. It is not easy [for converts] to believe in their new God. It takes much time." Laynez preaches that only Christ has power; the other evil spirits and alleged gods inhabiting streams and trees and hills are nothing. He jokes that his congregants are sometimes afraid to cut down a tree—but not because they believe it has a soul or fear that a god will punish the perpetrator. Rather, with the government's conservation efforts, the people fear possible punishment from DIGEBOS, the federal bureaucracy in charge of the regional reforestation program.

Neither do the Evangelicals fear the five days of taboo, according to Laynez. "If they do," he commented, "they don't change their behavior [to show it]." The Evangelicals work on the days when the traditionalists claim they are not supposed to, and they eat forbidden foods on days when this is discouraged. "I don't think the Evangelicals even know which days are what," Laynez says flatly.

To the extent that Chajul's Evangelical laity are like this pastor, they seem to know where they are going. Laynez encourages a forward-looking mentality, a hopefulness, an ambition in his congregants. He himself is articulate, literate, educated through the sixth grade, and speaks Spanish proficiently. Perhaps even more impressive, his wife and daughters speak Spanish, too. In my informal interactions with the women in his family, I was struck by their intellectual sharpness and curiosity. Laynez is enthusiastic about education and encourages such an attitude in his congregation. "I see from my personal experience that it is better to go to school. It is good for the children to go to school, to meet new people, to learn new ideas. That's good!" This openness carries over into other areas as well: when asked the same question presented to Gaspar Mendosa about the two farmers who are discussing how to improve their corn yield, Laynez immediately chose the path of innovation. "The farmer [who suggests change] is better. New methods are good. If you plant the same way as always, you'll get what you have always gotten. If you try something new you may have some gain." Although he now farms only corn and beans—the traditional crops—he says that he would like to try growing broccoli. His hesitation is not that this is a new and relatively strange crop in the area; rather, it is that at present he considers the seeds too expensive.

Laynez has seen positive changes in the lives of the converts in his church and believes that the Evangelical community in general is influencing some broader changes in the town. He says the townspeople are more open to outsiders than they were 15 years ago. With Christians of different races visiting Chajul from other parts of the country and the world, the townspeople's horizons have been broadened. The church, Laynez thinks, has made a contribution in this regard. He also believes that the Ixil are generally less fearful of evil spirits now and that this, too, is due, at least in part, to the growth of the Evangelical community. (He credits other institutions, such as the school and the health post, as well for this change.) Non-Evangelicals still go to the curanderos, he reports, but less frequently than before the growth of the Protestant community. Now more go to the doctor. As for the believers in his church, he says when someone is sick "we pray, and we also believe that God, through the means of the doctors and medicine, can bring healing." He thinks only three or four individuals in his large congregation still visit the curanderos. In addition to these changes in the area of health, he reports on positive economic changes in the lives of the believers: "They dedicate their resources to the family; they don't waste it (*sic*); they have good administration of their family resources."

## Religious Life in the Highlands

The comments of the two Gaspars capture an important snapshot of religious life in rural Guatemala and exemplify the socioeconomic effects of two contrasting worldviews. This contrast between adherents of different religions in Guatemala is set in sharpest relief when an orthodox Evangelical like Laynez is compared to a highly syncretized Cristo-pagan Catholic like Mendosa. As was discussed in previous chapters, the attitudinal and behavioral differences between the orthodox and the animist peasants of Guatemala are substantial, and such differences have significant implications for these individuals' prospects for development.

But even as the story of the two Gaspars highlights the very real and positive effects of Christian orthodoxy (e.g., increased literacy, openness to innovation, renunciation of alcohol), it neither tells the *whole* story of the Protestant revival in Guatemala nor reflects the complicated, messy picture of religious life in the rural highlands. The religious drama there has more than two roles. Not all the actors can be typecast as a Cristo-pagan like Gaspar Mendosa or an articulate, orthodox Protestant like Gaspar Laynez. The cast includes weak, syncretized Evangelicals who have not abandoned completely their former animist ways and Catholics who have successfully purged the Mayan elements out of their faith. In other words, the differences between Catholics and Protestants are not always as pronounced as they appear in the comparison between Mendosa and Laynez. In Guatemala, religious life and its effects are surprisingly diverse.

So are the wares in Chajul's market stalls. One day I went to snap a photograph of an eight-year-old Ixil girl in front of her mother's booth. As I focused the lens, I realized that the picture's backdrop included a row of machetes hanging from a rope strung across the stall; the tips of the machetes nearly touched the neatly arranged cartons of Colgate toothpaste displayed below. This blatant juxaposition of ancient and modern startled me then. Later, it became such a common sight that I began to overlook the irony of it all, like little barefoot boys leading mules laden with firewood past bright signs announcing "Orange Crush Sold Here." I never stopped being startled, though, by the persistence of Cristo-paganism throughout Guatemala's villages and hamlets. It was tough to grasp that the same places where you could get Coca-Cola and CNN, you could also get fingered for witchcraft.

Many of the Evangelical residents of La Tinta, in the department (province) of Alta Verapaz, a tiny hamlet along the jarring, tiresome bus route to Lake Isabella in eastern Guatemala, for example, refer to the Polochic Valley, in which the village sits, as a "valley of darkness." People in this region of the country, my informants reported, "talk to the spirits." They "burn fires and garlic on the four corners of their houses" to ward off evil spirits. They offer incense before planting their fields, petitioning permission from the dios el mundo to use the land and plead to him for a good harvest.[4] The curanderos in La Tinta enjoy a steady stream of customers: according to the Worldview and Development Survey, more than 40 percent of people seek their aid when sick. For me, the most frightening thing about La Tinta was the black, oversized spider I met in the latrine in the dead of night, whose diabolical presence was made more hideous by the flickering light of the candle I was holding. But for many villagers, the fickle activities of the earth god and of the lingering and often vengeful spirits of the dead inflict a far greater daily anxiety.

The Polochic Valley, I discovered, is not the only place of darkness in rural Guatemala. The Cristo-pagan rituals common in La Tinta are practiced regularly in other lowlands and highlands hamlets as well. Undoubtedly, of course, there are fewer Cristo-pagans in rural Guatemala today than in years past. Stepping into La Tinta in 1992, even with its thatch huts and mule-driven corn grinders, is not like stepping into La Tinta half a century ago. Some villagers are not much interested in the ancient customs, and they ridicule the old fears. In this village as

well as others, the combined influence of increased educational opportunities, greater exposure to the rest of Guatemala, and the growth of
Protestantism, has begun to erode the once common pagan/animist
beliefs. Nevertheless, as many contemporary accounts attest, Cristo-
pagan ideas continue to wield significant influence.

In La Tinta there are few orthodox Catholics; rather, most who call
themselves Catholic are highly syncretized in their religious beliefs, in-
corporating many common traditional Mayan ideas about ancestral
souls, nature gods, and sacred places. When the respondents in the
W&D Survey sample for La Tinta were divided into the worldview
groups using the criteria established by the cosmovision variable, the
category "Cristo-pagan" included the largest number of people (this
label fit 45 percent of those able to be classified). Only 3.6 percent of
sampled residents in La Tinta were classified as orthodox Catholics.

I did not conduct formal survey work in the Ixil Triangle—the name
given to three neighboring villages of Chajul, Nebaj, and Cotzal in the
central highlands of Quiche—but chances are high that such a study
would have revealed a significant number of Cristo-pagans there as
well. Gaspar Mendosa is not alone in his beliefs. The doctor at Chajul's
health post reports that he still sees patients complaining of susto (para-
lyzing fright often resulting from having been the recipient of the so-
called evil eye). And according to my informants in neighboring Nebaj,
blood sacrifice is still practiced at the traditional sites in the mountains.
Animistic beliefs, including the idea that trees have spirits, persist
among non-Evangelicals.

The same day I saw the machetes and toothpaste in Chajul's market, I
also met Marcos, an enthusiastic, fifty-something vendor of "Ropa
Americana" (secondhand clothing from the USA), at his corner stall.[5]
He reminded me of a barker from the gaming booths that line small
county carnivals. Marcos's evangelical fervor was not limited to the
blue jeans, little girls' jumpers, and rubber boots he hawked; he was
eager as well to sell me on the virtues of his church—called
*Renovación*—a large, Bible-centered, charismatic Catholic fellowship.
Marcos wanted to make clear that not all Catholics in Chajul were
syncretized traditionalists like Gaspar Mendosa. He claimed that Renovación had 800 members (I later found out this was exaggerated). The
*Renovacionístas*, Marcos explained, had become dissatisfied with the
dull worship of the Catholic mass and hungered for deeper Bible knowledge. They disapproved of the Church's seeming indifference to the
syncretism of so many of the town's Catholics, and they were uncertain
about its promulgation of infant baptism.

In their concerns for a purer Catholicism, the Renovacionístas of
Chajul (I also met these charismatic Catholics in other villages) are
similar to Catholic *Accionístas*, members of a lay Catholic fellowship

begun in the mid-1950s called Catholic Action. With the blessing of the Church hierarchy, priests trained lay believers in the orthodox Catholic catechism and instructed them to discard their animistic Mayan ways. These lay catechists then went out and taught other peasants, serving on the frontline of Catholic Action's battle against syncretism. The Accionístas have enjoyed a more stable and pleasant relationship with Church authorities than have the Renovacionístas: the latter's enthusiasm for Pentecostal-like forms of worship and openness to speaking in tongues is not shared by many priests.

Some Catholics in rural Guatemala, of course, are neither particularly syncretized in their beliefs nor members of Catholic Action or the Catholic Renovación. They are nominal Catholics: baptized and perhaps married in the Catholic church, they baptize their children as well and attend mass only on Christmas and Easter. Other Catholics do not belong formally to either the Accionístas or the Renovacionístas, and yet they share those groups' concerns for Christian orthodoxy. These Catholics, though, think that such groups have not gone far enough, and thus they adopt the rigorously ascetic ethic espoused by many Evangelicals (no drinking, gambling, womanizing, cursing, or fighting) without formally joining a Protestant congregation. Anthropologist Liliana Goldin, who has conducted substantial research in the highlands communities of Almolonga and Zunil, calls these individuals "hidden converts" to Evangelicalism.[6]

But some Catholics actually do convert to Protestantism: for them, Catholic Action and Catholic Renovación serve as "way stations" on the journey to a final break with Catholic faith. In the highlands town of Almolonga, several of the largest Evangelical fellowships were founded by charismatic Catholics who took the jump to Pentecostalism in a major revival that swept the town some 18 years ago. At that time, an extraordinary number of Catholic faithful had become ill with a rare disease. The local priest, a German, obtained special medicine from Europe to fight the scourge, but even this was not effective. Then a Canadian Pentecostal missionary from the Church of God named Norman Parish passed through town, preaching publicly and meeting with several leading Catholic catechists. Parish argued that the illness was the result of demon possession; he stayed three days, preaching about the Holy Spirit and the need for repentence and conversion to Christ. A dramatic revival ensued, and large groups of Catholics (several hundred people at a time) converted en masse, received the Holy Spirit, and were healed miraculously from their diseases. The large Pentecostal fellowships they established are now scattered throughout Almolonga.

The proliferation of Evangelical churches—some 13 denominations are represented—is one of the first things I noticed upon entering Almolonga after the 30-minute bus ride from nearby Quetzaltenango (Guatemala's second largest city). Another thing that catches the eye in this town is the proliferation of pickup trucks. In most rural towns one sees perhaps a handful of motor vehicles throughout the day, and most often these are large trucks just passing through. But Almolonga is different. It is noisy and bustles with traffic from early in the morning until 6:00 or 7:00 at night; it is always advisable to look both ways before crossing the main highway that cuts through town.

The town's nickname—"Garden of the Americas"—and the long, narrow, verdant valley of vegetables around which Almolonga's economic life is ordered, help explain the traffic. This little town is known throughout the country for its productivity in vegetables, and Almolonga's traders carry produce countrywide and across the borders to Mexico and parts of Central America. The wealth generated by the sale of Almolonga's vegetables is readily evident: the omnipresent pickups and larger trucks travel on asphalt or stone roads, there are many two-story homes in town, teenagers sport U.S. brand-name sneakers, and I noticed few barefooted women. I saw more television sets in Almolonga than any place else I visited in rural Guatemala, and a cable company and video shop have set up business there. Goldin reports the town's mayor as saying that Almolongueños are called the "Jews of Guatemala" because of their riches.[7]

Local informants estimate that close to of 50 percent of Almolonga's residents are Evangelicals, and it is tempting for neo-Weberian scholars to assert a connection between the town's prosperity and its Protestants. Ironically, most of the local Evangelicals do not make grandiose claims in this regard: they credit the town's wealth to its fertile land, sophisticated irrigation system, and hard-working citizenry. Economists point to the easy access to markets in Quetzaltenango and, via decent bus routes, the capital. Of course, neighboring towns enjoy these same advantages but do not appear to have exploited them to the degree Almolonga has. This may have something to do with the quality of the Almolongueños themselves, and *that* may have something to do with the enormous size of the Evangelical community there.

On the whole, Almolonga's Protestants do epitimize Weber's hard-working, entrepreneurial, thrifty folk. The Evangelicals though, are not the only ones to have adopted the Protestant work ethic; as Goldin discovered, many of the town's Catholics have, too:

> [Protestant values] extend beyond formal converts to Protestantism, but also directly affect Catholics who retain traditional affiliation. Thus, there are "hidden converts" who have adopted many aspects of the Protestant philosophy but who choose not to publicly commit to membership in the Protestant community.[8]

Many of those who have remained Catholic, Goldin continues, "hold positive views of [converts and] have 'accepted' (in the language of the Protestants) the new moral code, and have reshaped their world views to coincide with those of Protestants."[9] The stricter moral code exhibited today in Almolonga is "contradictory to the traditional lifestyle" and is legitimated or "validated" by the "broader Protestant belief system."[10] In particular, the Protestants have brought a new definition for "appropriate investments." A good investment is "one associated with material gains"; a bad investment (such as participating in fiestas) "does not generate economic rewards." These definitions have greater acceptability among Evangelicals and some Catholic hidden converts today, and they "represent a significant cultural shift from earlier views of fiestas and the *cofradias*."[11]

An irony in Almolonga is that while the Evangelicals there have adopted a set of reformed behaviors and practices that have paid off economically, they have not, as a group, made decisive breaks from several traditional Cristo-pagan beliefs. Several Protestant pastors with whom I spoke noted with sadness the serious problems of nominalism and syncretism in the Evangelical community. They admitted that Almolonga's impressive quantity of Evangelicals was not matched by an equally impressive quality of orthodoxy—though "orthopraxis," or correct moral behavior, was common. As one put it bluntly, "There is still idolatry and superstition here." The W&D Survey showed that only 45 percent of Almolonga's Evangelicals disagreed with the statement that it is necessary to make costumbre before planting a field or cutting down a tree. Almost half of the Evangelicals disagreed with the statement that "praying to the saints is wrong," and 40 percent admitted that "sometimes when I am sick, I go to the *curandero* for help."

Such doctrinal uncertainty characterizes Evangelicals in other areas of rural Guatemala as well, as one particularly tragic story I heard attests. The local missionary from a hamlet in mountainous Quiche who related the incident to me did so to support her frank declaration that "Evangelicals [in this village], when the rubber hits the road, will return to their old [Cristo-pagan] ways."[12] In the fall of 1992 in her village, a seventeen-year-old boy sustained a serious head injury as a result of an accidental firecracker explosion. The boy, badly bleeding and unconscious, was immediately taken to the nearest hospital—on a protracted, toilsome, bumpy mountain ride. After examining the young man, the doctor on duty (whose competence was questioned by the missionary) pronounced the boy dead. The family then brought the young man back to the village. According to eyewitnesses, as the family and other village members were gathered around the body, the boy's stomach growled, he moaned incoherently, and he reached out and took his mother's hand. The villagers mistook the semiconscious groaning and other actions as signs that the "dead" teenager had become inhabited by an evil spirit, and they buried him alive.

For the missionary, one of the most regrettable aspects of the tragedy was that one of the community's few Evangelicals—who happens to be the local rural health promoter—was on the scene when the "dead" boy was pronounced by villagers to be possessed by an evil spirit. Fearing the spirit would haunt and bring harm to the village, the people rushed to complete the funeral rites and bury the body without delay. Following local traditions, the boy's casket was carried to the outskirts of the village and spun around several times to "confuse" the spirit so that it would have difficulty finding its way back to the village. The missionary was terribly upset that her Evangelical friend—who works with her in the local Bible-translation project—had not intervened and stopped the villagers from burying the teenager. Her friend admitted that he had had doubts that the boy was truly dead but had not been particularly certain he was still alive, either. Moreover, he had feared incurring the wrath of the villagers if he told them there was no evil spirit and later it turned out he was wrong.

The ambiguity of this Protestant health promotor's convictions—and that of many rural Evangelicals—is a result of the weakness of many churches in the isolated hamlets of the outback. In some instances, the persistence of Cristo-pagan beliefs in the villages puts pressure on Evangelicals and makes it difficult for them to discard their pre-conversion animist beliefs. But other factors beside the local religious atmosphere affect the strength of Evangelical congregations in rural communities, such as the tendency of the laity to become easily disenchanted with particular aspects of a congregation or denomination and leave that group in order to found a new fellowship. Factionalism has long been a bugaboo of Protestantism: without the authoritative word from a governing body to settle theological and ecclesiastical disputes, Protestants have tended to part company, each faction asserting that its interpretation of the disputed issue is correct and establishing separate individual churches or whole new denominations to propound its specific interpretation.

In the villages I visited, church splits did not usually have their genesis in serious theological disagreements. Rather, arguments over worship styles or the appropriate personal conduct of believers were more commonly the root of the problem. Throughout rural Quiche, I found congregations plagued by internal problems. Churches had split over personality conflicts between church leaders and, on one occasion, even over the issue of where the church choir would practice. In one instance, a pastor became angry with some of the young people in his church and locked their group out of the sanctuary. (They promptly sawed through the lock, purchased another, and locked out the pastor.)[13] In another instance, a congregation was in conflict with their pastor because he had allegedly participated in a fiesta by making a donation toward the hiring of a marimba band.[14]

Far from these highlands communities of Quiche, in tropical little La Tinta, factionalism is a problem as well—fully 19 separate Evangelical churches have been established there. The extent of factionalism in the Protestant community of La Tinta was brought home to me with particular clarity one day while my assistant and I were traversing the village's dusty roads. At one point, we were surrounded on three sides by cornfields—we felt very much "in the boonies"—when we happened upon a one-room wooden shack with a large sign saying something like "Church of God of Universal Prophesy—Pentecostal of the Complete Gospel, No. 2." I was astounded that a church with such an elaborately defined identity could sport two separate congregations in such a small hamlet.

La Tinta's Evangelical community is divided into Pentecostal, neo-Pentecostal, and historic mission denominations. The largest fellowship in La Tinta, a Nazarene church, claims 337 adult members. Most churches, though, have between 70 and 100 members. Three of the pastors I interviewed noted that there had been at least one spin-off from their congregation; in one instance, former members had, at various times, started four new churches in the community. The Nazarene Church, which excels at statistics, reported that in 1990 (the most recent year for which the pastor had data on hand) 148 new members had been added to the congregation's rolls, but 98 had left the church to join other congregations or to start new ones. Other churches reported steady, but often, slow growth. One pastor, after noting that only two to three new families joined his congregation each year, shrugged his shoulders and commented, "Here there is much competition."[15]

Factionalism and church splits have also plagued the Protestant community in the Ixil Triangle. Nebaj's Protestant community is loosely divided into charismatic and noncharismatic groups, and about half of the churches are quite small, according to Summer Institute of Linguistics (SIL) linguists Ray and Helen Elliott, who have lived and worked in Nebaj for nearly four decades.[16] In the five-part division of Guatemala by the historic mission societies in the early twentieth century, the Ixil area was given to the Primitive Methodists, and many of the town's churches originated in that denomination. Over the years, the Methodist church has endured a variety of splits; when members left, they often started small new congregations. The impression I received in Nebaj is that church splits and "church hopping" (congregants changing churches frequently) is a common problem. I interviewed a pastor of a small congregation of about 30 families, for example, who was facing serious opposition from a few of the church's six elders. A split seemed imminent.

A further problem contributing to the qualitative weakness of the churches in rural villages is the lack of pastoral training. Where pastors are unable to understand and clearly articulate Scripture, the laity tend to see Evangelical affiliation as a list of "do's and don'ts," and they continue to practice some of the "don'ts." Several rural pastors I interviewed admitted (and lamented) their lack of theological knowledge and pastoral training. As one commented, "We are struggling to preach the word of God; we are far away from the capital. We are more isolated; there is no Bible institute nearby. It is very difficult for the people here to learn the word of God. Seminaries are far away, and there is no money to pay for teachers to come here."

The lack of sophisticated Bible knowledge and pastoral training has in some instances manifested itself in strange, obscure teachings by rural pastors. A medical doctor with Fundación Contra El Hambre (a private development organization) who visits the hamlet of Las Pacayas in Alta Verapaz once every two months told me of a radical Pentecostal congregation there that preaches against the use of any kind of medicine. They argue that such use shows a lack of faith in God.[17] I discovered a similar teaching six hours away in the *Iglesia Agape* in the village of El Pinal in the north-central highlands. As one of the elders of that church explained to me:

> In Exodus God promised that obedience would mean protection from the diseases and plagues that He sends on the wicked. Also James and Paul counsel the laying on of hands and prayer for the sick—and confession of sin. Confession brings healing. If a child is sick, then the parents must have sinned, and they should confess their sins to God and to the pastor.[18]

A member of the church, who was with us at the time of this interview, interjected at this point that his daughter had been sick with intestinal worms but that after he and his wife had confessed their sins, she had improved in a few days and passed all the worms in her stool.[19]

As these accounts attest, the qualitative weaknesses of the Protestant churches are real. But there are also many individuals, like Gaspar Laynez, who experience a clean break from animist ways, grasp the central truths of Christian orthodoxy, and live their lives in accordance with practical biblical principles concerning work, child-rearing, marital relationships, business relationships, and so forth. I remember being impressed with young Jonahata, a nineteen-year-old "pastor's assistant" from the Monte Sinai church in Zunil (a town neighboring Almolonga). He reported that his congregation emphasized the doctrine of regeneration and the new life available to converts through a personal relationship with Christ. The moral life demanded of Monte Sinai's members is strict: drinking and smoking are not allowed, and the group fasts and holds lengthy prayer vigils every two weeks. "Evangelicalism," Jonohata told me earnestly, was not "just another religion," but a "new life, a whole change of life."

The pastors from a variety of churches in Chimaltenango, a bustling town just an hour's bus ride from Guatemala City, told me similar things. Several churches there emphasize discipleship and training in Christian doctrine. The Alfa y Omega church, for example, requires converts to participate in an eight- to ten-week doctrinal course before being baptized and accepted as full members of the congregation. This class teaches "the elementary principles of salvation, devotional life, confession, and duty to the church," the pastor reported. The local Elim fellowship sponsors weekly discipleship groups of ten people each that meet in private homes. Other churches hold Bible study classes by age group, in order to gear the teaching to particular levels of understanding. The Church of God Evangelio Completo congregation has seven cell groups, each with its own leader, that meet regularly to study principles of Christian discipleship. The pastors I interviewed in Chimaltenango, with two exceptions, were articulate and seemed well-versed in scripture. When asked to describe the themes that dominate their preaching and teaching, none offered strange and peripheral subjects. Rather, several said they attempt to provide practical and biblically based instruction on such matters as child-rearing, family relationships, and money management.

The pervasive presence of Pentecostal, charismatic churches in rural Guatemala might lead one to suspect that the believers are "escapist" or focused excessively on the life to come rather than on this world. Their worship services are estatic, with great emphasis on the miraculous and supernatural workings of the Holy Spirit. One pastor gleefully reported that his congregation worships *con gusto* (with great enthusiasm). Every service I attended was remarkable for its volume, both in the music and in the initially disconcerting spontaneous vocal prayers that break out several times in the course of the culto (worship service). The lively music is exciting in the midst of an otherwise hum-drum life, and the dynamism of Evangelical church services is certainly one reason why they are so appealing to the Indians. But as researcher David Stoll reports, "Protestantism in Nebaj does not seem markedly otherwordly. Rather it is 'presentist,' focused on day to day needs."[20] He also notes:

> Like traditionalists, [E]vangelicals seek a feeling of human solidarity and trancendence in their group rituals, but they do so in a way that avoids the pernicious after-effects of heavy drinking. True to a long-standing paradox of Protestant revivalism, the *emotion in a worship service encourages a more controlled life*. The members of [E]vangelical congregations are disproportionately in their 20s–40s, couples with young children and heavy family responsibilities. What they have in common is, not a certain position in the Nebaj class structure, but the wish to husband their resources for what they call "the ordered life." They don't waste money on drink.[21]

The "presentist" character of Evangelical preaching in Nebaj matches that found in Chimaltenango, Almolonga, and Uspantan, a small village on the other side of the mountains from Chajul. As the crow flies, it is short trip from Chajul to Uspantan; I had the privilege of making it in a six-seater charter plane and thus avoided the tortuous seven-hour bus ride across the mountains. By the time I visited Uspantan (during my third month in Guatemala), all the small towns of the highlands were beginning to look alike, and the most attractive thing about Uspantan was its colorful cemetry. Guatemalan peasants appear not to stint on the dead: the hefty, elaborate mausoleums adorning gravesites reflect an ostentation rarely displayed on the living. There is one exception—the mint green, pink, and sky-blue paint splashed on the tombstones is also used on several of the Evangelical churches dotting the town's landscape.

Uspantan's congregations have fairly well established ministries and relatively articulate trained pastors. As is its custom, the Nazarene church has several "commissions" in the church to oversee educational, visitation, Bible study, evangelism, and youth programs. The Evangelio Completo church has separate men's, women's, and youth fellowship groups meeting regularly, as did the Primitive Methodist church. The latter also has an established vacation Bible school program for children and a twice-weekly visitation ministry to the sick and to those church members who had missed three or four Sunday worship services. All the pastors I interviewed reported high rates of church attendance, and according to the W&D Survey, Uspantan's Evangelicals are less syncretistic in their faith than their more rural brethren in the town's outlying *aldeas*. Fully 77 percent of Uspantan's Evangelicals scored low on the survey's Traditional Beliefs Index (TBI), and 82.4 percent gave the most orthodox response to the question on life after death.

As in Uspantan, Zunil's few Evangelicals are orthodox in their faith. Zunil is overwhelmingly Catholic: perhaps only 2 to 5 percent of the population is Protestant. Potential converts perhaps see the Protestant option as more clearly defined, and thus the Evangelical minority is more deliberate in its rejection of Cristo-pagan thinking. In neighboring Almolonga, where the majority is Protestant, conversion is easier and perhaps means less, and thus many of the believers are half-hearted in their religious commitments.

This diverse picture of the rural Evangelical church—with its orthodox and its tentative adherents, its competent and its well-intentioned but under-trained pastors, its factionalism and its "presentist" solidarity—highlights the mixed effects of Evangelical conversion. For converts like Gaspar Laynez, the difference between preconversion and postconversion life is dramatic. In other instances, conversion has had a less conspicuous impact. Similarly, not all Catholics are as syncretized as Gaspar Mendosa, and so the influence of their remaining animistic beliefs and practices is diluted. I met two women in Zunil one day who symbolized these realities.

Isabelle Blanca[22] is the wife of one of Zunil's Evangelical pastors.

She lives in a small, three-room home that her family rents for 300 quetzales ($60) annually. It has electricity, a tin roof, and a cement floor—by local standards, it is a better-than-average dwelling. Nonetheless, Isabelle is relatively poor: we sat on the floor because there were no chairs; there were two beds and a few cooking utensils scattered about. Isabelle was neatly though poorly dressed; her children wore dirty clothes and ran about barefoot. Her husband's certificate for having completed one year's training in a biblical studies program in Almolonga hung proudly on the wall—this and a colorful calendar were the only decorations in the sparsely furnished house. Isabelle converted to the Pentecostal faith ten years ago and said that it had changed her life considerably. She got up and pulled a bottle of pills from a wooden shelf and explained that she had just been to visit the doctor for her anemia and stomach problems, and that she was taking this medicine to alleviate her symptoms. She grinned sheepishly and commented that before her conversion she went to the curanderos for help for such problems, but they were not able to make her well. She grew up in an extremely poor family and did not go to school, and she remains illiterate. However, her children and all those of school age in her congregation are enrolled. All but one member of her church is a farmer, and most, she said, are poor. She explained that she is happier now because her husband no longer drinks.

Maria Sanchez[23] lives in a smaller and darker home than Isabelle does, though it is considerably more decorative. A household altar stands in one corner, resplendent with candles and various religious paraphernalia. A large image of Christ dominates another corner (apparently Maria belongs to one of the eight functioning local cofradias). Her home lacks electricity. Like Isabelle, Maria is illiterate. In addition to her duties as a mother and a housewife, Maria is a curandero. She explains that she is able to cure *mal de ojo* (the "evil eye"), susto, and various stomach ailments. She uses natural medicines but has also received some limited training at the local health post (as a midwife). She has had a little schooling, and appears knowledgeable about the causes of illnesses and the need for sanitary conditions and boiled water to avoid dysentery. She comes across as more educated than Isabelle, and her children are better dressed.

Maria attends mass faithfully but says she feels "empty and sad." She becomes increasingly depressed as we speak with her. Mostly she talks of marital trouble, being beaten by her husband, and having to protect her children from his physical abuse. Her husband is around only sporadically; he works as a *mozo* (day laborer) on other people's lands and also commutes to the coast to work on plantations there. The household is more tranquil when he is away, but her financial situation is precarious. He turns over only a small amount of his earnings to her and the children; much, she says, he spends on alcohol. She is first willing to admit her husband's drinking problem, and then as the conversation progresses, she confesses her own struggles in this regard. She asks us whether we have a medicine that can cure her of her drinking and other problems. My translator says she knows of no such pill, but suggests Maria contact one of the town's Evangelical pastors for counsel.

The differences between the two women's lives, resulting in part from their different worldviews, are not dramatically evident upon initial observation. Isabelle's house is more comfortable, but Maria is better dressed and more educated. Socioeconomically, both are poor, but Maria's situation is more tenuous. Isabelle has more security and greater domestic peace in her home. Conversion has not brought Isabelle and her family significant wealth, but it does seem to have brought an increased order and predictability. Maria's essentially Cristo-pagan worldview has not led her to reject modern medicine completely (as mentioned, she was an eager participant in preventative health care training at the local health post). Her education, though, has not induced her to stop worshipping the wooden "saints" and spending money on candles and other offerings, nor to reject her customs as a *curandero*. Isabelle's conversion to Evangelicalism has not encouraged her to learn to read and write, though it has led to behavioral changes (including a renunciation of drinking and an avoidance of shamans). For both women, religious worldview has had a *partial* influence on their thought and behavior.

## Orthodoxy and Transformation

The subject of alcohol came up frequently not only in my conversations with Maria and Isabelle but during the course of almost every interview. Tales of the beneficial effects of sobriety, on both family and economic life, dominate Evangelicals' conversations with outsiders. My visits to Almolonga and Zunil provided some interesting anecdotal impressions of the impact of Protestant revival on alcoholism. Neither my translator nor I saw even one drunk person in Almolonga during our visits there, whereas on a single weekday in Zunil, we saw two drunk women and four drunk men staggering about or passed out on the streets. Zunil also had far more liquor stores than Almolonga. Our anecdotal impressions were reinforced by testimony from staff at the health posts in the two towns. In Almolonga, my informant (who has worked in 15 other villages and has labored in Almolonga's health post for five years) stated matter-of-factly that "there are fewer people who drink here."[24] The doctor at the health post in Zunil, in contrast, reported, "The problem of alcoholism is very big. Everyone drinks and smokes excessively at funerals and fiestas. There are a lot of alcohol-ics—both males and females."[25] The decline in alcoholism in Almo-longa may stem both from the prohibitions issued by the Evangelical community and from the general decline in cofradia activity as a re-sult of dramatic Protestant growth. This in turn has led to an em-phasis on alternative forms of leisure, away from drunken fiestas and toward "sports, games, travel to visit nearby sites, or time spent with family."[26]

## Reformed Families

Transformations in family life are the most immediately evident mani-festations of conversion to orthodox Christianity. During the course of my research, I was most interested in discerning the economic effects of conversion, but these were not typically the first kinds of change noted by the converts themselves. Instead, informants emphasized such do-mestic transformations as fewer incidents of spouse and child abuse, less drinking, more attentive child-rearing practices, a reduction in the popularity of gambling, fewer incidents of marital infidelity, and a gen-erally enhanced status for women.

In La Tinta, one pastor told me that many of his congregants "fought and drank [before conversion]. They did not have peace in their homes or work. The people were very poor and had many problems. The wives would often complain regarding their husbands, and put their husbands in jail." After conversion these husbands "no longer beat their wives" and, now, he said, they enjoy "peace in [their] homes."[27] Another church leader there noted that conversion has in many instances im-proved relations among neighbors.[28] A third emphasized the difference between converts and others in regard to marital infidelity. His church confronts members suspected of infidelity, to discipline them and bring them to repentance.[29]

Throughout rural Guatemala I discovered that the Evangelical com-munity generally insists that its members formalize their relationships with their spouses. In Mayan culture it is fairly common to find couples living unidos. Most Evangelical fellowships, though, encourage their members to be formally and legally married, and statistics show that the laity follow these instructions. The W&D Survey found that fully 25 percent of Catholics live unidos while only 11.6 percent of Protestants do. A massive survey of more than 2,500 individuals in three rural municipalities of Quiche, conducted by a nonprofit group called FUN-DEQI, revealed that over 40 percent of Catholics reported living unidos while only 27 percent of Evangelicals did so.[30]

In other villages my informants mentioned the positive effects of conversion on child-rearing. As one put it, "As [Evangelical parents] begin to learn the Bible, they pay attention to teaching their children appropriate manners and how to relate properly with each other."[31]

Pastor Antonio Caso of Chimaltenango emphasized the importance of domestic transformation as we sat sipping lemonade in his handsomely furnished living room. Caso had been a successful businessman (the two cars in a Florida-style carport, the large television, and the fancy telephone attested to this) before he "heard the call of the Lord" to become a Protestant preacher. Clearly he was an advocate of the possibilities for change and improving one's life. During our conversation he stated, "More than anything when I [preach], I touch on the area of regeneration." To illustrate the regenerations he had witnessed among his congregants, he related the following story:

> In the time of the violence [i.e., the early 1980s] a family came to our church from Quiche. They had five or six children, and they came to Chimaltenango and did not know the Lord. God allowed us to bring the [Gospel] message to them. First the wife converted. They almost never bathed; they were always dirty. The children did not take baths, they did not wash their faces in the mornings. This was normal for them. That's how they lived. The wife almost never combed her hair. She worked, but her husband did not work. But when the Lord performed a work in this family, they started to change. The woman started to change her clothes, to bathe, to comb her hair—she looked totally different. She started to take her children to church, she bathed them and changed them. Then the husband converted and started to work. . . . [In our society] the woman works and takes care of the children and the man only plants his corn . . . and that's what they have to last them the year. The man does not take an interest in whether the woman has clothes, the children have shoes—the children go barefoot. This family came here this way but after a year and a half there was a total change. [They used to] live in a place on the outskirts of town. Now God has blessed them with a nice house [in a neighborhood in urban Chimaltenango]. It's very clean; the children have gone to school, they have shoes, and they live very well and all of it is because of the Gospel.[32]

In rural Quiche, Evangelical pastors recited similar accounts of improved family relationships and credited Evangelical faith for encouraging people to be "more joyful," "more peaceful," and "more upright" than non-converts. "Christians have more love of their family," these pastors asserted, and also enjoy freedom from evil spirits. ("The Christians know that God is their strong helper, stronger than the evil spirits.") All the pastors in the villages I visited emphasized that converts were different from non-Evangelicals because they left worldly vices—drinking, smoking, dancing, and participating in the fiestas—behind.

Time and again during interviews, I heard positive reports about the conversion of husbands leading to considerable improvements in women's lives; the most immediate improvement was that husbands stopped drinking and stopped beating their wives. In addition, as greater emphasis is placed on the importance of the family, women's status is elevated. Inside Evangelical churches, women take on positions of authority and responsibility, usually participating in the life of the church far more than they did in the Catholic congregation. Special women's ministries and women's Bible studies further enhance women's sense of importance in the church. And greater activity in the church, according to various analysts, produces two economically beneficial results: women are encouraged to learn to read (so that they may study the Bible) and they learn Spanish.

The credibility of these accounts of an improved social status for women is reinforced by the results of the previously mentioned FUNDEQI survey from the Uspantan and Chicaman municipalities. In the rural villages of the Uspantan municipality, approximately 25 percent of indigenous Evangelical wives are literate, compared to only about 18 percent of Catholic wives. Over 80 percent of Evangelical wives speak Spanish, compared to 73.5 percent of Catholic wives. The data are even more significant in Chicaman. There, Evangelical women are twice as likely to be able to read than are Catholic women. Moreover, more than two thirds of Evangelical women speak Spanish, compared to only half of the Catholic women.

### Economic Changes

In addition to these changes in marriage and family relations, conversion seems also to inspire a pattern of household budgeting that better manages a family's scarce resources and contributes to modest "microeconomic" improvements. As one pastor said in response to my query as to whether he had seen changes in converts' lives:

> Yes, there are changes. They've prospered; they now have a house and their children go to school; they have land and better clothes. They're still poor, but they're not in patched clothes. They've been taught that as children of God they should dress better. Before they did not wear shoes. . . . They have more money now because before they wasted it on drink, sins, vices.[33]

In Chajul (as elsewhere) informants emphasized the positive economic effects of male sobriety resulting from Protestant conversion. The Evangelical prohibition against drinking means that more income is available to save or to invest in additional land, better housing, newer clothing, and more nutritious food. Most of the Evangelicals I interviewed in Chajul said they were drunks before their conversion and lamented the money they wasted in those days. Several mentioned that they had purchased school supplies or new clothes for their children, or spent money on repairs for their homes, with the savings they had accumulated as a result of avoiding drink. None claimed dramatic postconversion economic improvements, but most emphasized that *poco a poco* ("little by little") their economic situation was improving.

Reports from La Tinta echoed these findings. All the pastors whom I interviewed claimed that conversion led to better management of domestic resources. The phrase, "the people don't waste their money any more," came up regularly in the context of discussing converts' freedom from alcohol, from the obligations of the fiesta system, and from the expensive and time-consuming rituals of Cristo-pagan religion:

> Conversion has made a big difference. Before people had no fear of God, and now they do. This means they no longer participate in the fiestas and the drinking. Catholics make rituals at plantings and harvests. During these seasons, they make offerings and sacrifices. They kill chickens and burn candles and copal. The Evangelicals do not do these rituals because the Bible says that we're not under the law of this world but under grace.[34]

Protestants also save money by making use of public medical clinics rather than witch doctors when they are ill. This contributes to their physical as well as financial health. As one observer from La Tinta reported: "Evangelicals here are more healthy than Catholics. The Catholics drink, they don't have sufficient money for food, their children are malnourished, and their wives are, too. The father wastes money on alcohol, festivals. The Evangelicals have sufficient food and eat together as a family."[35] The W&D Survey reinforced this informant's testimony: it indicated that only 18.7 percent of Evangelicals in La Tinta visited curanderos when ill, whereas nearly 60 percent of Catholics continued this practice.[36]

The FUNDEQI survey uncovered similar evidence in the surveyed villages of the Chicaman municipality. Evangelicals were more likely to use modern medicine and shun the *brujas* (female witch doctors) and *medicina naturala* (natural, herbal medicines). Of Evangelicals, 41.3 percent said they sought the aid of a doctor when ill, compared with 33 percent of Catholics. Whereas 11.6 percent of Catholics said they made use of witch doctors and natural medicines, only 4.3 percent of Evangelicals reported doing so.

According to the Acting Director of the Chajul Health Post, Antonio Rivera, there is also less drinking and smoking in Chajul "because of all the conversions to Evangelical religion."[37] The chief doctor at this health post, who had previous experience in several rural villages in Alta Verapaz, said he believes that fewer Evangelicals in Chajul visited witch doctors than was common among non-Evangelicals there and in other areas where he had worked. He reported that the health center had conducted a survey in 1989 in the village and found "a lot of Evangelicals, and they don't go to the curanderos."[38] Of course, he said, more villagers generally, regardless of their religious affiliation, were beginning to take advantage of the health post. This he credited to the increase of health education programs in the Ixil language. He did comment, though, that the Evangelical churches had helped the situation by encouraging their congregants to make use of the facilities.[39] The Verbo church in Chajul has set a particularly good example in health, since its pastor has one son and two daughters who work full time in the community health post. The family has long promoted good health, sold medicines, and given shots.

In addition to savings from decreased alcohol, ritual, and curandero expenses, some Evangelicals may be moving up the economic ladder poco a poco because of their greater propensity for occupational diversity. Evidence of this is admittedly scanty, but research completed thus far has been intriguing. According to researcher David Stoll, some occupational differences exist between Evangelicals and traditional Catholics in Nebaj. "It is not hard to find associations between Protestantism, thrift, and successful entrepreneurship," Stoll writes, nor "to find young Evangelicals venturing into new businesses and fitting the image of the innovative, hardworking Protestant entrepreneur."[40] According to a questionnaire administered by the Ministry of Development in 1987– 88, Evangelicals were more likely to be involved in nonagricultural occupations: 14 percent of Evangelicals versus 9 percent of Catholics reported a nonfarm occupation.[41] Stoll administered his own small survey of 261 individuals in Nebaj and found slight differences as well. Among Evangelicals, 46.8 percent were involved in nonagricultural, skilled labor compared to 36.2 percent of "traditionalists"; 37.5 percent of Evangelicals were involved in teaching, compared to only 21.9 percent of the traditionalists; 50 percent of the Evangelicals were engaged in commerce, compared to 30 percent of the traditionalists; and only 35.6 percent of the Evangelicals were involved in agriculture, compared to 46.2 percent of the traditionalists.[42]

Unfortunately, I could find no similar occupational studies for Chajul. I was told by a villager that the only *transportistas* there were Evangelicals; that is, that all the town's trucks (probably about four) were owned by Evangelicals. But I was not able to confirm this. As noted in chapter 2, researcher Sheldon Annis found, in a study of a village near Lake Atitlan, that Protestants were more likely than Catholics to develop nonfarm sources of income and that Protestants were more often engaged in business activity.

In addition to research studies, anecdotes indicate that Protestants may be more diversified in their commercial pursuits. I discovered an interesting pattern in an admittedly limited and somewhat informal study of small businesses in Almolonga. Of the shops where I interviewed, 52.8 percent were owned by Evangelicals; 41.7 percent were owned by Catholics.[43] On the whole, the Protestant-owned businesses were more lucrative than Catholic-owned ones. Over half of the Catholic owners lamented that their monthly profits were "extremely small, just enough to live on." Two Evangelical businesses were extremely profitable, garnering over 1,350 quetzales per month, and the rest earned on average between 300 and 400 quetzales a month (or 3,600 to 4,800 quetzales annually, an income higher than nearly 80 percent of all the families in Almolonga, according to the W&D Survey data). While 60 percent of the Catholics owned small, traditional *tiendas* selling basic articles—foodstuffs, candy, cigarettes, soda pop, soap, etc.—only 26 percent of the Evangelicals were involved in such businesses (and even these businesses tended to be larger shops with more extensive inventories). Evangelicals owned restaurants, tailoring shops, agricultural supply stores, barbershops, pharmacies, the local mill, and bakeries.

I conducted a similar (and larger) survey of more than a hundred small businesses in downtown San Pedro Sacatepequez in Guatemala's San Marcos department and uncovered similar results. As in Almolonga, more of the Protestants had become owners of their own businesses after their conversion. The Protestant-run businesses were slightly more likely to be larger, in terms of the number of employees, than were the Catholic-owned businesses. And only 6.6 percent of the Evangelicals owned traditional *tiendas* selling *articulos basicos*, while fully 18.3 percent of the Catholic-owned stores were of this type.

### Schooling and Literacy

Though the evidence at present for greater occupational mobility among Evangelicals is sketchy, it is possible that in the future such a trend could become clearer. This is because Evangelicals are preparing their children to be equipped for opportunities beyond traditional agricultural work by emphasizing literacy and formal schooling. Considerable enthusiasm for schooling exists in Nebaj's Evangelical community: I heard of a number of instances in which Ixil Evangelicals were even sending their youth to schools outside of Nebaj. Stoll reports: "In town, many of the young Ixils pursuing their education and dreaming of escaping subsistence agriculture were [E]vangelicals."[44] Similarly, several Evangelical families in Chajul were sending their children outside the town for higher schooling, despite cultural pressures against this.

According to long-time Nebaj residents Ray and Helen Elliott, "the first readers in Nebaj were the Christians."[45] They learned to read because they wanted to read the Scriptures for themselves. Additionally, with the development of roads and an increase in trading, Nebaj has become less isolated, making literacy and numeracy more practical (i.e., economically valuable) skills than previously. "Literacy rates are distinctly higher among Evangelicals," the Elliotts claim.[46]

Various data from the W&D Survey confirm such assertions. In Uspantan, for example, Evangelicals were more likely than Catholics to be literate (86.5 percent versus 67.5 percent).[47] In La Tinta, 80 percent of orthodox Evangelicals and 75 percent of orthodox Catholics, compared with only 47 percent of Cristo-pagans, were literate. In Zunil, 94 percent of orthodox Evangelicals could read and write compared with only 64 percent of Cristo-pagans. Moreover, in Chimaltenango, orthodox Christians have obtained higher levels of schooling: orthodox Evangelicals and orthodox Catholics have completed on average between eight and nine years of formal education, whereas Cristo-pagans on average have completed just through the sixth grade.

In Uspantan, the Evangelical pastors told me that education was highly esteemed by both Christians and non-Christians alike. The Nazarene pastor there, though, is convinced that the children of Evangelical families perform better in school than children of non-Evangelicals:

> There is a marked difference in how the children do in school. Christian children are more exposed to school discipline and have learned to read and write, to memorize, in Sunday school, and this improves their performance. The Christian parents take a more active role, more responsibility for the education of their children. The Evangelicals expect their children to do better and learn more.[48]

This pastor's contentions are shared by a local (Catholic) Ladino schoolteacher in Chajul. She credits Evangelicals with spurring greater enthusiasm for education. When she began teaching six years ago, she estimated that about 50 percent of the families were sending their children to school; in 1992 she estimated the figure was closer to 70 percent. She continues to be frustrated that more families do not take advantage of the school and that many who send their children do so principally because the children receive a mid-day snack. She reports that Catholics and Evangelicals demonstrate an equal propensity to send their children to school but that Evangelical conversions have "helped a lot." This is because, she believes, Evangelicals do a better job of disciplining their children, making them into more teachable students. She comments that the pastors tell their congregants that it is important for them to send their children to school and that they encourage them to learn Spanish so that they "can read and understand Spanish and be better prepared to preach."[49]

Enthusiasm for education was high among La Tinta's Evangelicals as well. As one Pentecostal pastor there put it, "We have a very high view of education because it is important to read the Bible." This pastor backs up his words by teaching the unschooled children in his congregation how to read, while a female member of the church teaches literacy classes to about 70 children and adults. In another instance, the new pastor at the Prince of Peace church tries to inculcate a positive attitude toward education among his congregants. He told me that he had not been able to send his own children to school in the village where he had lived previously because the school was five hours away. He taught his children at home himself. He says education is very important even though he himself has had no formal schooling. He taught himself to read and is very articulate; he struck me as a man who could inspire others to take learning seriously.[50]

Despite this apparently high regard for education, though, poverty still prohibits some parents in La Tinta from giving their children the opportunity to attend school. In two of the churches whose leaders I interviewed, many children were not enrolled in school. The pastors regretted this but reported that the congregants simply were too poor to send their children to school. Children were needed for work in the fields, and money was unavailable for school supplies. In the other churches, most families had sent their children to school at least through the third grade, though fewer had the financial wherewithal to allow the children to continue further than this. In contrast, in Uspantan, pastors boasted that youths from their churches were enrolled in high school.

### Agricultural Changes

While some converts are seizing the opportunity for a better education and a chance for nonfarm employment, others remain in agriculture. But even these farmers demonstrate some of the effects of their worldview change; specifically, some converts seem more open to innovation. In La Tinta, for example, the W&D Survey revealed that Evangelicals were more likely than Catholics to use fertilizer: 42.1 percent of Evangelicals reported doing so, compared with 30.4 percent of Catholics.[51] The difference between the two groups is not accounted for by varying levels of production: over 80 percent of both groups report growing some crops. Moreover, slightly more Evangelicals than Catholics reported growing "nontraditional crops" (as that term was defined in the W&D Survey). This difference was not statistically significant, but some additional evidence supports it. In November 1992 I conducted a survey of the village market in La Tinta to determine whether Evangelicals were more likely than Catholics to be dealing in nontraditional goods. My assistants and I briefly interviewed 264 vendors on a single market day (this represented about 90 percent of the total vendors there). Of those polled, 58 percent of the vendors said they were Catholic; 50 percent were Evangelical; and 16.3 percent claimed "no religion." Whereas 47.4 percent of the Evangelicals dealt in nontraditional produce and goods, only 28.8 percent of the Catholics did.

We conducted a similar market study in Chajul as well, which yielded similar results. We interviewed 135 vendors, representing 88 percent of the total vendors there that autumn day. We asked each one what they were selling (and then characterized the produce as traditional or nontraditional based on the information we had about local crops from a local agronomist) and what religion they claimed (Catholic, Evangelical, Renovación Catholic, or none). Of those marketing nontraditional goods, 57 percent were either Evangelical or Renovación charismatics, while only 32 percent were Catholic traditionalists. Though not dramatic, this notable difference may be suggestive—at least, anecdotally—of a propensity toward innovation among those who reject Cristo-paganism. My informants in the Ixil Triangle have observed that Evangelicals there have begun to make changes in their agricultural practices. Methodist pastor Miguel Santiago was among the first Indians in Chajul to plant such a radical, "off-the-wall" crop as carrots and to sow his corn less than the standard distance between rows. According to a local missionary, he is one of the few locals willing to try fertilizer.[52] In Nebaj, most Ixil would not pick corn before it was totally mature or beans before they were completely dry, because this would be an offense to the dueños of corn and beans. But the Evangelicals sell roasting ears for eating (which are harvested earlier than is the custom) and sell young green beans.[53]

In the AGROS village outside Chajul, which is populated exclusively by members of the Verbo church, villagers grow a variety of nontraditional crops. As a result of a wrong turn on my way to the AGROS village in the fall of 1992, I had a firsthand look at the crops in AGROS members' fields: broccoli, cabbage, squash, radishes, lettuce, beets, and potatoes, in addition to the traditional corn and beans. Here the connection between conversion and innovation was indirect: conversion brought the willingness to receive the "outsiders" from the AGROS Foundation (an agronomist from Quetzaltenango and the Foundation's director from Guatemala City) and to join the development project. Under the auspices of AGROS, new crops were introduced and new technologies such as terracing were taught.

### Development-Enhancing Attitudinal Change

The innovations practiced by Evangelicals in agriculture suggest their greater willingness, in general, to change traditional ways of doing things. Though it is impossible to document with systematic, empirical rigor, the Evangelicals among the Ixil do seem more open to innovation than their non-Evangelical neighbors. Some of the changes appear inconsequential at first glance, but in light of the strong cultural proclivity against change of *any* sort, such transformations are noteworthy. In Chajul, Presbyterian missionary Vilma Avila notices that "the Evangelicals wash their clothes more often. They bathe more frequently. They have more variety in their cooking." She thinks this is less a theological phenomenon than it is a matter of imitation. "The Evangelicals have had relationships with missionaries, like those from the United States. They observe what these families do and then they make those habits a part of themselves."[54] In Nebaj, the Elliotts report that "Evangelicals are in the forefront of changes. Others watch and then imitate them. Evangelical women were the first to wear their hair differently than the traditional style."[55]

Evangelicals in Chajul are bucking other traditions as well. In 1990, an El Salvadoran dental team visited the town (unknowingly) during the "five days of taboo." As noted earlier, these are frightful days for Cristo-pagans. During these days traditional Ixils, following the sorts of prohibitions mentioned by Gaspar Mendosa, will not work, do laundry, cook special meals, or take baths. It is considered unlucky to take any major actions during these days; most traditionalists stay quietly indoors. Several of Chajul's Evangelicals, though initially somewhat uncertain, decided to "brave it" and visit the dental clinic. "Let's try it and see what happens to us," they said. When nothing bad occurred, the women decided to sweep their houses and go out and do their laundry—to the chagrin and amazement of other townsfolk.[56]

In Almolonga, orthodox Evangelicals and orthodox Catholics were more likely to legitimate change than were Cristo-pagans. According to the W&D Survey, 100 percent of the orthodox Catholics and 85.7 percent of the orthodox Evangelicals, compared with 53.3 percent of Cristo-pagans, said that it was permissible to change old ways of doing things. Evidence from Zunil on this question was similar; over 90 percent of the orthodox Evangelicals and over 80 percent of the orthodox Catholics considered innovation legitimate, compared to just under 60 percent of Cristo-pagans.

In addition to openness to change, Evangelicals in the rural villages I visited differed from non-Evangelicals on other development-enhancing attitudes as well. Evangelicals in La Tinta, for example, were less likely to say that laziness is related to a person's fate or destiny. Only 28.4 percent of Evangelicals, compared to 37.8 percent of Catholics, affirmed this notion.[57] Similarly, in Chimaltenango, Cristo-pagans were nearly four times more likely than orthodox Evangelicals to say that peoples' behavior was simply part of their fate. In Uspantan, twice as many Catholics as Evangelicals affirmed this idea.

Moreover, to a small degree orthodox Christians in some of the rural villages I visited seem to be breaking out of the Limited Good mindset that pervades peasant communities. For example, Vilma Avila reported that some Evangelicals in Chajul were sending their children outside the village for secondary education, even though this was viewed by towns-people as an ostentatious display of initiative. A variety of questions in the W&D Survey addressed attitudes related to the underlying assumptions of the Image of Limited Good. One such question concerned attitudes towards achievement and initiative. It asked whether respondents thought they should "always try to do better economically than their parents." In Almolonga, nearly 90 percent of orthodox Evangelicals, compared with about 64 percent of Cristo-pagans, agreed with this statement. Another survey question probed for respondents' attitudes toward merit and equality. It asked whether a just economic system was one in which everyone earned the same amount or one that rewarded people differently according to their varying skill levels. In Zunil, three quarters of the orthodox Evangelicals affirmed a merit-based economy as just, whereas about half of the Cristo-pagans preferred an equality-based distribution. Another item in the survey asked respondents whether they believed the free-market system "usually gives everyone the chance to succeed" or "is unjust because it exploits the poor." Evangelicals in La Tinta were more likely than Catholics to affirm the former statement (44.6 percent of Evangelicals, compared with 34.8 percent of Catholics).

## Summing Up

One day, while driving at a frustratingly slow pace on the muddy, pock-marked mountain trail connecting various tiny villages in rural Quiche, my helpers and I were on the lookout for a particular Evangelical pastor whom I wished to interview. We passed by a construction site. It was difficult to discern what exactly was under construction—a larger-than-average home? A storehouse? A church? Only the foundation and the beginnings of two walls had been laid. After passing by it several times, our curiosity got the better of us, and we pulled into the site. When we got out of our truck, we were fortunate to happen upon an attractive Indian woman of thirty-something doing some chores outside her small, cement block home adjacent to the building site. We asked her about the project next door and she explained that it was going to be a church, for which her husband, Luís,[58] would be the pastor. It was Luís who had been the object of our search, and so we settled down to await his return, engaging in a lengthy talk with his wife. She was uncharacteristically loquacious (for an indígena) and inquisitive, her Spanish proficient, though not fluent. She had lively eyes, a quick smile, and a generally optimistic attitude.

Two of her eight children dashed in and out of the yard where we sat. They were, by local standards, relatively well dressed. She warmed to the subject of her husband and his evangelistic work, and punctuated her remarks with familiar quotations from the Bible. From all appearances, her domestic life seemed pleasant (again, by local standards), despite the hardships of the obvious poverty she and her large family endured. She was looking forward to the completion of the church building; after this, she and her husband would be moving into more spacious living quarters.

When her husband finally arrived and we began talking with him, we gradually realized that he had been the source of a serious dispute in another local church whose leaders we'd interviewed; indeed, Luís's former church had split into two factions because of him. Now we understood the reason for the partially constructed building next door: it was to be a new congregation comprised of the disgruntled who had, following Luís, left their previous fellowship. This was not Luís's perspective, of course. He seemed to bear no particular ill will toward the co-congregants he left behind, and insisted that his church was simply a purer branch from the same denominational tree. Once again, I was face-to-face with the problem of divisiveness among rural Protestants.

Luís was an enthusiastic evangelist and told us of his itinerant travels throughout Guatemala. But from what he related, it became clear that the evangelistic message he carried was skeletal, a "bare-bones" Gospel of sin and redemption through Christ. Neither he nor his wife really had a fully developed Evangelical worldview—their faith, much like the partially constructed church next door, had a foundation and the beginnings of a wall or two. Its transformative power in their personal and family lives was evident, and they were both uncharacteristically forward-looking and enthusiastic about the future. They (especially Luís) had been exposed to life beyond tiny El Pinal, and they had begun to integrate into Ladino society (they were literate and spoke passable Spanish, and they had a few years of formal schooling). Their home life seemed well ordered; they laughed at the notion of evil spirits and going to the witch doctors, and they criticized an Evangelical leader they knew in a neighboring village who had participated in a cofradia festival. But their religious understanding seemed to be limited to the narrow theme of salvation through Christ and a few moral regulations. A transformation in their understandings about themselves, about the universe, about the supernatural, and about their family life, had begun and, by all appearances, had enhanced their lives. A process of change, a process of constructing a new world and life view, had started, but it was not by any means completed.

This couple's experience reflects the connection between Evangelical faith and cultural, behavioral, and ideological change I uncovered in

Guatemala. As is the case with many believers, their conversion had brought positive domestic changes: increased literacy and educational attainments, less alcoholism, stronger marriages, fewer incidents of abuse, wiser budgeting, and better healthcare. Beyond this "package" of changes associated with domestic life, conversion may also be contributing to opening up the vision of converts. As noted earlier, orthodox Evangelicals and Catholics are more open to change and less enslaved to a fatalistic worldview than are Cristo-pagans. They may be better positioned for social mobility, and they are equipping themselves with the skills, and the openmindedness, for integration into the Ladino culture. They legitimate wealth differences and encourage, rather than hinder, personal initiative.

But these two clusters of changes (improved domestic life and a more ambitious vision of the future) are like the foundation and walls of the unfinished church next to Luís's home: they are partial and anticipatory. The influence of Evangelical conversion (and Catholic conversion to a more orthodox and less traditional worldview) is not yet in full bloom. Among the Quiche, for example, the more orthodox do not yet universally embrace the notion of a merit-oriented economy, and while sympathetic to profit, they are not substantially more so than their less orthodox neighbors. Nonetheless, considering the thousand individuals from various villages interviewed for the W&D Survey, orthodox Evangelicals and orthodox Catholics, more than Cristo-pagans, are beginning to escape the Limited Good mindset. As a group, the orthodox are wealthier than their nonorthodox neighbors, though not dramatically so. Similarly, as a group, they have attained higher levels of education, though again the difference is not dramatic.

The socioeconomic and attitudinal differences between the orthodox and nonorthodox of rural Guatemala are, in short, subtle. This does not, however, make them insignificant. At least among some of the orthodox, a process of development has started, and in future generations it is likely to manifest itself in even more readily observable ways.

# PART III

# ORTHODOXY
# AND
# DEMOCRATIC
# CAPITALISM

## SIX

# Evangelicals and
# Civic Culture

W hile the previous two chapters have examined some of the "private" effects of Christian orthodoxy (i.e., those on individuals
and families), the next two look at "public" effects (i.e., those related to
political and economic life).

The most serious defenders of democratic capitalism assert that it
requires a certain moral-cultural soil in which to flourish. They are
interested in discerning what the likely impact of the Evangelical explosion in Latin America on the region's prospects for consolidating democracy and capitalism will be. With some exceptions,[1] the prevailing
view in the elite media (and parts of academia) is that Protestant growth
will, at worst, actively threaten democracy or, at best, hinder its development.

One common stereotype is that of the apolitical Evangelical, who
considers politics a "dirty business" with which he ought to have no
contact. Another stereotype could be called "the Romans 13:1" view.
Critics of *los evangelicos* cite this verse (which commands obedience to
political authorities because they are "ordained by God") and accuse
Protestants of refusing to defend democracy and human rights. These
observers assert that Evangelicals give uncritical support to the governing authorities, whatever their political stripe or repressive nature. A
staffer from the Washington Office on Latin America, a left-leaning
human rights group, for example, claims that "the fatalism embodied in
[Evangelical] doctrine is a near total acceptance of authority" that pre-

cludes criticism of government human rights abuse.[2] Still other analysts tend to pigeonhole Evangelicals as representatives of the far right: a *Los Angeles Times* writer worried that "unless the fundamentalist trend is reversed," Central America would face "a strong likelihood of increased military dominance and of economic power remaining in the hands of a wealthy oligarchy."[3]

This chapter argues on theoretical and empirical grounds that such interpretations are wide of the mark, at least in Guatemala. Rather than inhibiting the institutionalization of political and economic liberty, the Evangelical growth in Guatemala is likely to make at least a modest contribution to the nurturing of the moral-cultural soil that is conducive to the consolidation of democratic capitalism.

This is true in part because Evangelical theology contributes to the "fertilization" of that soil through the Evangelical challenge to modernity, to liberation theology, and to religious hegemony, as well as by the encouragement of democratic habits through the life of the church. Such theoretical issues are taken up in this first section of the chapter.

But what about the actual *practice* of Evangelicals in Guatemalan politics? Critics point to the stormy presidency of self-proclaimed Evangelical General Efrain Rios Montt as proof of the negative consequences of the Protestant revival on Guatemalan democratization. The second section of this chapter revisits this abrupt baptism of Evangelicals in Guatemalan politics, arguing that Evangelical political thought and action cannot be equated exclusively with Rios Montt and that, besides, the general's own political philosophy is not necessarily threatening to democracy.

The third section of the chapter explores a variety of findings from two surveys—the W&D Survey noted earlier and a survey of Evangelical alumni of a prestigious urban high school—that relate to the political behavior and attitudes of Guatemalans of varying religious persuasions. As the reader may now suspect from earlier arguments, these data generally suggest that it is not so much the growth of Protestantism per se that offers support for the enhancement of the moral-cultural soil undergirding democratic capitalism, but rather religious orthodoxy as expressed by strict Evangelicals *and* Catholics.

Legitimation of market institutions is also likely to reinforce the political culture in which democracy can flourish. As sociologist Peter Berger asserts in his powerful book *The Capitalist Revolution*, "capitalism is a necessary but not sufficient condition of democracy."[4] If this proposition is true (and it enjoys considerable confirming empirical evidence), it follows that when Evangelicals show support for the norms animating the market, and hence facilitate its institutionalization, they are contributing indirectly to the consolidation of democracy. The following chapter takes up this line of inquiry. It examines the evidence from the W&D Survey and the Evangelical Graduates Survey concerning religious worldview and attitudes toward the free market. It does so in the context of a larger discussion of the Evangelicals' redefinition of how to order community and economic life. In general, the empirical data suggest that orthodox Evangelicals (and orthodox Catholics), in comparison to other worldview groups, hold relatively favorable attitudes toward capitalist institutions and norms.

## Evangelical Theology and Church Life and the Strengthening of Democracy

Evangelical theology's first contribution to the consolidation of democracy is a metaphysical one: it asserts that humans are sinful. This claim is basic to the ordering of democratic institutions; it underlies constitutional democracy's notion of accountability. In light of people's fallenness, government must be accountable to the governed, by way of such Madisonian institutions as limited authority, separation of powers, federalism, inalienable human rights, and equality before the law. These checks and balances deny the concentration of unaccountable power in the hands of any one individual or group. They deny as well the possibility of constructing an earthly "City of God" through human efforts in the political realm. Instead, these institutions affirm that government is under a Higher Law (though that particular term may not be employed).

### The Evangelical Challenge to Modernity

The ethos of modernity—and specifically, its claims about moral relativism—challenge these propositions of Madisonian (or limited, constitutional) democracy. Modernity, if it can be summarized so simply, reflects a certain zeitgeist which rejects traditional claims about absolute truth, universal standards of right and wrong, and the idea of transcendence. This modern moral relativism attacks the core of democracy, for without absolute standards of right and wrong it is impossible to make a case for inalienable human rights. Without transcendence, it is difficult to prevent the state from asserting that it is *the* highest authority, a claim that is the very foundation of totalitarianism. Evangelical theology refutes the claims of modernity. It is quick to acknowledge human sinfulness while also affirming that humans were created in the image of God and endowed with dignity—an assumption that is the basis for claims to *inalienable* human rights.

## *Evangelicalism and Liberation Theology*

The Evangelicals' second contribution toward the consolidation of democracy is their resistance to liberation theology. While the various theologies of liberation have evolved toward a more tempered view of Marxism after the fall of the Berlin Wall, they nevertheless continue to assert various propositions that are corrosive to constitutional democracy. For one thing, some of the theologies of liberation reject (or at least de-emphasize) the traditional Christian view of the nature of man as imperfect: in them, sin is not so much part of the human heart as it is part of the social structure. Since evil resides in unjust structures, once these are destroyed and replaced by "just" ones, evil will be eradicated. In addition, liberation theology offers the prospect of the Kingdom of Heaven coming to earth—specifically, through this process of revolutionary transformation of the unjust political and economic systems.[5]

This utopianism leaves little room for political pluralism, for all must stand on the side of the oppressed by participating in the social liberation project. There can be no criticism of this project; from the liberationists' point of view, it is the revealed will of God and the only legitimate political activity. This attitude is authoritarian and tends to give the government (as long as it proclaims itself the vanguard of the liberation project) absolute power to usher in—with coercion if necessary—the Kingdom of God on earth. Hence, many liberation theologians enthusiastically supported Sandinismo in Nicaragua, where Daniel Ortega and others implemented an oppressive, centralized political and economic regime at a terrible cost to the citizenry. As noted, some rethinking is currently underway in liberationist circles. But the liberationists' strict "for or against the poor" dichotomy (the criteria of which only they may define) sows the seeds of class conflict and undermines the cause of pluralism.

In contrast, Evangelical theology is antiutopian and permits no political apparatus to be put in the place of God. Rather, politics is always "under God." Moreover, Evangelical churches offer an alternative source for fellowship and community life to the liberationists' "Christian base communities." Even committed liberation theologians, such as Phillip Berryman, acknowledge that several times as many people belong to Evangelical fellowships as to the *communidades eclesiales de base* that put liberation theology into practice.[6] Commentator David Stoll admits that "liberation theology has been overemphasized as the vanguard of religious reformation in Latin America."[7] Simply put, the *really* significant religious story in Latin America (and specifically, in Guatemala), in terms of numbers at least, is not liberation theology but the Evangelical explosion. The former, of course, has had a large and disproportionate influence on Latin American religion, politics, and economics. But the influence of the latter in these spheres is growing. Evangelicalism serves, in short, as a form of institutionalized resistance to liberation theology, and the attitudes it injects into the political sphere may counterbalance those inserted by liberation theology.

### Church Life and Democracy-Building

As commentators Christian Smith[8] and David Martin[9] have noted, the growth of Protestantism also contributes to democracy-building by creating "open spaces" in the civil society. Churches are mediating structures, relatively independent of political control, and are places where democratic habits can be instilled. While Evangelical pastors do often wield significant authority, active lay leadership and participation are encouraged. The Protestant belief in the "priesthood of all believers" also generates an egalitarian sentiment, and decisions are often reached through a process of dialogue which includes the laity.

### Evangelicalism and the Rule of Law

Evangelicals may also contribute to the growth of democratic political culture through their high regard for the rule of law. Their respect for the law stems from their "law-based understanding of God's will for human behavior" and from direct commands in scripture regarding obedience to political authorities.[10] Though some have argued that this respect leads Evangelicals to countenance *any* political authority, democratic or not, this concern is overstated. The very biblical passages that command submission to authority also indicate the criteria by which such authorities should be judged. If authorities fulfill their role as agents of God's justice, then they are owed allegiance. If not, the opportunity for criticism of or protest against unjust regimes exists. And, as Smith points out, the Protestants' perspective is that "ultimately, it is the law itself that must be obeyed, not the person who wrote it." This transfers the Evangelicals' allegiance from specific rulers (the basis of *caudillismo*, or "rule of the strong man," in Latin America) to the set of political institutions or system of laws. The stress on law-based rather than person-based authority undermines the caudillo mentality and holds political authorities "accountable for their own legal violations."[11]

### Evangelicalism and Religious Diversity

Finally, democratic *theory* notes a positive connection between religious pluralism and political pluralism: people who are able to tolerate others whose fundamental first principles are different from their own may have a greater capacity to tolerate those who dissent from their political beliefs as well. In historical practice the connection also seems to hold: some of the strongest and oldest democracies, such as the United States and Great Britain, are religiously pluralistic. In contrast, states where one religion has asserted monopoly control (e.g., Orthodoxy in some Eastern European countries) have had more violent and tortured political histories. In this light, the religious diversity in Guatemala brought about by rise of Protestantism may be a significant source of strength for democratic institutions *in the long term*. The latter phrase is crucial because it must immediately be admitted that in the Guatemalan situation, at least in the short term, Evangelical growth may be increasing religious tensions (and by extension, political tensions).

## Assessing Evangelical Political Behavior

Contrary to the prevailing stereotypes that depict Evangelicals as excessively quietistic, escapist, or uniformly conservative, careful studies of Evangelical political behavior, such as Martin's, demonstrate the diversity of Protestant attitudes and practices present. Martin concedes that Evangelical theology tends to foster a suspicion of political activity, but notes that Evangelicals do vote in numbers comparable to nonEvangelicals. Some display traditional *hacienda*-type political styles, where the pastor directs his flock's votes much like the patron did his workers'. Others support populist leftists, and still others support candidates pledging anticommunism, strict law enforcement, and national security.[12] Though their political involvement varies, Martin does note important similarities in Evangelical attitudes. Most significantly, their God-centered theology makes them anti-Marxist[13]—an attitude that is certainly conducive to the stability of democracy.

It would be an overstatement to suggest that Latin Evangelicals have a well-developed philosophy of the relationship between religion and democracy or even a mature conception of their public role. This should not be surprising; after all, Evangelicals have had a long historical presence in the United States, but only in recent decades have they begun to grapple seriously with their role in public life.

### The Evangelical Arrival in Guatemalan Politics

Guatemala may be *the* country in Latin America where such a public philosophy of Evangelicalism will develop: it is, in the words of one scholar, "the crucible where the public role of Evangelicals will be forged."[14] Evangelicals are more numerous, relative to total population, in Guatemala than anywhere else in Latin America. And they have been in the political limelight ever since Efrain Rios Montt, a conservative, anti-Communist military general and self-proclaimed Evangelical, assumed the presidency in March 1982. (Younger military officers staged a coup against the ruling regime and invited Rios Montt to take the helm. Rios Montt himself was not involved in the coup.)

By their own admission, Guatemalan Evangelical leaders had until that time largely avoided the "dirty arena" of politics. The events of March 1982 startled them; they felt God had "called" their Evangelical *hermano* (brother) to the presidency, and, respecting him as a man of God, they supported him. When Rios Montt looked to the Evangelical community for counsel, despite their previous discomfort with political activity, Evangelical leaders felt they could not refuse to help.

Rios Montt initiated the process toward democratization and civilian rule in Guatemala. But his controversial "beans and guns" program of pacification of the rural areas during some of the worst violence of the early 1980s led to charges that he was overseeing a slaughter of Mayans. Moreover, his evening television broadcasts, in which he would openly preach to the nation, were an affront to those who felt religion and politics should not mix (at least, not *Protestant* religion and politics in this predominantly Catholic country). Rios Montt's ouster in 1983 did not terminate Evangelical involvement in politics; indeed, Evangelicals have tossed their hats into the ring in the most recent presidential elections, and Rios Montt has remained an important political player.

For some commentators who question Rios Montt's democratic commitments, Evangelical sympathy toward the general (which in fact is not limited only to Evangelicals and not inclusive of all Evangelicals) is potentially worrisome. Rios Montt's ire at being excluded from the political process in the 1990 presidential election had him making some comments then that were not comforting to Latin democrats. Ten days before the election, for example, Rios Montt asserted that conditions were ripe for a coup because of his exclusion from the race. He also urged his supporters to annul their ballots and stated publicly before the election that Guatemala's next president would be the nation's legal, but not legitimate, leader. Several Evangelical leaders did issue strong, public criticisms of Rios Montt when he ordered his supporters to annul their ballots. They charged that his action undermined the democratic system and stated that Evangelicals had a civic responsibility to vote—and not waste their vote—under the instruction of Romans 13:1.[15]

Those sympathetic to Rios Montt, however, argued that the constitutional injunctions against his candidacy were illegitimate. Their support of Rios Montt's activities, therefore, should not be interpreted necessarily as anti-democratic. They felt that a valid democratic process would have allowed the general to participate. Moreover, in contrast to the stereotypes of Rios Montt's followers that were common in the prestige media, I found his advisors articulate and sincere in their defense of political and religious pluralism during interviews I conducted with them in the summer of 1992. I asked them polite but very direct questions about government's responsibility to protect the religious freedoms of groups teaching different worldviews than their own. In response, they adamantly declared that any democratic administration in which they served would defend and guarantee the rights of, for example, Mormons to run their own schools. Rios Montt's supporters also candidly admitted that the Rios Montt administration had made faulty policy judgments, suggesting that some of these were the result of their inexperience in the political arena.

In short, the Rios Montt wing of the Evangelical movement in Guatemala did not appear to be the fanatical, near-fascist bunch that some in the academic community perceive them to be. They are concerned about the influence of secular humanism in the schools and the media, but they do not wish to set up a theocracy or impose Christianity on anyone. They affirm the division of powers, the right of private property, the principle of limited government, the importance of controlling inflation (so the "weights and measures of the society are just"), and the need to protect the environment. They believe the Bible (particularly the laws of the Old Testament) offers principles for a just society, but that in advocating such principles they need not make narrow, exclusively religious claims. Rather, they believe that biblical principles are enshrined in other sources of political philosophy; they are not exclusive to Christianity. Rios Montt's followers are conservative in their political philosophy—in particular, they believe the government has assumed responsibilities in areas that more appropriately belong to the private sphere. They are, as well, concerned about the gap between the rich and poor of their society, and they want the churches to become more intensively involved in meeting social needs.[16]

The general himself, though forceful and overly dramatic, was hardly fanatical in his political views when I interviewed him in his home in July of 1993. Rather, the themes which emerged in our conversation were those of decentralized authority, limited government, and the rule of law.

"The basis of democracy is the rule of law," Rios Montt told me. "When there is no respect for law, democracy loses its reason for being."[17] He defined politics as the art of governance. His philosophy of government, it seemed to me, rests on a sort of "sphere sovereignty" theory akin to that of the Dutch theologian and statesman Abraham Kuyper.[18] For democracy to flourish, Rios Montt argued, individuals must demonstrate the capacity for self-restraint and self-governance. Families must be allowed authority over the matters affecting their well-being; the church should have the freedom to oversee its own affairs without interference from the government; the economic sphere should operate under the self-governing norms of free market interplay under the rule of law; and the state should have limited authority, acting as "the servant of the people." Rios Montt criticized the Guatemalan constitution for "telling people what to do" rather than "setting the limits of government."[19] None of this sounds particularly threatening to constitutional democracy.

## Evangelicals and Political Pluralism

The Evangelicals' political savvy has matured since the early days of Rios Montt, and Evangelicals acknowledge that they have learned some lessons. The most important concerns the value of political pluralism. In years past, Evangelicals assumed that their best political strategy was to create a unified movement or party behind one chosen candidate.[20] But this approach tended to alienate many voters. Marco Tulio Cajas, a middle-class Evangelical who formerly headed the Guatemalan Civic Organization (GCO), explains how the Evangelicals' strategy changed.

Cajas was Jorge Serrano's campaign manager in the 1985 presidential election, and, like most other Evangelicals, was surprised by Serrano's dismal showing (he received only 12 percent of the vote). Cajas realized that his candidate's chief failure was his imitation of Rios Montt's earlier self-styled image as God's anointed political leader for Guatemala, as *the* Christian candidate. Having absorbed this lesson, Evangelical political advisors counseled their candidates in the 1990 election to avoid making narrow religious appeals and to refrain from employing messianic language about their candidacies. Furthermore, Cajas remembers how pleased Evangelicals were to have three candidates in the race, thereby suggesting an acceptance and appreciation for pluralism. The GCO, a nonpartisan round table of Evangelicals, reflected this attitude: it met regularly with political leaders from many different parties to discuss pressing issues. Though several of the GCO's members were sympathetic to Rios Montt or to Serrano, the organization as a whole gave no endorsements.

Critics might argue that this evolution reveals only that Evangelicals have become more sophisticated in politics, not that they have a new-found commitment to pluralism. But Cajas, at least, suggests differently. His democratic commitments stem from a religiously informed, "Federalist papers" defense of democracy. He supports democracy as the form of government best suited to the reality of human fallenness and the need to keep power limited, divided, and accountable. His defense of pluralism is linked to his understanding of the need for a strong civil society to buttress stable democratic institutions. Other Evangelicals are less sophisticated in their support for democracy. For many of them, political participation is less a philosophically informed exercise than simply a way to promote honest, clean government and support political leaders who are expected to uphold the rule of law impartially.

Meanwhile, Cajas continues to press for a maturation among Guatemalan Evangelicals in understanding their civic responsibilities. He cites the participation of Alianza Evangelica, a national group of Evangelicals representing most of the Protestant denominations, in the peace talks between Guatemala's leftist guerrillas and the government as a great step forward in this regard.

Manuel Conde, a young, articulate Evangelical from a family of political leaders, was the Alianza's delegate to the talks.[21] He later became the chief government negotiator with the guerrillas under President Jorge Serrano. He agrees with Cajas that the Evangelical community has learned important lessons about political participation and that Protestants are unlikely to retreat from political activism despite their ambiguous experiences with the political limelight during Rios Montt's and Jorge Serrano's presidencies. Speaking shortly after the coup in Guatemala and Serrano's exile, which embarrassed many Evangelicals, Conde said:

> In the Evangelical community today there is a new vision of politics. The two political experiences at the highest levels of government have not been very good for the church. But we are convinced that the presence of Evangelicals is needed in the political sphere. We need political reform in Guatemala, and the Evangelicals are able to do much to help with this. The Evangelical community is assuming more responsibility regarding life in this world; before, the emphasis was more on life in the next. The Evangelical church is learning about participating.[22]

Conde believes that Evangelicals learned from Rios Montt's tenure not to place Evangelicals exclusively in positions of influence and counsel. In Conde's opinion, the Verbo Church[23] was far too influential during Rios Montt's presidency, when the opinions and input of other groups ought to have been sought. By contrast, Serrano went too far the other way, strictly limiting the participation and leadership of Evangelicals, leaving very few Protestants in his administration.

## The Evangelical Example and Political Culture

The real political importance of the Evangelicals goes beyond their potential electoral strength and even their ability to field candidates for the highest offices. The Protestant explosion is a *cultural* phenomenon, not a political movement. The changes it sparks in the cultural sphere may resonate powerfully, if gradually, to the political sphere.

Conde believes that Evangelicals set a good example as people of self-discipline and moral rectitude. And, therefore, they may be contributing to wider cultural change:

> The Evangelical community is making a positive contribution by changing lives and increasing respect for law. We are told to be salt and light in the world, not only in the church. The Gospel is transforming culture: it's a new culture. The church is not a political party; it is maintaining an ideologically balanced position and it identifies with the rich and the poor. The Evangelical church has presented a new model of life, and in political offices both high and low, people know whether the person [holding the office] is a Christian or not.[24]

According to Conde, Evangelicals exemplify the transformation that can occur with conversion. Before, he says, Evangelicals were the poorest and least educated community. Now this is changing. "The Evangelicals are not hiding their Bibles or their lifestyles; they are proud of their identity. They're punctual, they work hard, they maintain an attitude of service," he comments. The important thing for Evangelicals, he maintains, is to persuade others by example, not to try to force their ways upon others or attempt to set up an unhealthy establishment of the church in the political order. The point is not to politicize the church nor to invest the church with political authority. Rather, the church must set an example apart from the political realm, but an example that penetrates and speaks to the political realm.

Marco Antonio Rodriguez, current president of the Alianza Evangelica, shares this view. In an interview in 1993, he explained that "the Alianza Evangelica, as the Alianza, does not participate in politics. We are a religious, not a political, group. But we are totally open to supporting development and peace." His emphasis, like Conde's, was on the personal and familial changes that Protestant conversion brings and on the ripple effect that such changes make in the society at large. Evangelicals, he argued, contribute to the peace process simply by being pacific individuals. The church, institutionally, has contributed to the society through its promotion of health—through setting up medical clinics and holding medical campaigns. "The criticism of Evangelicals as only 'heaven-bound'," he argued, "is unfair. The press is against the church, and no one hears about the church's social work. And we don't go around publicizing it." But even Rodriguez's discussion of the church's social impact first emphasized individual and family transformation: "When the Gospel comes in, it transforms the whole family. There is less drinking and more time for the children, stronger marriages. This contributes to economic gain."[25]

Rafael Escobar Arguello, editor of the most important Evangelical publication in Guatemala, *Hechos* magazine, makes a similar argument. He, too, sees the Evangelical community's political contribution largely in terms of the individual reformations it encourages. In an interview, he stressed the importance of electing individual Christians to office:

> We [Evangelicals] believe that in all Latin American governments there is too much corruption. If Christian men, honest men, men who give good testimonies, come to be part of the government, the corruption will stop. If we have Evangelicals in charge of social programs (housing construction, building roads, setting up hospitals), we will limit the corruption.[26]

Arguello's definition of the appropriate intersection of religion and politics, however, may be more sophisticated than this initial interview suggested. I completed a content analysis of two years' worth of issues of *Hechos* (1991 and 1992) and found a considerable amount of political commentary that went beyond calls for electing honest, Christian men to office. Roughly 20 percent of the articles were devoted to political subjects, ranging from the predictable (reports on individual Christians in office, the problem of corruption, religious liberty issues) to, among other things, commentaries on the death penalty, Christianity and patriotism, human rights, the peace process, and the Palestinian refugees. Moreover, out of 12 editorials, nearly half were devoted to political matters and three to the necessity of greater "social responsibility" on the part of Evangelicals (Arguello encouraged intensified activism in the fight against cholera, against AIDS, and against materialism/consumerism).

Generally, the philosophy of Evangelical elites seems to be that the church must be the church, and from its being so, it will set in motion a process of personal transformation. Then, regenerated individuals with new lifestyles will be able to contribute to societal reform. As Conde sums up: "The most important thing is that the Evangelical person, day by day, has a testimony. We are learning something. The church has a theme: "transform your life." But if the church wants to establish a church in my [political] office, that's a mistake. The change in my office will come from my transformed life."[27]

## Evangelicals and Civil Society

While personal transformations and bustling activity may be occurring inside the church walls, Evangelicals have nonetheless been chided for their apparent lackadaisical involvement in social and political affairs outside those walls. An Evangelical Guatemalan businessman lamented to me, "The vast majority of traditional Evangelical churches share little interest in politics."[28] This view is not unfounded: political action is not high on the agenda of most of Guatemala's Evangelical churches.

Fernando Solarez, a popular evangelist and pastor of one of Guatemala City's mega-churches, spoke for many pastors when he told me: "I am a pastor of the Christian faith, and I do not believe in mixing the Christian faith and politics."[29]

Other powerful pastors in the capital, though, disagree. Harold Caballeros, pastor of the large El Shaddai congregation (several thousand people attend, including Jorge Serrano while he was still in Guatemala), began a "Jesus Is Lord of Guatemala" prayer campaign to reform the nation.[30] Caballeros's approach to religion and politics is similar to Pat Robertson's: a combination of spiritual tactics for influencing national change (prayer, revival campaigns) as well as willingness (eagerness?) to comment publicly on political questions. Edmundo Madrid, former president of the Alianza Evangelica, wishes there were greater Evangelical input in contemporary political debates. "The Evangelical community is now more respected by the political authorities," Madrid says, "but the Evangelical voice is not being heard as much as is necessary."[31]

Clearly, the Protestant community in Guatemala is still debating the legitimacy and appropriate nature of political engagement. But it would be inaccurate to paint Evangelicals as completely uninvolved in the public square. At the institutional level, a variety of Protestant organizations have been established, and at the personal level, evidence suggests that in some towns Evangelicals are more engaged in community affairs than are non-Evangelicals.

Evangelical groups such as the 500-church Indigenous Association for the Evangelization of Guatemala and various Christian relief and development agencies are overseeing micro-enterprise development projects, literacy programs, and agricultural teaching. Evangelicals are also influencing the media: Christians own one television station and broadcast on others.[32] Christian radio stations can be heard throughout the country, the most important being Radio TGN in the capital. The director of TGN also serves as president of the Commission on the Social Responsibility of the Evangelical Church, a small group of pastors, church leaders, and Evangelical professionals who hold seminars on political topics and publish position papers. The group was founded in 1983 to counteract the perception among Evangelicals that politics is sinful, and to demonstrate that Evangelicals have a legitimate role to play in public life.[33] Finally, the Evangelical community has been very active in education, establishing numerous youth and student organizations and founding more than 210 private Evangelical schools.[34]

These institutional expressions of social action by the Evangelical community demonstrate that the criticism of Guatemalan Protestants as being completely detached from public life is overstated. Additionally, outreach by Evangelicals on an individual level is less visible than that being conducted under the auspices of Protestant associations, but it, too, is nevertheless real. In various rural communities I visited through-out 1992 and 1993, Evangelicals were in the forefront of local affairs. Evangelicals had served or were serving as mayors and assistant may-ors, heads of parents' councils, directors of local cooperatives or devel-opment initiatives, and members of volunteer firefighting brigades.

Evangelicals are particularly active in community leadership in Nebaj and Chajul. According to researcher David Stoll, "Charismatics and pentecostals include much of the community leadership [in Nebaj] . . . their members [are] involved in the same kinds of activities as the [Catholic] catechists before the war and now. These include pursuing school educations, starting new business, managing aid projects, orga-nizing cooperatives, and running for office."[35] One tangible contribution of the Evangelicals to Nebaj is Radio Ixil, a Christian radio station established a few years ago. In addition to specifically religious program-ming, the station broadcasts short educational programs on the family, health, and hygiene and carries the government's literacy program, CONALFA, in the Ixil language.

Evangelicals in Chajul have also made important civic contributions. They are among the most active of local residents in community im-provement projects: they led the initiative to construct homes for wid-ows left homeless following the war; they are working the AGROS agricultural development project; they work with SIL's literacy pro-gram for youth (along with Renovacionístas); and they hold or have held many important local political and administrative offices. Indeed, since the time of the violence, the Evangelicals, and to an extent the Renovacionístas, have emerged as the community's leaders. The pas-tors' committee wields significant influence locally. The pastor of the Methodist church served several years as mayor during the most diffi-cult reconstruction period, and a key Evangelical figure won the most recent mayoral elections in May 1993. This same individual has headed Chajul's volunteer firefighters' brigade. In addition, a local parents' group is headed by an Evangelical; an Evangelical serves as treasurer of a local cooperative; and Evangelicals dominate the civil patrols.[36] With Evangelicals in the civil patrol, fewer abuses have been reported—fewer than occur in other towns.[37]

In short, despite common impressions of Evangelicals as quietistic and escapist, at both the institutional and individual levels, Evangelicals are active in social outreach. The mistaken stereotype of Evangelicals as being completely uninterested in community affairs has arisen in part from some Evangelical churches' reluctance to become involved in com-munity development projects because they suspect the leaders of such initiatives of corruption.

And in some cases, these suspicions are justified: development com-mittees may extract resources from community members while promising various projects and programs which never materialize. Hence, the Evangelicals' unwillingness to support such projects may not be an indication of social irresponsibility or a lack of initiative.[38] David Martin, relying on the research of Johannes Tennekes, who studied Protestants in Chile in the early 1970s, offers similar arguments. Martin writes:

> Whereas participation in community organizations might be for social benefit, the life of [politics is] inevitably bound up with sordid bargains and self-interested considerations. So it is not that [Evangelicals believe that] positions of responsibility in society are to be abjured automatically. It is rather that the conditions of contemporary politics make the participation of Christians difficult.[39]

## Voting, Elections, and Participation

The significance of these anecdotal impressions about Evangelical participation in civil society is reinforced by the findings from two surveys I conducted in Guatemala in 1993. Both surveys explored the relationship between religious convictions and political behavior and attitudes. The W&D Survey polled 1,000 rural Guatemalans from five towns; the Evangelical Alumni Survey polled 122 mostly urban alumni of a well-respected, private Evangelical high school in Guatemala City. (These alumni represent a younger generation of Evangelicals: the median age of the respondents was 28.)

The W&D Survey revealed that orthodox Christians in the rural areas had higher voting rates than traditional Mayan animists: about half of the latter voted in the 1990 presidential elections while fully two thirds of the former claimed to have done so. Orthodox Christians in the urban areas (as represented in the Evangelical Alumni Survey) showed even higher voting levels: nearly three quarters (73 percent) of them cast ballots in the 1990 elections. These findings are especially important in light of polling data published shortly after the elections that revealed that, nationwide, only 47 percent of eligible voters showed up at the polls. As one reporter put it, "The majority of Guatemalans were indifferent to the elections."[40] Evangelicals, it would appear, were more interested than most.

In late 1990, the Free Enterprise Chamber in Guatemala sponsored a poll of 1,000 Guatemalans that asked: "What would be the best type of government for Guatemala?" In answering, respondents were allowed to select from a variety of options (e.g., military government, democracy, Communist government, undecided). Only 31 percent of the respondents chose democracy.[41] My surveys included a similar item. Respondents in both the W&D Survey and the Evangelical Alumni Survey were asked with which of the following statements they most closely agreed:

1. Competitive elections, though not perfect, are the best method for selecting our political leaders.
2. In the Guatemalan context, competitive elections are not an appropriate method for choosing our political leaders.

Sixty-five percent of the Evangelicals in the W&D Survey and nearly 80 percent of the Evangelical Alumni agreed with the first statement. Though the items in the Free Enterprise Chamber's study and my own two surveys were not exactly alike, both probed respondents' enthusiasm for democracy. The varying results suggest that Evangelical Guatemalans, as a group, may be more predisposed than the average Guatemalan to democratic institutions.

Traditionally, many Evangelicals have avoided the realm of dirty politics. Since the 1980s, though, they have been more willing to entertain ideas of political involvement. One very important indication of this evolving attitude was the decision of the Alianza Evangelica to participate in the peace talks between the government and guerrilla forces. Some findings from the Evangelical Graduates Survey also reinforce the claim that Protestant attitudes are changing. Fully 62 percent of the graduates said yes when asked, "Should Christians run for political office?" Nearly 14 percent reported that they had personally contributed time or money to a political campaign. And nearly 65 percent said, in answer to a hypothetical question, that it was "somewhat" or "very likely" that they would get personally involved in efforts to stop a law that they felt was unjust or detrimental to their community.

Indeed, the quantitative and anecdotal evidence I gathered throughout the country indicates that the more integrated respondents are into the Evangelical subculture (*integration* being defined as frequent church attendance, membership in a prayer or Bible study group, and frequent exposure to Christian radio and magazines), the higher their voting and community participation rates are. In this sense, for many believers, the more Evangelical they are, the less likely they are to conform to the common, negative stereotypes of Latin Protestants as escapist and politically disinterested, or alternatively, as bent on theocratic triumph. Rather than rallying their followers to a partisan political agenda, the Evangelical churches are encouraging their followers to become more Evangelical. And it's likely that this will *not* produce individuals who are so heavenly minded that they are no earthly good.

## Recapitulation

Some analysts of religion and politics worry that the revival of conservative religion bodes ill for democratic prospects. They conclude pessimistically that such revivals will lead toward traditionalism, backwardness, and authoritarianism and away from progressive strides toward democracy, tolerance, pluralism, and development. It may be that such observers are inappropriately extrapolating from their examinations of Islamic fundamentalism (another religion that, like Pentecostalism, is growing dramatically throughout the world). *That* form of conservative religion frequently has shown itself hostile to democracy. Many forms of militant Islam demonstrate authoritarian and theocratic political tendencies, and although they resist forces of secularization, they are inimical to pluralism.

In contrast, many Evangelicals who staunchly proclaim that their message is the one "true truth" nevertheless support religious freedom, and by extension, pluralism. This is particularly true in Latin America, where Evangelicals are in the minority and face a cultural climate where one religion—Catholicism—historically has asserted a monopoly position. The fight for religious freedom is, therefore, at least in part, rooted in self-interest.

Evangelicals in Guatemala seem to appreciate democracy and pluralism. Their theologically informed understanding of human nature provides the theoretical basis for constitutional democracy, and their own church life nurtures democratic "habits of the heart." As Martin observes, Evangelicals "set up communities, the political implications of which are fraternal, participatory, and egalitarian." Pentecostalism, he contends, is "sociologically consonant with democratic politics and provide[s] part of the popular cultural base on which such politics might rest."[42] As mentioned earlier, for Martin it is highly significant that Evangelicalism has created "free social space."[43] In the midst of stratified, hierarchical Latin America, where democratic culture is fragile and democratic experience weak and uncertain, the movement allows for the development of a participatory and individualistic ethos with affinities to the spirit of democracy. The active participation of laity in the social organization of the church provides a place for individual expression, for dialog, and for consensual forms of decision-making. Congregants can attain status, are encouraged to take on responsibility, and have an opportunity to voice their testimonies and their opinions. They may gain greater self-esteem and self-confidence because the church gives them a sense of belonging and a role to play. Often the Pentecostal emphasis on the empowerment of the Holy Spirit reduces attitudes of fatalism and increases the sense of human dignity and initiative.[44] Over time, these various attitudes may spill over into the Evangelicals' social relations outside the church walls.

Outside the church, Evangelicals model a kind of respect for the rule of law that undercuts caudillismo. They do not appear eager to establish their churches as political entities, but rather, to allow the churches' moral voice to speak to the political sphere. While some Evangelicals continue to view politics as dirty business, such separatist attitudes have begun to wane, and more Protestants now consider it legitimate for Christians to run for political office. Evangelicals appear to vote as often as non-Evangelicals and they hold relatively favorable attitudes towards competitive elections. While Evangelical involvement in public life is largely individualistic, a small but important number of Protestant institutions have been established that influence public discussion of politics, social action, and education. In sum, from a long-term perspective, it seems likely that the theological and sociological dynamics of the Protestant community will contribute to rather than detract from the growth of a democratic political culture in Guatemala.

SEVEN

# The Evangelicals' Alternative Communitarianism

The word communitarianism never came up in any of my conversations in Guatemala. As an idea, though, communitarianism is ubiquitous. In popular tourist travel guides, North American gringos visiting Guatemala are reminded that the Mayan Indians are more community-focused, avoiding the dog-eat-dog individualism alleged of the residents of *El Norte*. In more sophisticated literature, anthropologists exalt the community-mindedness of traditional Mayan villagers and worry about the consequences of an encroaching modernity. A liberal Guatemalan churchman I interviewed lauded the Maya for their solidarity and group consciousness. The same churchman extolled the Guatemalan Marxist guerrillas as bearers of this sense of community: the socialist revolution, he said, would bring in a new, more just society that would more fully embody the communitarian ideals of the indigenous peoples. An encounter one day in the early 1990s between some indigenous Evangelicals and a band of guerrillas on a dirt-packed trail in the highlands of the Ixil Triangle casts doubt, however, on the argument that *all* Mayans long for this brand of communitarianism.

## Rejecting Marxian Communitarianism

The indigenous Evangelical villagers live together in a hamlet a few kilometers outside Chajul where they are participating in an agricultural development project called "AGROS." One afternoon they

147

were cutting a road between their tiny village and the entrance to Chajul. For this project, they were using a tractor on loan from the Guatemalan government. As they were clearing the roadway, they were sud-
denly confronted by the guerrillas, who had come down from hiding in
the nearby mountains. The guerrillas announced that they were going
to burn the tractor since it belonged to "the enemy." "It doesn't matter
who it belongs to," the villagers replied, "because it's helping us build
our road. And we have to have the road," they continued, "because it's
the only way we'll be able to take our produce out. If you destroy the
tractor we won't be able to finish and we'll probably never get another
one again." According to the man who related the story to me, at this
point the guerrillas sought to persuade the villagers of their good inten-
tions:

> Then the guerrillas started to say, "Well, you guys should be with us.
> We're trying to fight for you and defend your interests and what we do is
> for you. You should be with us rather than the government." But the
> village members told them they didn't want to join them. "You've
> achieved almost nothing over the years," they said, "and a lot of people
> have been killed. You don't eat well, you sleep in the woods, you're under
> attack constantly, you have abandoned your families. Look at the life we
> have here! This is our home, this is our land. See that," they said, pointing
> up the hill, "that's our school there and there is our church. We have
> broccoli here, we've got lots of different crops, and we're building this
> road here, and we are doing well." Well, this really angered the guerrillas,
> but later the AGROS men told me that they could see the envy in the eyes
> of the rank-and-file members of the squad. It was like they were saying,
> "Yeah, they're right!" But the guerrilla leaders were mad, only they didn't
> know what to do. So they said, "All right, we won't burn the tractor but
> we're going to take the battery." So they took out the battery—probably
> to use in making a bomb or something.

According to my informant, this was the final clash between the
AGROS villagers and the local guerrillas. It was as though the two sides
reached a tacit agreement that day, whereby the guerrillas decided to
leave the villagers alone, seeing as they could not convince them to rally
to their cause.[1]

The story reveals that times are changing in the once bloody Ixil
Triangle, where nearly every family lost a son, father, or husband—or
personally knew someone who had—during the long guerrilla war of
the late 1970s and early 1980s.[2] Signs of the previous nightmare are
still evident in the town of Chajul today—not only in the disproportionate number of widows and orphans, but also in the distant shots one
sometimes hears echoing in the hills, and in the heavily armed government soldiers who ran to meet our little six-seater Cessna aircraft when
my colleague and I arrived there.

The violence and resulting fear have calmed down considerably in the Triangle in the last few years. On my first visit to Chajul in June 1992, a group of guerrillas came into the town and commandeered a truck—promising they would borrow it for only a day. My translator and I had planned to hire a truck to take us to the neighboring town of Nebaj, but our Ixil host explained that that would be inadvisable. A "wait-and-see" attitude prevailed in the town that day, and no trucks went in or out. We were advised not to walk outside the town limits. At around 4:00 P.M. we heard some commotion in the street. Opening the door, we saw a bunch of men running toward the town square, which overlooks the market area below. Curiosity rather than fear appeared to animate the men, and so we followed along, learning that the excitement had been stirred by the arrival of guerrillas who were returning the truck (less a few parts, if I remember correctly). Having followed some of the horror stories reported from Guatemala by a Washington-based human rights group I'd worked with a few years back, I was surprised at how calm the atmosphere was in town that day. In the early 1980s, the arrival of guerrillas would have inspired terror. Ten years ago villagers were caught in the crossfire between the military and the guerrillas. Now the people are relatively safe inside town; the fighting that does continue is limited to direct confrontations between the guerrillas in the hills and the soldiers stationed in barracks on the outskirts of town.

With the relatively more peaceful years has come an increased self-confidence on the part of local residents. But the courage the AGROS villagers displayed in standing up to the guerrillas that day on the roadway reveals more than this. The manner in which the villagers challenged the guerrillas is instructive. When they pointed to the new community they had built at the AGROS hamlet, they were rejecting both the guerrillas' method for seeking a new communitarianism and the Marxist vision of community. "What we have—land, a school, new crops, a church—is better than what you promise," the villagers in effect told the guerrillas. And judging by the reaction, at least some of the ordinary guerrilla foot soldiers seemed persuaded that this community was indeed more attractive than the one for which they were fighting.

The AGROS Evangelicals are not the only ones who have rejected the Marxian version of communitarianism. In the tiny village of Las Pacayas, outside beautiful Coban in Guatemala's Alta Verapaz department, the Evangelicals I hoped to interview initially declined; they viewed my assistant and me with suspicion. I quickly found out that in the local dialect, the word for "guerrilla" is basically synonymous with the word for "foreigner": my blond-haired, blue-eyed assistant was considered by locals a likely guerrilla sympathizer or perhaps a fighter herself. The Evangelicals of this village had little affection for the guerrillas, and I was able to talk with them only after convincing them that neither I nor my colleague was a Marxist. Several hours to the north-west, in the town of Uspantan, a local Assemblies of God pastor I interviewed spoke disparagingly of the guerrillas and of the attempts by liberation theologians to mix Marxist and Christian thought. "Death and destruction were the result of that theology," he commented bitterly. Even farther north, in the Ixil area, some townspeople had sympathized initially with the guerrillas, but later felt betrayed by their empty promises.

## Rejecting Traditional Communitarianism

The Marxian version of communitarianism is not the only social arrangement, though, that the Evangelicals have rejected. They have also broken with the notions of community forwarded by Catholic traditionalists (who, as explained earlier, are more accurately called "Cristo-pagan"). Much has been written, by anthropologists and more casual observers, about the Cristo-pagan form of community, with its cof-radias, its principales, and its fiesta system. All three of these institutions began to erode before the dramatic increases in the size of the Protestant community; their current weakness cannot be attributed solely to the gains made by Evangelicals. But even though the membership of these Cristo-pagan groups has decreased (and with this some of their authority), it is still the case that the worldview undergirding these institutions continues to wield influence. Traditional community structures and norms are still evident in rural Guatemala. The Protestants opt out of these, and encourage others to do so as well.

Since for some observers Protestantism is considered right-wing or excessively individualistic, or destructive of traditional community, the rapid growth of the Evangelical movement is viewed as regrettable. Coming to such a judgment, though, requires demonstrating, first, that the existing Cristo-pagan communitarianism is genuine and desirable, and second, that Protestantism is producing atomistic individuals. In fact, neither proposition is defensible. The communitarianism of Mayan traditionalists is more apparent than real, and it results in a pernicious egalitarianism that hinders socioeconomic development. And, while Protestantism does open the way for personal initiative and achievement, while legitimizing a greater role for the individual, it also creates an alternative community differing from both those of the Marxists and the Cristo-pagans.

## Traditional Communitarianism Examined

As anthropologist George Foster has persuasively argued, peasant societies are characterized by their belief in a "fixed pie" world in which all desirable goods—land, opportunity, wealth, respect, friendship, and so on—are limited. He calls this mindset the Image of Limited Good (see chapter 2 for a more detailed discussion). In response to this alleged reality of a finite universe, peasants can choose either to maximize cooperation, and perhaps even impose a communistic system, or to pursue the path of excessive individualism. Despite the popular perception of traditional societies as highly communitarian, Foster argues that peasants typically choose the latter response.

### Excessive Individualism

This choice is based on at least two factors. First, cooperation requires leadership, and peasant societies have difficulty delegating authority because it is seen as still another finite good. Individuals are reluctant to assume leadership for fear that they will be seen as overstepping their rightful bounds by trying to get too great a share of the scarce good called leadership. Second, typical subsistence-level peasant economic activities usually require little cooperation with others outside the family unit. Families are able to work their own small plots of land, make and mend their clothing and shelter, and otherwise provide for most of their own basic needs. As Foster puts it, peasant families "take care of themselves with a degree of independence impossible in an industrial society, and difficult in hunting-fishing-gathering societies."[3] He continues:

> Whatever the reasons, peasants are individualistic, and it logically follows from the Image of Limited Good that each minimal social unit (often the nuclear family, and, in many situations, a single individual) sees itself in perpetual, unrelenting struggle with its fellows for possession of or control over what it considers to be its share of scarce values. This is a position that calls for extreme caution and reserve, a reluctance to reveal true strength or position. *It encourages suspicion and mutual distrust, since things will not necessarily be what they seem to be.*[4]

If Foster is correct, clearly the community spirit attributed to peasant societies is somewhat superficial, since distrust predominates. Peasants do display a certain community-mindedness as they make decisions, but the motivation behind this seems not to be a concern for the community per se as much as a concern for the ways in which the community will judge the decision and whether the individual is likely to suffer any retribution from the community for taking a particular course of action. The peasant's motivation, in other words, is individualistic. His behavior appears communitarian, in the sense that he is unlikely to act in ways that will be disparaged by his neighbors, for he wishes to avoid their wrath (expressed, for example, in ridicule or physical persecution or witchcraft). As anthropologist May Diaz explains, the peasant is essentially a conformist, submitting to the rules set out by his neighbors: "The area in which [the peasant] can decide how to run his economic enterprise and how to dispose of his income is limited by the expectations shared with his fellow villagers and by the regulations imposed by the larger society. . . . the nonconformity of one frequently is seen as a threat to the cohesion of the whole.[5]

## Economic Costs of Traditional Communitarianism

As Diaz elaborates in a later section, the peasant's need to conform in order to avoid negative sanctions hinders the possibility for capital accumulation and productive investment:

> [S]ocial commitments often limit the capital which [peasants] can acquire, what they can spend, and how they can invest. Thus in "closed" communities—and often in "open" ones as well—egalitarian styles of life are insisted upon. Acquiring more wealth than one's fellows suggests that one has somehow robbed them and snatched more than one's fair share.[6]

Diaz's point is, of course, essentially the same as Foster's about the pernicious egalitarianism fostered by the peasants' "fixed-pie" view of the socioeconomic universe. Since peasants view everything as finite, the belief prevails that someone can get ahead only by putting someone else out. Any individual's gain is seen as the community's loss; in Foster's words, "someone is being despoiled whether he sees it or not."[7] Consequently, getting ahead is delegitimized and even considered to be dangerous, since it could make one the target of the neighbors' envy, malice, and even witchcraft. Thus families must hide any gain they do make, avoid consumption that would reveal the family's true economic position (e.g., making housing improvements, purchasing new clothes, or paying school tuitions), and be willing, if found out, to expend their surplus in socially approved ways.

In Mayan society, the fiesta system provides a face-saving way for an individual's financial gain to be poured back into the community. Those who have done particularly well are invited to sponsor the village's major saints' festivals; such sponsorship requires purchasing food, drink, entertainment, and necessary sacrificial items for ritualistic purposes. The system thus acts as an economic leveling mechanism that restores the individual to a more equal position with the rest of the community. And what individuals lose in material wealth they gain in social prestige for having fulfilled their civic duty. In Foster's words, "these practices are a redistributive mechanism which permits a person or family that potentially threaten community stability gracefully to restore the status quo, thereby returning itself to a state of acceptability."[8]

## Social/Familial Costs of Traditional Communitarianism

The problems with such institutions and the mentality underlying them are numerous. As already mentioned, the possibilities for capital accumulation and productive investment are severely limited, which thus restrains economic growth. Moreover, the suspiciousness that pervades peasant society because of peasants' perception of a limited good universe fuels the male's machismo image. Honor and respect, as well as material wealth, are viewed as finite; competition among men for these goods is intense, if somewhat veiled. As Foster explains, the Image of Limited Good "encourages a male self-image as a valiant person, one who commands respect, since he will be less attractive as a target than a weakling."[9] To foster this image, men are quick to fight to protect their sense of honor and to prove their bravery. They may abuse their wives or pursue sexual quests outside marriage as a way of demonstrating their manliness. Such behavior is clearly destructive to the family. Finally, the conformity enforced by a false communitarianism frustrates individual initiative and stifles personal achievement, invention, and aspiration, thus reinforcing the fatalism common in many subsistence economies.

## Creating an Alternative Community

Once it is understood that aspects of Cristo-pagan communitarianism are unhealthy and they discourage development, it is easier to recognize some of the motivations behind Evangelicals' disrespect for the traditional system. Their desire to escape an enforced egalitarianism is not merely a wish to avoid the expenses of community service and fiesta sponsorship. It is more broadly a desire to break free of the constraints of a system that suppress individual expression and initiative. Entrepreneurial types chafe under the restrictions of the Cristo-pagan community, and those who have prospered may view the conspicuous consumption of fiesta sponsorship as a wasteful, nonproductive expenditure. The discomforts one may experience under the system are, in short, both psychological and economic.

### *Escaping Cristo-pagan Constraints*

Conversion to Protestantism can relieve both sorts of discomforts. Most immediately, the financial burdens of the fiesta system specifically, and of Cristo-pagan religion more generally, are alleviated: converts are discouraged from visiting witch doctors, from making regular costumbres to various Mayan deities, and from participating in fiestas. A new attitude toward financial stewardship dominates: the goal is to make good investments. This means curtailing expenditures on alcohol, shamans, and various animist rituals and redirecting funds towards home and land improvements and educational opportunities for children. Rather than being scorned, the desire to improve oneself is encouraged, and Evangelical pastors preach that the empowerment of the

Holy Spirit can help parishioners achieve personal transformation. As long as converts remember to render to God what is His due, they are encouraged to save, work hard, grasp new opportunities, and climb the economic ladder little by little.

Often, Pentecostal pastors teach that God will bless those who are faithful in giving to Him the biblical tithe, or 10 percent of one's income. In wealthy Almolonga, a town known countrywide for its prosperity derived from vegetable trading, some Protestant leaders give this sort of explanation for their congregants' prosperity. As one explained with contagious enthusiasm:

> Here in the local church brothers who have paid their tithe now have double [what they had before] in four years time. Not long ago I did a survey to see who is more poor today. When they [his congregants] accepted the Lord, they were poor. [I asked] do they have more or less now? And there was not a single person to say that now that they are in the Gospel they have less. Everybody has more. They have more, they're better off economically. They have learned that giving is better than receiving. They have seen that he who gives the tenth part of their income God will multiply for them. It's an act of faith, right? . . . I have seen how some brothers have started a tiny store and at the beginning they sell just a carton of eggs or little bags of soap, some very few small things. But from that little bit they give their tithe, and economic prosperity [follows]. The key has been making offerings and paying the tithe. Those who haven't paid the tithe haven't stopped having things, but they kind of stagnate, like water that doesn't run.[10]

Whether or not this pastor has accurately captured the exact dynamic explaining the economic improvements enjoyed by converts, there does seem to be a correlation between conversion and improved socioeconomic well-being. In 1990, anthropologist Liliana Goldin interviewed at length several Almolonga families who, in their grandparents' generation, had shared similar economic positions but then became differentiated by the end of the 1980s. She reported: "Most respondents who had experienced what they considered beneficial economic changes in their lives had also converted to Protestantism."[11]

### Support for Free-market Norms

Beyond the microlevel differences in socioeconomic well-being existing between Cristo-pagans and orthodox Evangelicals, certain attitudinal differences are evident that bear upon the prospects for macrolevel economic development. In brief, while the presuppositions underlying Cristo-pagan communitarianism are inherently anti-capitalist, those animating the Evangelicals' alternative community resonant more freely with free-market norms. Cristo-pagan peasants assume a finite universe and insist on economic egalitarianism, even though this comes at the expense of economic growth. They are suspicious of individual initiative and criticize financial stewardship that is nonconformist. Their emphasis is on tradition rather than innovation. Economic improvement is seen as the result of an individual's luck or fate rather than as a somewhat predictable outcome of hard work, careful investment, thrift, and delayed gratification. Such attitudes nurture the belief that economic justice is synonymous with economic equality and that profit-making is a harmful pursuit.

Now, anyone who has been in a Mayan marketplace may be quick to dispute such assertions. There, an intense haggling occurs that clearly demonstrates that peasants have as sophisticated an understanding of profit (and desire for it) as any Western businessperson. Moreover, private property is the norm: the Mayans' traditional notions of community do not require communism. And, any visitor quickly recognizes that Mayans are hard working, resourceful and inventive, and in many ways, frugal. Anthropologist Sol Tax calls the Guatemalan indigenous "penny capitalists," and the label fits.

The point is not that Mayans demonstrate an anticapitalist behavior. It is, rather, that Cristo-pagan suppositions about natural resources, about justice and fairness, about the proper ordering of relationships among humans and between humans and nature, and nature's deities, neither offer strong support to nor legitimate the norms animating free-market systems. In contrast, the values undergirding the Evangelicals' alternative community are more harmonious with those norms.

These attitudinal differences between Cristo-pagans and orthodox Evangelicals regarding the free market were evident in the results of the W&D Survey. Though not dramatic, these differences are very important in light of the general cultural suspicions many Guatemalans have of the free market and its underlying values. Considering the entire sample of individuals interviewed in the W&D Survey, just under half (48 percent) agreed with the statement that "the free market usually gives everyone the opportunity for success." The fact that over half of the respondents failed to endorse the free market reveals the society's considerable suspicion of this way of ordering economic life. The source of such suspicion is open to interpretation. My own belief is that Guatemalans share a general misconception of the market system. *Capitalism* is a dirty word in much of the Third World, largely because the dislocations and pains of statist economies are often mistakenly blamed on capitalism. Recently, at a conference in Costa Rica, I was reminded afresh of the ubiquitous nature of this misunderstanding. After presenting a paper defending a variety of market-friendly policies, I was confronted by one audience participant who said, "What I have heard sounds persuasive, but it is difficult for me to embrace capitalism after all the suffering and injustice it has [caused] in, for example, Nicaragua under [Anastasio] Somoza and the Philippines under [Ferdinand] Marcos." I responded by agreeing that the economic systems to which he referred were undeniably discriminatory, inequitable, and inefficient. But, I said, these economic systems were not capitalist, but interventionist or statist.

Since the overall sample of Guatemalans surveyed by the W&D study was hardly enthusiastic in its support of the free market, the greater affection shown toward the market by the most orthodox respondents is notable. Put simply, orthodox Evangelicals demonstrate a greater sympathy for the norms undergirding a free-market, merit-based economy than do Cristo-pagans, who remain tied to egalitarian sentiments. In the survey, respondents were asked whether the free market "was unjust because it exploits the poor" or whether it "usually gives everyone the chance to succeed." Fully 46.8 percent of orthodox Evangelicals, compared with 38.8 percent of Cristo-pagans, endorsed the latter statement. Similarly, orthodox Evangelicals and Cristo-pagans differed on a survey item designed to assess respondents' views on the possibility of an individual attaining greater prosperity without harming other members of the community. Evangelicals were more likely to legitimate profit-making than were Cristo-pagans. Most important, the two groups differed substantially on a question evaluating respondents' definitions of a just economy. This survey item asked respondents to choose one of two statements: that a just economy was one in which everyone earned the same amount or one in which people with greater skills would earn more. Fully 70 percent of the orthodox Evangelicals, in contrast to only 50 percent of Cristo-pagans, legitimated a merit-based distribution.

## Redefining Gender Relations

In addition to the way the alterative community of Protestantism legitimates free-market norms, it alters male behavior. Evangelicals criticize the drinking, gambling, and womanizing of "machismo" culture by drawing on scriptural injunctions against such behavior. But the Evangelical community also limits these activities by removing the underlying suppositions that encourage it. With greater scope allowed for personal initiative without fear of reprisal or criticism, and with the idea that getting ahead is possible without inflicting harm on the community, males need not be so quick to defend their actions and protect their gains by asserting their manliness.

Moreover, the alternative community of Evangelicalism elevates the status of women. Women directly benefit from the changes encouraged in male behavior and indirectly enjoy enhanced status as wives and mothers because of the tremendous emphasis Evangelical churches place on stable marriages and solid families. Women also attain positions of influence and authority within Protestant churches. This is not necessarily a dramatic change from Cristo-pagan society, where women could serve as *daykeepers* and could be members, with their husbands, of the cofradias. It is, though, somewhat different from the spectator role most women played previously in the Catholic church.

### Increased Inclusiveness

This greater openness to the role of women suggests that an increased inclusiveness marks the Protestants' alternative community. In addition to welcoming women as full participants, the Evangelical community also opens its arms to those who have difficulty fitting into the traditional society and its institutions. As Annis has reported from his fieldwork in villages around Lake Atitlan (see chapter 2), the most common converts to Evangelicalism are those at the two extremes of the local socioeconomic ladder. Those at the bottom lack the resources for an effective participation in the traditional society: they have little hope of attaining social status by serving in cofradias or helping with fiestas because they cannot afford such activities. Those at the top wish to escape the economic leveling of the fiesta system and enjoy the freedom to prosper without being viewed as selfish and evil.

Apart from welcoming members from all social strata, in some instances the Protestant churches are also more open to bi-ethnic relations than traditional Cristo-pagan groups. The case should not be overstated, though; there are villages where one finds churches strictly divided along ethnic lines. In Coban, for example, a Nazarene pastor told me that Ladino Nazarenes will not attend social functions or ministry outreaches coordinated by indigenous Nazarenes, and vice versa. But there are also numerous examples of bi-ethnic congregations, and various studies indicate that indigenous Evangelicals show a greater willingness than indigenous Cristo-pagans to participate in bi-ethnic organizations. As anthropologists Sol Tax and Robert Hinshaw uncovered in their study of Panajachel, indigenous Protestants showed a greater informality and intimacy in their relations with Ladinos. Moreover, the Protestant churches at the time of Tax and Hinshaw's study each consisted of approximately equal numbers of Indians and Ladinos.[12] In Brazil, a researcher found that the Evangelical church provided a place for the establishment of new relations between dark-skinned and light-skinned Brazilians:

> Pentecostalism's vision of transformation forges the possibility for negroes [dark-skinned Brazilians] to be treated as equals—even better than equals—with light-skinned *crentes* [Protestant believers]. Pentecostal

doctrine proclaims that the Holy Spirit is no respecter of persons. In fact, *crentes* commonly claim that the lower and humbler one is in the world, the more open one is likely to be to the power of the Spirit. Based on this principle . . . negroes discover that Pentecostalism allows them to develop a degree of authority impossible in any other social arena.[13]

Similarly, research by David Stoll in his recent study of Nebaj suggests that the growth of the Evangelical community there has contributed to better ethnic relations and to a greater sense of equality between the Ixils and the Ladinos. "Race or stature doesn't matter, the Gospel is for everyone," proclaims a popular refrain in evangelistic campaigns.[14] This has a special resonance in a place like Nebaj, which has been characterized by Ladino discrimination against Ixils.[15] "Ethnic equality is a common theme in preaching in [E]vangelical churches," Stoll writes, "despite their conservative tone." He continues:

> The contribution of reformed religion to ethnic egalitarianism is several. First, keeping young males off the bottle contributes to their efforts to move into new occupational roles. Second, [E]vangelical churches introduce a new language of equality backed up by the practices of born-again churches. The fraternal discourse of "brothers" and "sisters" in Christ recasts the old moral economy in more egalitarian terms across ethnic lines.[16]

### Broadening the Circle of Responsibility and Trust

The new language of brotherhood indicates a further aspect of the alternative communitarianism of Evangelicalism: it reveals that Protestants are broadening their notions of social responsibility. In traditional societies, obligations to help others in times of need are typically limited to the immediate and extended family. The radius of trust in such societies is similarly limited to clan ties. Protestantism puts a new cast on the idea of family, because co-congregants from different families now consider one another brothers and sisters in the Lord. This redefinition then widens the circle of responsibility, care, and trust and establishes a fraternal network of support. As described in the previous chapter, this manifests itself in the variety of mercy or social ministries congregants undertake on one another's behalf.

## Conclusion

The alternative community created by the Evangelicals is distinct from both the Marxist and Cristo-pagan forms of community. It legitimizes personal initiative without encouraging an excessive individualism. The convert is simultaneously liberated to pursue personal goals and anchored in a community of fellow believers to whom he is responsible and accountable and from whom he receives moral support, encouragement, and often, practical assistance. As Goldin summarized in her study of Protestantism in Almolonga:

> [The individualism of the Evangelicals] is fostered by an appeal to community support and solidarity. Thus, shared community ideals, in the past fulfilled through *cofradia* activities, are now being fulfilled through the participation in the new community of "brothers and sisters" who work towards the common goal of self-betterment. It is paradoxical that while the new ideology emphasizes individualism, competition, personal improvement, and social and economic progress, among other values, it does so by appealing to fundamental Maya values associated with community solidarity, support, and guidance.[17]

The Protestant community, in short, nurtures microlevel economic growth by removing the cultural constraints to self-improvement, innovation, and ambition. In addition, the alternative communitarianism of Evangelicals may also modestly contribute to the growth of a moral-cultural climate conducive to the consolidation of free-market institutions—and this bodes well for the prospects for macrolevel economic development. Evangelical theology affirms biblical principles that undergird the market system. The orthodox believer can provide scriptural justification for such free-market propositions as private property, economic initiative, and man's creative capacity. Evangelical conversion does, in some instances, permit the convert to appreciate profit, merit, initiative, innovation, and entrepreneurship. Moreover, the orthodox believe that the Bible encourages personal transformation as a prelude to societal reform, not the reverse. They stress the first principles of personal commitment to Christ and moral regeneration, over economic and political concerns. This has won them the ire of Christian-Marxist liberationists who support wide-ranging economic redistribution projects. As David Martin summed up his reflections on the connections between the Evangelical explosion and democratic capitalism, "by molding individuals with some sense of their own self-hood and capacity to choose, [Pentecostals] may well be building up a constituency well-disposed to a capitalist form of development."[18]

# A Third Reformation?

## Prelude: Ligia's Story

Ligia Col Alva[1] is about sixteen years old, slight, with jet-black hair and piercing, deep brown eyes. She is shy but curious, methodical, and well organized. We are sitting in her 6-foot-by-8-foot office at the local, cement-block elementary school in Las Pacayas, a hamlet about a 25 minutes' drive outside Coban in Guatemala's Alta Verapaz department. Ligia is the community's health promoter and one of the principal contacts between the villagers and a private Christian development agency operating several projects in Las Pacayas. Ligia and her family are Evangelicals, and the ways in which their faith has changed their lives reflect many of the themes raised in this book.

As Ligia, my colleague, and I walk down the muddy main road in the village toward her home on a gray, drizzly day in July 1992, Ligia tells us about her family. When she was a little girl, she says, her father was an alcoholic. He "kept six women" in addition to her mother and was notorious for fighting when drunk. Her mother sometimes bore the brunt of this violence, and I had the sense that Ligia and her siblings had not been spared either, though she did not admit this openly. About six or seven years ago, Ligia's father got into a particularly bad brawl at a village carnival. Some Evangelicals came to visit him while he was recuperating from his injuries, and, she says with a shy smile, "shared the Gospel with him." He converted to Evangelical faith then, stopped drinking, terminated his extramarital affairs, and eventually became a deacon in a local Pentecostal church. But, Ligia reports, he continued to fight with her mother. She had converted before him, Ligia explains, and participated actively in the church. Her mother confided her continuing marital troubles to the elders of the church, and Ligia remembers the elders often coming to her home. They would talk with her father, admonishing him to change his ways and to be a better husband, applying the Bible's teaching on marriage. Now, Ligia says, her parents' relationship is much better—there are no more fights. The changes from her father's conversion, as she puts it, "became certain" (or "solidified") about four years ago.

Ligia's story captures one of the main findings of my research: as is typical of the experience of many of Guatemala's Evangelicals, the primary benefits Ligia's family enjoyed as a result of her father's conversion were domestic. He curtailed his drinking and forsook his extramarital relations, focusing his attentions on his family. Gradually, he reformed his abusive behavior, and marital and family ties were strengthened. When I interviewed Señor Victoriano Col Alva,[2] he told me he lamented his sinful past and "all the money I wasted on drink," and thanked God for giving him a patient wife.

According to Ligia, her father's transformed behavior brought notable economic benefits as well. At about this point in our conversation, we arrived, damp and chilled, at Ligia's home. It was a modest, three-room adobe hut with a dirt floor, four beds, three chairs, and the typical, on-the-ground cooking fire. Ligia's mother was crouched by the fire, attending a young child with one hand and cooking corn tortillas with the other. She gave us a friendly, gap-toothed grin and motioned for us to warm ourselves by the fire. I looked around me: the home was neatly kept, the beds carefully made, cooking paraphernalia hung on a variety of hooks protruding from the walls or set on homemade wooden shelves. Ligia, her mother, and the two younger siblings present were neatly groomed and dressed in clean, though slightly worn clothes. Ligia's four-year-old sister played with a new plastic necklace of the sort children get out of gumball machines in the United States, and Ligia dutifully admired it. Their mood was happy—but the stark reality of their poverty depressed me; my mood was as gray as the thin smoke that hung in the air of their cottage. Ligia sat down, gently pulled her younger sister onto her lap, and said expressively to me, "Things are so much better for us now!" I smiled weakly, swallowed hard, and pondered the fact that their living conditions were even meaner before her father's conversion.

Ligia's humble home reflects another theme of this book, namely, the reality of the *discernible though partial and anticipatory* nature of the economic changes introduced by Evangelical conversion. Again, as is typical, conversion for Ligia's family meant modest, not radical, economic gains. Still, from their perspective, the savings they have gained from a disciplined, "reformed" lifestyle have had a significant impact: the children, for example, have adequate food, clothing, and shoes and are able to attend school. Ligia has an sixth-grade education—a rare achievement for girls in rural, isolated villages. And, unlike some homes I visited in rural Guatemala, Ligia's roof did not leak.

Throughout Guatemala I met Evangelicals who were much better off than Ligia and her family: people who lived in large homes with televisions and even telephones, drove decent cars, and sent their children to private schools. But in most of the places I visited, the economic differences between Evangelicals and their non-Evangelical neighbors were more subtle. The beneficial effects of conversion on the status of women and children, however, were readily evident just about everywhere I went.

Beyond behavioral changes that influence family life, conversion to a biblical worldview can also lead to a new engagement in community affairs.[3] Once again, Ligia's family's experience is somewhat representative. Her father is a deacon of the Pentecostal church that introduced him to the faith, and his responsibilities to the 120 members of this congregation keep him busy. But Victoriano is also the president of the community's nine-member development committee. (In fact, seven of the nine members are Evangelicals.) The committee oversees a revolving agricultural credit fund and a potable water project and is the intermediary with government agencies working on an electrification scheme for the village. Victoriano is also one of the principal contacts from the village with Fundación Contra El Hambre (FH), an Evangelical development agency overseeing the community's agricultural training projects and child sponsorship program. Indeed, when FH first entered the community, Victoriano was one of very few people who expressed willingness to cooperate. Other villagers were uninterested at best and hostile at worst. Judging by the many appointments Señor Col Alva kept, and the numerous interruptions we experienced one day while walking to the school, he is a man actively sought out by the villagers because of his high level of community involvement.

His daughter Ligia is also a key activist in the village in her role as health promoter. The position is funded by FH and involves an assortment of responsibilities. Ligia was trained in basic preventive health care by a nurse from Chimaltenango and travels periodically with her, visiting families throughout Las Pacayas, giving health tips to pregnant mothers, teaching about hygiene and safe cooking procedures, and encouraging childhood vaccinations. Ligia reports that initially the Evangelicals in town were more open than the Catholics were to her teaching because it was reiterated by Evangelical pastors. Now, she reports, most families, regardless of their religious affiliation, are improving their health habits.

Ligia is an evangelist for innovations in other areas beside health and hygiene. Along with an agency staff member from Coban, she is one of the promoters of FH's agricultural and micro-enterprise programs. In this role she encourages widows to join the potato growing project (potatoes are a nontraditional crop in this region) and she teaches young children to embroider flowered designs on blouses that are later sold in nearby markets. Ligia is also responsible for keeping the records for FH's child sponsorship program. Inside her office, sitting at her battered desk, Ligia shows me her files, cards, and papers with a subdued but noticeable sense of pride and self-confidence.

The way Ligia and her father think epitomizes another theme raised in this study, namely, that of the attitudinal changes that a profound and serious conversion to Christian orthodoxy appears to encourage. Ligia and Victoriano are open to innovation, to new ideas, and to outsiders. They affirm the importance of education and of modern medicine. They legitimize personal initiative, ambition, and leadership. They have escaped the pervasive, fatalistic mindset prevalent in traditional agrarian cultures. And in a village where fear of evil spirits—and of government soldiers and armed guerrillas—is common, they exhibit a quiet confidence and sense of optimism.

## Behavioral and Attitudinal Change

Throughout Guatemala, in places as diverse as urban Chimaltenango and isolated La Tinta, my fieldwork and the empirical data from the W&D Survey indicates that joining an Evangelical church leads first to behavior modifications, and then, for true converts who adopt a biblical worldview, to attitudinal transformation as well. The adoption of a morally rigorous Protestant ethic (by both Evangelicals *and* some orthodox Catholics) frees believers from alcohol addiction and encourages careful, disciplined investments in family well-being. It also encourages families to avoid potentially harmful traditional remedies for illness and saves money previously expended for costumbres and the services of curanderos. Some converts, it appears, pursue literacy and Spanish-speaking ability with a new energy, at least partly as a result of being in Evangelical churches where Bible reading is encouraged and the singing is in Spanish. The reformed lifestyle common among Evangelicals usually brings modest, not dramatic, socioeconomic improvement. Families are able to save more of their income, which is then often invested in housing improvements and children's education.

Moreover, they enjoy stronger family relationships and avoid the expenses often formerly incurred by the husband's fighting, gambling, and loss of work time following drinking binges.

This evidence of Evangelical affiliation leading to behavioral change that produces socioeconomic benefits at the micro or family level reinforces Max Weber's argument about the socioeconomic influence of the Protestant ethic. Numerous testimonials from Evangelicals indicate that behavioral changes follow conversion even when converts retain some of their previous animistic religious beliefs. This is so at least in part because membership in a Protestant church disciplines converts in ascetic practices, keeping them accountable for their actions. This finding reinforces Weber's emphasis, in his essays on the sociology of religion, on the social dynamics of Protestant churches. Weber, it will be recalled, argued that Protestant membership was probationary: members had to remain in good moral standing in order to enjoy access to communion. In the small villages of Guatemala, membership in an Evangelical church is a public declaration that commits the affiliate to the well-known code of Protestant behavior: sobriety, marital fidelity, chastity for the unmarried, and avoidance of gambling, fighting, and witchcraft.

Though membership in a Protestant church clearly encourages behavioral transformation, it does not ensure broad-ranging attitudinal change (in the sense of rejecting all animist beliefs). The empirical evidence from the W&D Survey indicates that serious attitudinal shifts are contingent upon a profound conversion whereby animistic religious ideas are decisively rejected. This kind of substantial attitudinal change is facilitated in places where at least some of the Bible has been translated into the indigenous languages and where pastors have completed at least some measure of formal training. This was the case, for example, in Chimaltenango, where the level of orthodoxy among converts was high. Chimaltenango's pastors are well trained, and the churches emphasize discipleship and Bible study. In addition, the area is relatively more urban than the other case sudy communities, and the congregants have obtained higher levels of education than residents of the other communities (and literacy rates are higher). These factors also contribute to the strength of the Evangelical community there.

I found profound conversions and highly orthodox believers in poorer, more isolated areas as well, though, such as La Tinta and Zunil. An important factor influencing the levels of orthodoxy in these two villages was the fact that Cristo-pagan beliefs were held with particular intensity by local Catholics. This meant that the Protestant option was clearly defined and conversion was, in a sense, costly in terms of one's relations with one's neighbors. In contrast, conversion to Protestantism has become almost the norm in Almolonga, and while the pastors in many of Almolonga's churches are well equipped to disciple their congregants, many of the laity are lax in their commitment to doctrinal purity. It "costs" less to be a Protestant in Almolonga, where Evangelicals dominate, and the lack of depth among converts there reflects this.

In all these villages, weak or less orthodox Evangelicals could be found who adopted certain Protestant behaviors while maintaining some animist values and attitudes. These Protestants enjoyed modest socioeconomic improvements from their reformed behavior, but their prospects for significant economic growth may be limited because of their retainment of some essentials of the animist, zero-sum view of the world. Orthodox Evangelicals, in contrast, have more thoroughly rejected not only former behavioral patterns but also old religious and cultural values. These converts adopt important new attitudes— openness to innovation, to education, to personal initiative, to economic accumulation—that predispose them to capitalist development.

To reiterate, the behavioral changes resulting from Evangelical conversion produce socioeconomic results at the domestic level, while the attitudinal changes associated with serious conversion to orthodox Christianity portend longer term effects at the macro or societal level. The new attitudes and values affirmed by the orthodox Christian worldview (as embraced by Evangelicals, orthodox Catholics, and "hidden convert" Catholics) challenge traditional notions of the zero-sum economy, initiative, fate, social mobility, entrepreneurship, and innovation. As more and more people come to adopt the new worldview, the stifling grip of the traditional worldview can be loosed, making possible an economic takeoff.

Generalized economic development among the Guatemalan Maya is currently retarded at least in part by the traditional worldview that is based on the Image of Limited Good identified by scholar George Foster. The situation among the Maya is not unique; rather, other Third World agrarian societies exhibit similar cultural attitudes that hinder economic advancement. As one researcher noted recently:

> [P]re-industrial societies are zero-sum systems: upward social mobility can only come at someone else's expense. [In such societies] social status is hereditary rather than achieved, and the culture encourages one to accept one's social position in this life. . . . Aspirations toward social mobility are sternly repressed. Such value systems help to maintain social solidarity and discourage economic accumulation in a variety of ways, ranging from norms of sharing and charity, to norms of *noblesse oblige*, to the potlatch and similar institutions in which one attains prestige by giving away one's worldly goods. . . .
>
> Traditional cultures are geared to maintain social peace and stability in steady-state economies; social mobility threatens the system. . . . [T]raditional value systems of agrarian society . . . tend to discourage social

> change in general and accumulative entrepreneurial motivation in partic-
> ular, which is likely to be stigmatized and relegated to pariah groups if
> tolerated at all. Economic accumulation is characterized as ignoble greed.
> *To facilitate the economic accumulation needed to launch industrializa-*
> *tion, these cultural prohibitions must be relaxed.*[4]

The first wave of Evangelical revival—the Protestant Reformation—
played a key role in liberating northern Europe from the grip of traditional values that inhibited economic development and in legitimizing
economic accumulation. Indeed, as Weber noted, such accumulation
began to be highly respected as a sign of divine favor upon the elect.

Protestantism also freed poor people from an animistic worldview
that emphasized "equitable exchanges with nature, the dead, and fellow
humans."[5] As one scholar has observed, "Animism encourages an exaggerated sensitivity to the predicament of anyone, human or spirit,
who is pushed aside or marginalized by productive or reproduc-
tive activity."[6] This makes peasants reluctant to interfere with nature,
even though their survival depends on harnessing natural resources.
Consequently, peasants adopt various propitiatory rituals to seek permission from spirit owners and appease the gods of the natural environment.[7] According to this scholar, Protestantism "shatter[ed] equity-
consciousness."[8] By removing deity to a distance (emphasizing God's
transcendence rather than immanence), Protestantism permitted a new
conception of the human relationship with nature. Moreover, Protestantism's emphasis on original sin suggested that the misfortunes of the
poor and marginalized were not always tied to specific oppressive or
discriminatory acts by particular, responsible individuals. The poor
were not always victims of deliberate maleficence; rather, their misfortune could be rooted in the generalized depravity of the fallen world.[9]
Hence, the way was paved for believing that one person's economic
gain would not *necessarily* be interpreted as harming another person.
Personal initiative was legitimated.

The second wave of Protestant revival took place not in a setting of
peasant animism, but in gradually industrializing England in the eigh-
teenth and early nineteenth centuries. Consequently, the attitudinal
changes it encouraged were somewhat different, though the end result
was similar: Protestantism legitimated personal initiative. The discussion of the second wave of Protestantism focuses mainly on the behavioral transformations brought about by strict Methodism, transformations similar to those experienced by Pentecostal converts in Latin
America: sobriety, marital fidelity, discipline, punctuality, frugality.
Less attention has been given to the attitudinal changes encouraged by
Methodist revival. Martin's study notes briefly the way in which Evangelical conversion provided avenues for an assertion of the values of

equality of opportunity and merit-based, rather than heredity-based, social status in the midst of a rigidly stratified society. As he explains, some people on the margins of the English social hierarchy found that social order reproduced in the Anglican establishment, and "by joining the Methodists they were able to make their autonomy visible without directly challenging the whole political order."[10] Methodism, in short, provided what Martin calls "free social space" in class-based England. Inside the dissenters' fellowships of the 1800s there was freedom for self-expression, individualism, and participation in decision-making—in short, free space for personal initiative.

Importantly, as Martin argues, Pentecostalism—the third wave of Protestant revival—provides similar "free social space" today in Latin America and similar freedom for self-expression and initiative. The attitudes that the W&D Survey demonstrated to be correlated with Christian orthodoxy—legitimation of profit; of merit-based inequalities; of personal achievement; of innovation; and of the pursuit of education, literacy, and the skills required for integration into the formal economy—suggest that conversion to this worldview erodes attachment to traditional, animistic values that inhibit economic development. Consequently, this third wave may play an extremely important role not only in affecting the economic prospects of individual families but, over time, in influencing broader, society-wide progress.

## Looking to the Future

Many observers, of course, dispute that the Evangelical explosion in Latin America represents a third reformation that will produce the kinds of social, economic, and political changes associated with the earlier waves of religious revival. They usually offer one of three arguments.

First, many scholars who look at the intersection of religion and economics—and of culture and development, more generally—do so with an assumption that ultimately, the chief factor influencing a less developed country's prospects for advancement is the structure of the international economy. For these researchers, even if religious revival in poor nations produces socioeconomic change at the family level, it will be unable to do more than this because Third World societies are trapped in poverty by the international capitalist system. They believe economic development is principally a matter of a country's position in the global economy—an economy that is unjust and ordered in such ways that the increasing prosperity of the industrialized North is inextricably bound up with the diminishing prospects for the less developed South. Such views are not new; rather, they represent the old dependency school dominant in the 1960s and 1970s. Needless to say, if one believes that what happens inside a poor country has little relevance for that country's economic prospects, then one will have little appreciation for even significant cultural change in that country.

However, if one argues (as I do) that a country's prospects for development are a function primarily of factors internal to the country, rather than external to it in the global economy, then one must take cultural change seriously. My earlier book, *Preferential Option*,[11] argued that the evidence from the last five decades of development experience in the Third World shows that countries' economic prospects are more affected by their own internal economic policies, political and legal structures, and cultural values than they are by the trading patterns, power relationships, and economic arrangements of the global system. I will not repeat those arguments here; suffice it to say that those who view the world through the lens of dependency theory will not easily recognize the potential that broad-ranging cultural change, stimulated by the Evangelical explosion, creates for economic development.

The second reason that some scholars dismiss the notion that the third wave of religious reformation could produce social change and economic development is that they do not take religious beliefs seriously enough. As argued earlier, many studies of the intersection of religion and economics focus on religious affiliation. But since people may affiliate with a particular religion, without embracing that religion's worldview, comparisons based on nominal affiliation are usually unilluminating. When few differences between Protestants and Catholics can be found, many researchers conclude that religion is not an important causal variable. When we look beyond nominal affiliation to the content of one's religious beliefs, however, then important differences among people with varying worldviews appear. Consequently, it is significant that notable numbers of citizens are abandoning a traditional animist worldview and embracing a Biblically orthodox one.

The third possible objection to the idea of a third reformation is the most important and persuasive one. It is the contention that the historical context in which the Evangelical explosion is unfolding is remarkably different than that of sixteenth-century Europe or nineteenth-century England. Therefore, any consequences of the revival are likely to differ from those that characterized the earlier ages.

The theological centers of the earlier reformations—Calvinism, Lutheranism, and Methodism—took religious institutions seriously. The early reformers were concerned not only about evangelism and worldview change but about how to nurture converts and how to sustain the faith by transmitting it from one generation to the next. They wanted to help converts understand the ways in which their newly grasped faith was to be lived out in every sphere of life. Moreover, they were preoccupied with not only converting individuals but with the question of the church—its sacraments, creeds, and governing structures. They saw the church not only as the gathering place of the faithful, but as an influential institution in society.

By contrast, the theological center of the third wave—Pentecostalism —tends to be less interested in questions of institutionalization and more interested in the immediacy of God's presence. The emphasis on religious experience does not exclude concern for religious doctrine and teaching. But it can dilute interest in the task of creating institutions that embody the new worldview and that apply its truths to all fields of inquiry. Throughout Guatemala, one finds Pentecostals who spend far more time in evangelism (sharing the new faith) than in discipleship (teaching converts the rules of life that flow from Biblical principles).

To an extent, the profound changes associated with the earlier religious reformations were not only a product of many individuals embracing a new worldview, but also of institutions being shaped and transformed by that worldview. Consequently, if the third wave of Evangelical revival is to stimulate broad-ranging social change, Evangelicals will have to create institutions that can sustain and nurture converts over time.

In Guatemala, more institution-building is being done than immediately meets the eye. Most important, Evangelicals are establishing private schools (elementary through high school) for the inculcation of a Christian worldview in the coming generations. As noted earlier, there are already more than 200 private Christian schools in the country. In some of the schools I visited, a distinctively Christian worldview is not immediately evident. Teachers begin the day with prayer and there may be a specific chapel or devotional time, but biblical insights are not integrated into academic discussions. In other schools, by contrast, great attention has been given to constructing a comprehensive curriculum addressing the intersections of biblical faith and science, politics, economic life, the natural world, literature, and so forth. Most of these institutions are affiliated with the neo-Pentecostal churches. They are labeled "neo" because while retaining traditional Pentecostal emphases —on religious experience, the gifts of the Holy Spirit, and preparation for the next life—they also, unlike traditional Pentecostals, urge their congregants to be active in this world and to apply biblical truth to everyday life.

It remains to be seen whether biblically orthodox Christians in Guatemala and throughout Latin America will be able to create new institutions and reshape old ones to reflect the insights of their faith. To the extent that Evangelical revival produces large numbers of true converts who adopt and begin living out a new worldview *and* stimulates the growth of institutions that embody, nurture, and sustain that world-view, then it may stimulate socioeconomic change.

What is definitely unclear is whether the Christian orthodoxy that appears able to give rise to socioeconomic progress can automatically be sustained once that progress has been attained. One of the more sobering aspects of prosperity, at least for those who take religious conviction seriously, is that it can make cultures, like individuals, forgetful of their God. If Lawrence Harrison's contentions in the latter part of his book *Who Prospers?* are correct, one reason for the economic decline of the United States is that the moral-cultural values that underpinned its astounding rise to prosperity have eroded under the forces of modernization and secularization unleashed by that very prosperity.[12]

Guatemala has not yet experienced such a prosperity nationwide. Guatemala's orthodox Christians may point to a verse of scripture that encourages them to "be not conformed to the patterns of this world, but be ye transformed by the renewing of your minds," as one that helps explain their enhanced well-being following conversion. They rejected ancient, Cristo-pagan attitudes common to the surrounding culture that inhibited development and adopted new patterns of thinking and behaving that proved conducive to socioeconomic advancement. The challenge for them in future generations may be to resist other "patterns of this world"—namely, those of a secularized materialism springing from increased prosperity.

# Worldview and Development Survey Questionnaire

In developing this questionnaire, I drew from survey instruments employed by other social science researchers conducting work in the United States and Latin America. I am particularly indebted to the work of Mitchell Seligson and John Booth in Central America; James Sexton, Clyde Woods, Sheldon Annis, and Sol Tax in Guatemala; and Herbert McClosky and John Zaller in the United States. The full bibliographic citations for these works are in the bibliography.

Interview Booklet
Worldview and Development Survey
Guatemala

TO BE COMPLETED BY THE INTERVIEWER:
1. Interview Number: _____
2. Residence of respondent:
    1. La Tinta, Dept. of Alta Verapaz
    2. Uspantan, Dept. of Quiche
    3. Chimaltenango, Dept. of Chimaltenango
    4. Almolonga, Dept. of Quiche
    5. Zunil, Dept. of Quiche

INTERVIEWER'S INTRODUCTION: Good day. My name is _____
and I am working with CINASE, a private polling firm in Guatemala City. We

are conducting surveys in several towns in Guatemala on behalf of Lic. Amy Sherman, a researcher from the University of Virginia in the United States. This survey is about living standards, culture, and religion in Guatemala, and I hope you will be willing to help me by answering some questions in the survey. Before we start, let me mention that all your answers will be kept confidential, and nobody's name will be revealed. Also, I want to emphasize that this is not a political survey, and it is not sponsored by the government or any political party or group.

[If further explanation is necessary]: The results of this survey will be used to help Lic. Sherman in writing her doctoral thesis in order to graduate from the university. Again, all your answers are strictly confidential.

TO BE COMPLETED BY THE INTERVIEWER:
   3. Sex of Respondent:     1. male     2. female

INTERVIEWER: The first part of our survey has to do with information about your work and family.
   4. First, what is your civil status? Are you . . .
         1. married                     2. living together
         3. divorced/separated          4. widow/widower
         5. single (never married)
   5. How many children do you have living with you?
         _____ children
   6. What sort of school do your children of school-age (4–18 yrs) attend?
         1. I don't have school-age children.
         2. public school
         3. private school (but not Christian)
         4. private school (and Christian)
         5. My children do not attend school.

[INTERVIEWER NOTE: Ask question 7 only of respondents who have children living with them]:
   7. Have your children been vaccinated?
         1. yes     2. no
   8. Can you speak and understand Spanish?
         1. yes     2. no

[INTERVIEWER NOTE: If "yes," ask]:
         8b. Can you listen to a radio program in Spanish and understand most of it?
               1. yes     2. no
   9. And your spouse? Can she/he speak and understand Spanish?
         1. yes     2. no

10. Do you know how to read and write?
    1. yes    2. no
11. How many years of schooling in total have you completed?
    (note the number of years on the response sheet)

    _____

12. Where do you go for medical help when you or someone in your family is ill?
    1. health post or clinic
    2. pharmacy
    3. shaman/curer or use natural medicine
    4. health promoter
    5. other (specify _____)

INTERVIEWER: Thanks for answering those questions. Now we can talk a little about your work.
13. What has your principal occupation been? _____
    _____

14. Are you the head of the household?
    1. yes    2. no

[INTERVIEWER NOTE: If "no," ask question 14b and 14c]:
    14b. What has been the principal occupation of the head of the household? _____
    _____

    14c. What religion is the head of household? _____
    _____

[TO BE COMPLETED BY INTERVIEWER]:
Circle the correct category of the Head of Household's occupation and confirm your choice with the respondent:
    1. *mozo* (paid day laborer on another's land)
    2. farmer only
    3. farmer and trader
    4. trader only
    5. owns own business
    6. store clerk
    7. *transportista*
    8. artisan (shoemaker/repairer; carpenter; textile weaver; watch/jewelry repair; craftsman; leather worker; furniture maker/repairer, etc.)
    9. auto repair
    10. barber/hairdresser
    11. secretary/office worker
    12. manager
    13. government employee

14. professional (doctor, accountant, dentist, teacher, lawyer)
15. other (specify _____ )
15. Now can you tell me please, what was your father's principal occupation during the time you were growing up? (If your father did not live with you while you were growing up, or died when you were young, what was your mother's principal occupation?) _____

_____

16. Are you [and your family] raising any of YOUR OWN crops on any land (land that you own or land that you rent from someone else)?
    1. yes    2. no

[INTERVIEWER NOTE:—If "no," skip to question 20
        —If "yes," continue . . . ]
17. What kinds of crops do you grow? Do you grow . . .
    1. corn? (yes/no)
    2. beans? (yes/no)
    3. coffee? (yes/no)
    4. green vegetables (for example, broccoli)? (yes/no)
    5. carrots or radishes? (yes/no)
    6. others? (Please specify _____ )
18. Do you use any fertilizer on any of your crops?
    1. yes    2. no

[INTERVIEWER NOTE: If "yes," ask question 18b and 19.
        If "no," skip to question 19]:
    18b. What kind of fertilizer do you use?
        1. organic
        2. chemical
        3. other (specify) _____
19. Where do you sell your crops?
    1. local market only
    2. local and regional market—specify name of regional market

    _____

    3. Guatemala City
    4. places outside of Guatemala (for example, El Salvador)
20. Which range best describes your ANNUAL household income (including income from all sources)?
    1. less than Q3,000    5. from Q24,001–Q36,000
    2. from Q3,001–Q6,000    6. from Q36,001–Q48,000
    3. from Q6,001–Q12,000    7. from Q48,001–Q60,000
    4. from Q12,001–Q24,000    8. more than Q60,000

INTERVIEWER: Now I have some questions for you about religion.

21. First, religious faith is more important to some people than to others. How important is religious faith to you?
    1. very important
    2. somewhat important
    3. not very important
22. What is your religion?
    1. Catholic
    2. Catholic Action
    3. Evangelical
    4. other (for example, Mormon, Jehovah's Witness)
       specify _____
    5. I don't have any religion

[INTERVIEW NOTE: If respondent answers 4 or 5, skip to question 23. If respondent answers 1, 2, or 3, find the appropriate box and continue with question 22]:

BOX ONE: *Catholic*
    22a. What was your parents' religion while you were growing up?
        1. Catholic
        2. Catholic Action
        3. Evangelical
        4. other
        5. no religion
    22b. Are you now, or have you ever been a member of a *cofradia*?
        1. yes    2. no
    22c. How often do you make *costumbre*?
        1. more than once a week
        2. about once a week
        3. less than once a week
        4. less than once a month
        5. hardly ever
    22d. How often do you attend mass?
        1. more than once a week
        2. about once a week
        3. less than once a week
        4. less than once a month
        5. hardly ever
    22e. Have you changed your occupation in the last 10 years?
        1. yes    2. no

[INTERVIEWER NOTE: If "yes," ask, "What was your occupation before you changed it, and what is it now?"

BOX TWO: *Catholic Action*

22a. What was your parents' religion?
1. Catholic
2. Catholic Action
3. Evangelical
4. other
5. no religion

22b. Are you now, or have you ever been, a catechist?
1. yes    2. no

22c. How often do you attend mass?
1. more than once a week
2. about once a week
3. more than once a week
4. less than once a month
5. hardly ever

22d. Are you a member of a Bible study or prayer group?
1. yes
2. no

22e. In what year did you join Catholic Action? _____

22f. Since the time you became a member of Catholic Action, have you changed your occupation?
1. yes    2. no

INTERVIEWER NOTE: If answer is "yes," ask, "What was your occupation before you joined Catholic Action, and what occupation did you change to after you joined Catholic Action?" _____

22g. What percentage of your income do you give to the Church? _____ %

BOX THREE: *Evangelical*

22a. What was your parents' religion?
1. Catholic
2. Catholic Action
3. Evangelical
4. other
5. no religion

22b. What denomination is your church? (example, Nazarene, Pentecostal, Baptist) _____

22c. How often do you attend church services?
1. more than once a week
2. about once a week
3. less than once a week

4. less than once a month
5. hardly ever

22d. Are you a member of a Bible study or prayer group?
    1. yes    2. no

22e. In what year did you accept Christ? _____

22f. Since the time that you accepted Christ, have you changed your occupation?
    1. yes    2. no

INTERVIEWER NOTE: If "yes," ask, "What was your occupation before you accepted Christ, and what occupation did you change to after you accepted Christ?"

_____

_____

_____

_____

22g. Some Christians believe that it is important to tithe, but find that they just cannot afford to. In the past year, have you been able to tithe (that is, give at least 10 percent of your income to the church)?
    1. yes    2. no

INTERVIEWER: People hold different opinions about different religious matters like what happens after we die. I'm going to read you some statements that people sometimes make, and I'd like you to tell me which one of the statements best reflects your own opinion.

23. First I have four statements we sometimes hear about life after death. Which one best reflects your own opinion?
    1. There is no life after death.
    2. There is life after death—but what we do in this life has no bearing on it.
    3. Heaven is the reward for those who earn by it their good life.
    4. Jesus Christ is the only way to eternal life.

24. Now here are three statements that have to do with what people sometimes think about religion. Which one most closely reflects your own opinion about religion?
    1. Religion is a guide to help people get to heaven.
    2. Religion is a guide for transforming society.
    3. Religion not only helps people get to heaven, it also helps them change and improve their way of living here on earth.

INTERVIEWER: Thanks for answering those. Now I'll ask you some questions that are a little shorter. These are some statements we hear when we interview people about religion and spiritual matters. I'll read a statement, and then after each one, all you need to do is tell me whether you agree or disagree with the statement.

25. The first statement is: It is important to make costumbre before cutting down a tree or planting a field. Do you agree or disagree?
    1. agree
    2. disagree
    3. does not know/refuses to answer/unsure
26. The next statement is: It is important to read the Bible everyday.
    1. agree
    2. disagree
    3. does not know/refuses to answer/unsure
27. Praying to the saints is wrong.
    1. agree
    2. disagree
    3. does not know/refuses to answer/unsure
28. Certain places (such as certain hills or caves) are sacred.
    1. agree
    2. disagree
    3. does not know/refuses to answer/unsure

[INTERVIEWER NOTE: Ask questions 29 and 30 ONLY of Catholic and Catholic Action respondents]:

29. I try my best to follow all the teachings of the Catholic church.
    1. agree
    2. disagree
    3. does not know/refuses to answer/unsure
30. I try to always attend mass on the prescribed days.
    1. agree
    2. disagree
    3. does not know/refuses to answer/unsure
31. If angered or neglected, the spirits/souls of ancestors can cause their living relatives to become ill.
    1. agree
    2. disagree
    3. does not know/refuses to answer/unsure
32. If a person angers the earth god or mountain god, the god may punish him by making him sick or causing him to have an accident.
    1. agree
    2. disagree
    3. does not know/refuses to answer/unsure
33. The Bible helps me in practical ways—like instructing me on how to raise my children or manage my money.
    1. agree
    2. disgree
    3. does not know/refuses to answer/unsure

34. Sometimes when I get sick, I go to a curandero for help.
    1. agree
    2. disagree
    3. does not know/refuses to answer/unsure

INTERVIEWER: You're doing a good job. Now we're more than halfway through the survey. In this next section, I'd like to talk with you about some issues here in your community and your activities here.

35. First, have you ever participated in a project to improve your neighborhood?
    1. yes    2. no

36. Are you a member of a voluntary organization (such as the volunteer firemen)?
    1. yes    2. no

37. Did you vote in the most recent national elections?
    1. yes    2. no

38. Here are two opinions about the free market/free enterprise system. Do you think that . . .
    1. The free market system is unjust because it exploits the poor?
       —Or do you think that . . .
    2. The free market system usually gives everyone the opportunity for success.

39. And here are two different statements we sometimes hear from people about competitive elections. Which one comes closest to your opinion?
    1. Competitive elections, although not perfect, are the best system for electing our political leaders.
    2. Competitive elections are not the most appropriate method for choosing our political leaders in our country's context.

40. And which of these two statements about economic justice comes closest to your opinion?
    1. Under a just economic system, all people would earn the same amount.
    2. Under a just economic system, people with higher skills would earn more.

INTERVIEWER: Thanks for your answers to those questions. We're in the final section of the survey now.

Next I have some statements of opinions that people hold about some different interesting topics. As we did earlier, after I read each statement, I'd like you to tell me whether you agree or disagree with it.

41. The first statement is: "A man should always try to do better economically than his parents did."
    1. agree
    2. disagree
    3. does not know/refuses to answer/unsure

42. The next statement is "A man who advances economically probably was successful because he robbed, cheated, or otherwise hurt other people."
    1. agree
    2. disagree
    3. does not know/refuses to answer/unsure
43. "Being competitive is a positive trait." Do you agree or disagree with this statement?
    1. agree
    2. disagree
    3. does not know/refuses to answer/unsure
44. And do you agree or disagree with this statement: "Someone who has more than his neighbors will receive more respect."
    1. agree
    2. disagree
    3. does not know/refuses to answer/unsure


[INTERVIEWER NOTE: IF NECESSARY FOR CLARIFICATION OF "MORE," say "more money," "more economic wealth."]


INTERVIEWER: Now for this last series of questions, I'd like you to imagine that there are two farmers named Juan and Pablo talking with one another as they work. They have different opinions on some interesting topics.

45. For example, Farmer Juan says that if he could choose, he would rather have more money than more land. But Farmer Pablo disagrees; he says he'd prefer more land to more money. Which man do you think has the better opinion?
    1. Farmer Juan (more money)
    2. Farmer Pablo (more land)
46. Then the two farmers talked about how they might increase their harvests. Farmer Juan says that they should change their traditional way of doing things and try some new ways that might work better. But Farmer Pablo says that they should keep things the same because people who try to change the way things have always been done often end up making things worse. Who do you think is right?
    1. Farmer Juan (change old ways)
    2. Farmer Pablo (keep things the same)
47. Then Juan and Pablo started talking about luck. Juan says that a person who works hard can overcome whatever lies in his luck/fate. But Pablo thinks that if a person is born with bad luck, there is nothing he can do to change it. Who do you think is right?
    1. Farmer Juan (can overcome fate)
    2. Farmer Pablo (cannot overcome fate)
48. Then they talked about laziness. Juan said that he thought laziness was like

a sin. But Pablo said that if a person is lazy, he was probably born that way and it's not his fault. Who do you think is right?

    1. Juan (laziness is a sin)

    2. Pablo (born that way and it's not his fault)

49. Then the two farmers talked about school. Juan said that children should not attend school because it is more important that they learn the work of their fathers and mothers. But Pablo thinks that children should attend school because what they learn there is useful. Again, who do you think has the better opinion?

    1. Juan (don't send children to school)

    2. Pablo (send children to school)

INTERVIEWER: Thanks so much for your time. You have been very helpful. I just have one more question for you, and that is . . .

50. How old are you? _____ years

INTERVIEWER: Thanks again for helping us out!

*  *  *  *  *  *  *

[INTERVIEWER NOTE: Exit the home and then complete the following sections on the respondent and the status of the respondent's home. Do not ask these questions of the respondent.]

Exit Q1. Was the respondent indigenous or ladino?

    1. indigenous

    2. ladino

Exit Q2. Was the interview conducted . . .

    1. totally in the indigenous language

    2. partially in the indigenous language and partially in Spanish

    3. totally in Spanish

Exit Q3. How proficient was the respondent in speaking and understanding Spanish?

    1. very proficient

    2. somewhat proficient

    3. not very proficient

    4. spoke almost no Spanish at all

Exit Q.4 What kind of floor did the home have?

    1. dirt

    2. cement

    3. other

Exit Q5. What kind of roof did it have?

    1. tile

    2. tin

    3. thatch

    4. other

Exit. Q6. Did the home appear to have electricity?

   1. yes

   2. no

   3. unable to ascertain

Exit Q7. Was there a latrine?

   1. yes

   2. no

   3. unable to ascertain

# Selected Additional Tables from the Worldview and Development Survey

TABLE B-1 Female Literacy and Bilingualism by Worldview Type

| | Orthodox Evangelical (%) | Moderate Evangelical (%) | Weak Evangelical (%) | Cristo-Pagan (%) | Orthodox Catholic (%) | Traditional Catholic (%) |
|---|---|---|---|---|---|---|
| Able to read and write (N = 288)[1] | 77.3 | 44.4 | 49.0 | 47.1 | 65.9 | 75.0 |
| Able to speak and understand Spanish (N = 288)[2] | 89.3 | 80.0 | 93.9 | 68.6 | 86.4 | 83.3 |

SOURCE: W&D Survey, Guatemala, June 1993.

[1]Significant at $p$ = .000
[2]Significant at $p$ = .01

TABLE B-2 Attitudes Toward Education and Innovation by Worldview Type

| | Orthodox Evangelical (%) | Moderate Evangelical (%) | Weak Evangelical (%) | Cristo-Pagan (%) | Orthodox Catholic (%) | Traditional Catholic (%) |
|---|---|---|---|---|---|---|
| Affirming innovation (N = 623)[1] | 91.7 | 73.0 | 86.9 | 77.6 | 90.1 | 80.0 |
| Affirming children's education (N = 631)[2] | 82.4 | 77.5 | 79.8 | 62.8 | 79.8 | 71.0 |

SOURCE: W&D Survey, Guatemala, June 1993.

[1]Significant at $p$ = .005
[2]Significant at $p$ = .000

TABLE B-3 Attitudes Toward Profit by Worldview Type ($N = 594$)[1]

| Attitude | Orthodox Evangelical (%) | Moderate Evangelical (%) | Weak Evangelical (%) | Cristo-Pagan (%) | Orthodox Catholic (%) | Traditional Catholic (%) | Row Total (N) |
|---|---|---|---|---|---|---|---|
| Profit illegitimate | 9.4 | 20.2 | 17.5 | 16.5 | 9.3 | 16.9 | 87 |
| Profit legitimate | 90.6 | 79.8 | 82.5 | 83.5 | 90.7 | 83.1 | 507 |
| Column total (N) | 139 | 104 | 97 | 103 | 86 | 65 | 594 |

SOURCE: W&D Survey, Guatemala, June 1993.

[1] Significant at $p = .115$

TABLE B-4 Foster Index Score by Worldview Type ($N = 632$)[1]

| | Orthodox Evangelical (%) | Moderate Evangelical (%) | Weak Evangelical (%) | Cristo-Pagan (%) | Orthodox Catholic (%) | Traditional Catholic (%) |
|---|---|---|---|---|---|---|
| Average score (out of total score of 6) | 4.85 | 4.20 | 4.32 | 4.12 | 4.82 | 4.36 |

SOURCE: W&D Survey, Guatemala, June 1993.

[1] $F$ probability = .000

TABLE B-5 Rejection of Traditional Medicine by Worldview Type (N = 625)[1]

| Visit curanderos? | Orthodox Evangelical (%) | Moderate Evangelical (%) | Weak Evangelical (%) | Cristo-Pagan (%) | Orthodox Catholic (%) | Traditional Catholic (%) | Row Total (N) |
|---|---|---|---|---|---|---|---|
| Yes | 0 | 27.9 | 57.0 | 56.9 | 2.2 | 44.3 | 187 |
| No | 99.3 | 71.2 | 43.0 | 43.1 | 93.4 | 54.3 | 438 |
| Column total (N) | 144 | 111 | 100 | 116 | 91 | 70 | 625 |

SOURCE: W&D Survey, Guatemala, June 1993

[1]Significant at p = .000

TABLE B-6 Retention of Traditional Beliefs by Church Attendance (N = 437)[1]

| Retention of traditional beliefs | More than 1/week (%) | 1/week (%) | Less than 1/week (%) | Less than 1/month (%) | Hardly Ever (%) | Row Total (N) |
|---|---|---|---|---|---|---|
| Low | 53.9 | 50.4 | 46.4 | 33.3 | 0 | 226 |
| Medium | 24.8 | 24.3 | 21.4 | 55.6 | 66.7 | 111 |
| High | 21.3 | 25.2 | 32.1 | 11.1 | 33.3 | 100 |
| Column total (N) | 282 | 115 | 28 | 9 | 3 | 437 |

SOURCE: W&D Survey, Guatemala, June 1993.

[1]Significant at p = .23

# Notes

Preface

1. Wilton M. Nelson, *Protestantism in Central America* (Grand Rapids: Eerdmans, 1984), 37. It is possible, though, that this author means progress not so much in terms of quantitative church growth, but rather in the expansion of Protestant activity. According to scholar Virginia Garrard-Burnett, Protestant missions "introduced a vast network of Protestant-run development projects into the Guatemala countryside" during the first three decades of this century. Despite "this impressive flurry of activity," however, she says "none of the missions registered any significant growth in rural areas" during this time period. See Virginia Garrard-Burnett, "Protestantism in Rural Guatemala, 1872–1954," *Latin American Research Review* 24 (1989):127–142.

2. Nelson, *Protestantism in Central America*, 72.

3. Ibid., 58.

4. Ibid., 71.

5. According to Virginia Garrard-Burnett, the indigenous churches became particularly active beginning in the 1960s, though some were founded earlier. These indigenous denominations "embraced Pentecostalism" and "encouraged a native pastorate familiar with the customs, norms, and values of their own congregations, while retaining the theological fundamentalism and political conservatism of the missions." [See Garrard-Burnett, "Protestantism in Rural Guatemala," 140–141.]

6. Nelson, *Protestantism in Central America*, 72.

7. Ibid.

8. There are some radical or theologically liberal elements in the historic

Protestant denominations, and these believers would not necessarily affirm such doctrines as the historical veracity of the miracles described in the New Testament or the sufficiency of salvation by grace through faith in Christ. These Protestants, sympathetic to liberation theology, might deny the historical Jesus and focus on the idea of a "Christ figure" or "Christ myth." Some consider certain political stances—such as anticapitalism and a choice to "side with the poor" against the rich—as fundamental for salvation. Some might also deny the existence of hell, believing that there is sufficient evil in this world and there need be no hell in the afterlife. In some cases these groups exist within otherwise orthodox denominations: for example, certain synods of the Presbyterian church are more liberal than others (and the liberationists talk of separating from the Presbyterian denomination and forming an alternative, liberal, Presbyterian church). There are two confederations of Protestant churches in Guatemala: the more orthodox (and larger) Alianza Evangelica and the smaller, liberal Conference of Evangelical Churches of Guatemala. The Alianza is far more concerned than the Conference with the preservation of orthodox doctrine: I interviewed a high-ranking staff member of the Conference who told me that Guatemalan Protestantism needed to become "truly indigenous" and if this meant that Evangelicals wished to worship the traditional pantheon of Mayan deities as well as Jesus Christ, then that was acceptable. For an ideologically inspired commentary on the orthodox and liberationist Evangelical factions in Guatemala, see Rosemary Radford Ruether, "Ecumenism in Central America," *Christianity and Crisis* (10 July 1989): 208–212.

Introduction

1. James D. Sexton, ed., *Son of Tecún Umán: A Maya Indian Tells His Life Story* (Tucson: University of Arizona Press, 1981), 26, 151.

2. David Martin, *Tongues of Fire: The Explosion of Protestantism in Latin America* (Oxford, England: Basil Blackwell, 1990), 205.

3. Élie Halévy, *The Liberal Awakening 1815–1830*, vol.2 of *A History of the English People in the Nineteenth Century*, trans. E. I. Watkin (New York: Barnes & Noble, 1961), vi.

4. Herbert Schlossberg, unpublished bibliographic essay on the Evangelicals' effect on nineteenth-century England, quoting from J. L. and Barbara Hammond, *Age of the Chartists, 1832–1854: A Study of Discontent* (Hamden, Conn.: Archon Books, 1962), 238.

5. See Peter Berger in the foreword to Martin, *Tongues of Fire*, vii.

6. Robert Wuthnow, "Understanding Religion and Politics," *Daedalus* (Summer 1991), 14.

7. Ibid.

8. Ibid.

9. James F. Pontuso, interview by Kenneth A. Myers, September/October 1993, *Mars Hill Tapes* (Powhatan, Va.: Mars Hill Audio, 1993).

10. Richard Critchfield, *Villages* (New York: Doubleday, 1981), 252.

11. See Maud Oakes, *The Two Crosses of Todos Santos: Survivals of Mayan Religious Ritual* (New York: Pantheon Books, 1951), 170.

12. The phrase is Liliana Goldin's; for a discussion of her arguments, see chapter 5.

13. In studies from Bolivia and Guatemala, respectively, anthropologists Leslie Gill and Linda Green have found that individuals shift their affiliations among different congregations and sometimes hold more than one affiliation at a time. Green comments that scholars should differentiate between conversion and affiliation, since affiliations are not fixed, "nor do changes in membership necessarily represent [converts'] rejection of Mayan cosmology." See Linda Green, "Shifting Affiliations: Mayan Widows and Evangelicos in Guatemala," and Leslie Gill, "Religious Mobility and the Many Words of God in La Paz, Bolivia," in *Rethinking Protestantism in Latin America*, ed. David Stoll and Virginia Garrard-Burnett, (Philadelphia: Temple University Press, 1993), 174.

14. James Davison Hunter, *Culture Wars: The Struggle to Define America* (New York: Basic Books, 1991).

15. Hunter, *Culture Wars*, 42.

16. Ibid., 44–45.

17. Qualitative methods were extremely valuable for another reason as well. My interviews pointed to the significance of conversion as a change agent. Cross-sectional survey data reveal correlations between values and can suggest, though not prove, cause-and-effect relationships. In the absence of longitudinal data, the anecdotes and testimonies my informants related to me about changes in converts' lives *following* conversion suggest that religious worldview not only correlates with certain development-enhancing attitudes and behaviors and with various indicators of development, but actually encourages them.

18. Hunter, *Culture Wars*, 58.

19. Glenn C. Loury, "Ghetto Poverty and the Power of Faith" (Address to the Center of the American Experiment, Minneapolis, December 1993), 3–4.


Chapter One

1. Robert B. Edgerton, *Sick Societies: Challenging the Myth of Primitive Harmony* (New York: Free Press, 1992).

2. Ibid., 12.

3. Ibid., 205.

4. Max Weber, *The Protestant Ethic and the Spirit of Capitalism*, trans. T. Parsons (London: Unwin Paperbacks, 1984).

5. Jane Schneider, "Spirits and the Spirit of Capitalism," in *Religious Orthodoxy and Popular Faith in European Society*, ed. Ellen Badone (Princeton: Princeton University Press, 1990), 26.

6. Max Weber, "The Protestant Sects and the Spirit of Capitalism," "Religious Rejections of the World and their Directions," and "The Social Psychology of the World Religions," in *From Max Weber: Essays in Sociology*, ed. and trans. H. H. Gerth and C. Wright Mills (New York: Oxford University Press, 1964).

7. Weber, "Religious Rejections of the World," 325.

8. Ibid., 326.

9. Weber, "Social Psychology of World Religions," 274.

10. Weber, *Protestant Ethic*, 72.

11. Weber, "Protestant Sects," 305.

12. Ibid., 308, 312–13.

13. Herbert Schlossberg, "The Controlled Economy: Gunnar Myrdal's Subjective Conclusions," in *Freedom, Justice, and Hope: Toward a Strategy for the Poor and the Oppressed* (Westchester, Ill.: Crossway Books, 1988), 48, emphasis mine.

14. Gunnar Myrdal, *Asian Drama: An Inquiry into the Poverty of Nations* (New York: Pantheon, 1968), 937.

15. Joseph A. Schumpeter, *Capitalism, Socialism, and Democracy* (New York: Harper Brothers, 1950), 132. W. Arthur Lewis continued to emphasize the role of the entrepreneur in his exploration of development. In *The Theory of Economic Growth*, Lewis asked why some countries produced more entrepreneurs than others. He concluded that religion played a key role in the sense that persecuted religious groups—such as the Jews, Huguenots, and Quakers— tended to exhibit high rates of achievement. The society's legitimation of innovation was also key; entrepreneurs would tend to arise more in societies that respected and rewarded their efforts. See Lewis, *The Theory of Economic Growth* (Homewood, Ill.: Richard D. Irwin, Inc., 1955).

16. Amitai Etzioni, "Entrepreneurship, Adaptation, and Legitimation: A Macro-Behavioral Perspective," *Journal of Economic Behavior and Organization* 8 (1987): 175–89.

17. David C. McClelland, *The Achieving Society* (New York: Irvington Publishers, 1976), A.

18. Ibid., D.

19. Tomas Roberto Fillol, *Social Factors in Economic Development: The Argentine Case* (Cambridge, Mass.: MIT Press, 1961), 7.

20. Ibid., 9.

21. Ibid., 11–12.

22. In a 1974 work, Frank wrote: "[I]t is capitalism, both world and national, which produced underdevelopment in the past and *which still generates underdevelopment* in the present." See Andre Gunder Frank, *Capitalism and Underdevelopment in Latin America* (New York: Monthly Review Press, 1967), 1, emphasis mine.

23. See, for example, Bela Balassa, "The Adding Up Problem," *World Bank Working Paper #30*, and "Public Finance and Economic Development," *World Bank Working Paper #31* (Washington, D.C.: The World Bank, 1988); and Anne O. Krueger, *Perspectives on Trade and Development* (Chicago: University of Chicago, 1989); Krueger, *Liberalization Attempts and Consequences* (Cambridge, Mass.: Ballinger, 1978); and Krueger, *Political and Economic Interactions in Economic Policy Reform* (Oxford: Basil Blackwell, 1993).

24. See, for example, P. T. Bauer's *Dissent on Development*, (Cambridge: Harvard University Press, 1976); *Equality, the Third World, and Economic Delusion* (Cambridge, Mass.: Harvard University Press, 1981); and *Reality and Rhetoric: Studies in the Economics of Development* (London: Weidenfeld and Nicolson, 1984).

25. See, for example, *World Development Report 1992* (Washington, D.C.:

The World Bank, 1992), which summarizes the lessons learned in development economics since the 1940s.

26. *Development and the National Interest: U.S. Economic Assistance into the 21st Century* (Washington, D.C.: Agency for International Development, 1989). The report was nicknamed after Alan Woods, the Administrator of AID at that time.

27. Thomas Sowell, *The Economics and Politics of Race* (New York: Quill, 1983).

28. Ibid., 136.

29. Ibid.

30. Ibid., 23.

31. Ibid., 24.

32. Ibid., 49.

33. Ibid.

34. Ibid., 55.

35. Ibid., 83.

36. Ibid., 63.

37. Ibid., 73.

38. Lawrence E. Harrison, *Underdevelopment Is a State of Mind* (Lanham, Md.: Madison Books, 1985), 6.

39. Ibid.

40. Lawrence E. Harrison, *Who Prospers? How Cultural Values Shape Economic and Political Success* (New York: Basic Books, 1992), 10.

41. Ibid., 11.

42. Ibid.

43. Ibid., 12.

44. Ibid.

45. Ibid., 13.

46. Harrison, *State of Mind*, 164.

47. Ibid., 165.

48. Harrison, *Who Prospers?* 81–82.

49. Ibid., 85.

50. Ibid., 115.

51. Ibid.

Chapter 2

1. David Martin, *Tongues of Fire: The Explosion of Protestantism in Latin America* (Oxford: Basil Blackwell, 1990), 205.

2. Conversion testimony quoted in Martin, *Tongues of Fire*, 202.

3. James D. Sexton, "Protestantism and Modernization in Two Guatemalan Towns," *American Ethnologist* 5 (May 1978): 280.

4. Ibid., 287.

5. See Martin, *Tongues of Fire*, chapters 9 and 10.

6. June Nash, "Protestantism in an Indian Village in the Western Highlands of Guatemala," *Alpha Kappa Deltan* (Winter 1960): 50.

7. Elizabeth Brusco, "The Household Basis of Evangelical Religion and the

Reformation of Machismo in Colombia" (Ph.D. diss., City University of New York, 1986).

8. Liliana R. Goldin and Brent Metz, "An Expression of Cultural Change: Invisible Converts to Protestantism among Highland Guatemala Maya," *Ethnology* 30 (October 1991): 327–28.

9. Sexton, "Protestantism and Modernization," 287.

10. Benson Saler, "Religious Conversion and Self-Aggrandizement: A Guatemalan Case," *Practical Anthropology* 12 (May/June 1965): 107.

11. Ibid., 109.

12. Ibid., 112.

13. Richard A. Thompson, *The Winds of Tomorrow: Social Change in a Maya Town* (Chicago: University of Chicago Press, 1974).

14. Ibid., 103–04.

15. Ibid.

16. Daniel Wattenberg, "Gospel Message of Getting Ahead Inch by Inch," *Insight* (16 July 1990): 17.

17. Sexton, "Protestantism and Modernization," 287.

18. For example, Steve Bruce, "Protestant Resurgence and Fundamentalism," *The Political Quarterly* 61 (April/June 1990):161–168; David Clawson, "Religious Allegiance and Development in Rural Latin America," *Journal of Inter-American Studies and World Affairs* 26 (1984:4): 499–524; Peter Fry, "Two Religious Movements: Protestantism and Umbanda," in J. D. Wirth and R. L. Jones, eds., *Manchester and São Paulo* (Stanford: Stanford University Press, 1978), 177–202; Blanca Muratorio, "Protestantism and Capitalism Revisited, in the Rural Highlands of Ecuador," *The Journal of Peasant Studies* 8 (1980): 37–61; and Bryan R. Roberts, "Protestant Groups and Coping With Life in Guatemala City," *The American Journal of Sociology* 6 (May 1968): 753–67.

19. Martin, *Tongues of Fire*, 206, emphasis in the original.

20. Reviewing one such story, about a German immigrant enclave in Brazil, researcher F. Jongkind argued that Calvinist religion provided the social glue that held the community together. The rigorous ethical system encouraged a spirit of enterprise, innovation, hard work, and thrift and "largely activated the efforts which led to economic success." Explaining the "extraordinary success of the Calvinist Dutch colonies in Brazil," Jongkind wrote:

> In particular, religion, in its function as an orienting value system and an integrating factor, forms a central factor of explanation. In the early years, religious convictions prevented moral decline, and gave the people hope for a better future. The Calvinist denomination in a Catholic country strengthened ethnic identity and solidarity among the Dutch and thus formed the basis for social organization in associations informally. The closely-knit social organization made the highly flourishing cooperative possible. Hard work, frugality, honesty, ability to innovate and other characteristics held high in Calvinism united the individual colonists into a solid economic organization. F. Jongkind, "The Agrarian Colonies of Dutch Calvinists in Paraná, Brazil," *International Migration* 27 (September 1989): 467–86.

For an extended discussion of the mores of the Protestants' "alternative community," see chapter 7.

21. James D. Sexton and Clyde Woods, "Development and Modernization among Highland Maya: A Comparative Analysis of Ten Guatemalan Towns," *Human Organization* 36 (Summer 1977): 169.

22. Brusco, "The Household Basis," 2.

23. See, for example: Mary O'Conner, "Two Kinds of Religious Movement Among the Mayo Indians of Sonora, Mexico," *Journal for the Scientific Study of Religion* 18 (no. 3, 1979): 260–68; Paul Turner, "Religious Conversion and Community Development," *Journal for the Scientific Study of Religion* 18 (no. 3, 1979): 252–60; and Henry Wilbur Aulie, "The Christian Movement Among the Chols of Mexico with Special Reference to the Problems of Second Generation Christianity" (Ph.D. diss., Fuller Theological Seminary, 1979).

24. Brusco, "The Household Basis," iv–v.

25. Sol Tax and Robert Hinshaw, "Panajachel a Generation Later," in *The Social Anthropology of Latin America: Essays in Honor of Ralph Leon Beals*, ed. Walter Goldschmidt and Henry Hoijer (Los Angeles: Latin American Center at the University of California, 1970).

26. John D. Early, "Education via Radio Among Guatemalan Highland Maya," *Human Organization* 32 (Fall 1973), 223.

27. As reported in Martin, *Tongues of Fire*, 209–10.

28. Sexton, "Protestantism and Modernization," 293–94.

29. Sheldon Annis, *God and Production in a Guatemalan Town* (Austin: University of Texas Press, 1987), 102.

30. Ibid., 99–100.

31. As reported in Martin, *Tongues of Fire*, 210.

32. Nash, "Protestantism in an Indian Village," 50.

33. Thompson, *Winds of Tomorrow*, 103–04.

34. Sexton, "Protestantism and Modernization," 293.

35. Tax and Hinshaw, "Panajachel a Generation Later," 191.

36. Sexton and Woods, "Development and Modernization," 165, 168.

37. Ibid., 164–67.

## Chapter 3

1. Vera Kelsey and Lily de Jongh Osborne, *Four Keys to Guatemala* (New York: Funk and Wagnalls, 1943), 19.

2. *Milpa* is Spanish for the plot of land on which Indians typically grow the traditional crops of corn and beans.

3. Benjamin N. Colby and Lore M. Colby, *The Daykeeper: The Life and Discourse of an Ixil Diviner* (Cambridge, Mass.: Harvard University Press, 1981), 38. The term is employed by the Ixil; other Mayan groups have alternate names for the Christ figure.

4. Kay B. Warren, *The Symbolism of Subordination: Indian Identity in a Guatemalan Town* (Austin: University of Texas, 1978), 33.

5. Ibid.

6. Colby and Colby, *The Daykeeper*, 165–68.

7. Eugene A. Nida, *Communication of the Gospel in Latin America* (Cuarnavaca, Mexico: Centro Intercultural de Documentación, 1969), 28.

8. See, for example, Ruth Carlson and Francis Eachus, "The Kekchi Spirit World," in Helen Neuenswander and Dean E. Arnold, eds., *Cognitive Studies of Southern MesoAmerica* (Dallas: Museum of Anthropology, Summer Institute of Linguistics, 1981), 41–42.

9. Colby and Colby, *The Daykeeper*, 122.

10. Ibid.

11. Ibid., 123.

12. Paul G. Townsend, with Te'c Cham and Po'x Ich', eds., *Ritual Rhetoric From Cotzal* (Guatemala City, Guatemala: Instituto Linguistico de Verano, 1980), 27 and 43.

13. Carlson and Eachus, "Kekchi Spirit World," 42–43.

14. Warren, *Symbolism of Subordination*, 48.

15. Nida, *Communication of the Gospel*, 29.

16. Barbara Tedlock, *Time and the Highland Maya* (Albuquerque: University of New Mexico Press, 1982).

17. Ibid., 153–71.

18. Ibid., 106–31.

19. Ibid., 133–34.

20. Colby and Colby, *The Daykeeper*, 50.

21. Richard Adams, ed., *Political Changes in Guatemalan Indian Communities* (New Orleans: Middle American Research Institute of Tulane University, 1957), 4–6.

22. Catholic Action is a national group of Catholic layperson, which emerged in the 1950s with the blessing of the Catholic hierarchy. It aimed to purge Mayan Catholicism of its syncretistic elements and promote Catholic orthodoxy.

23. See, for example, Paul Deiner, "The Tears of St. Anthony: Ritual and Revolution in Eastern Guatemala," *Latin American Perspectives* 5 (Summer 1978): 92–116.

24. Warren, *Symbolism of Subordination*, especially 1–26.

25. Linda Greenberg, "Illness and Curing Among Maya Indians in Highland Guatemala: Cosmological Balance and Cultural Transformation" (Ph.D. diss., University of Chicago, 1984), 4.

26. Ibid., 50.

27. See, for example, Helen L. Neuenswander and Shirley D. Souder, "The Hot–Cold Wet–Dry Syndrome Among the Quiche of Joyabaj: Two Alternative Cognitive Models," in Helen L. Neuenswander and Dean E. Arnold, eds., *Cognitive Studies of Southern MesoAmerica* (Dallas: Museum of Anthropology Summer Institute of Linguistics, 1981), 112–13. Neuenswander reports that among the Quiche illness is perceived as the result of improper balancing of hot and cold foods or experiences. In the initial diagnosis, Indians also try to determine whether the particular illness is a wet or dry one. A wet illness can be inflicted by God and is usually not terribly serious or long term. A dry illness is more serious and less treatable; it often derives from the malevolent actions of men or from evil spirits. Dry diseases "require special rituals performed by native curers" (even though these ceremonies are "singularly unsuccessful").

28. Greenberg, "Illness and Curing," 184.

29. Colby and Colby, *The Daykeeper*, 42.
30. Townsend, *Ritual Rhetoric*, 18–19.
31. Ibid.
32. Nida, *Communication of the Gospel*, 31.
33. Warren, *Symbolism of Subordination*, 49.
34. Ibid., 82.
35. Tedlock, *Highland Maya*, 176.
36. Nida, *Communication of the Gospel*, 33.
37. Warren, *Symbolism of Subordination*, 26.
38. Waldemar R. Smith, *The Fiesta System and Economic Change* (New York: Columbia University Press, 1977), 2.
39. Ibid.
40. See, for example, Deiner, "Tears of St. Anthony," 97.
41. Ibid., 98.
42. Sheldon Annis, *God and Production in a Guatemalan Town* (Austin: University of Texas Press, 1987), 37.
43. Ibid., 10.
44. George M. Foster, "Peasant Society and the Image of Limited Good," in *Peasant Society: A Reader*, ed. Jack M. Potter, May N. Diaz, and George M. Foster (Boston: Little, Brown, 1967), 304, emphasis in the original.
45. Foster, 307.
46. Eric R. Wolf, quoted in Foster, "Peasant Society," 315.
47. Foster, "Peasant Society," 315–16.
48. Ibid., 317.
49. Ibid., 318.
50. For a discussion of McClelland, see chapter 1.
51. Foster, "Peasant Society," 319.
52. Ibid., 320.
53. Sol Tax and Robert Hinshaw, "Panajachel A Generation Later," in *The Social Anthropology of Latin America: Essays in Honor of Ralph Leon Beals*, ed. Walter Goldschmidt and Harry Hoijer (Los Angeles: Latin American Center at the University of California, 1970), 175–95.
54. Ibid., 184.
55. Ibid., 188–89.
56. James D. Sexton and Clyde Woods, "Development and Modernization Among Highland Maya: A Comparative Analysis of Ten Guatemalan Towns," *Human Organization* 36 (Summer 1977): 165.
57. Ibid.
58. James D. Sexton, "Protestantism and Modernization in Two Guatemalan Towns," *American Ethnologist* 5 (May 1978): 295.
59. See Richard Adams, ed., *Political Changes in Guatemalan Indian Communities* (New Orleans: Middle American Research Institute of Tulane University, 1957): 48–52.
60. Benjamin Paul, unpublished paper, quoted in June Nash, "Protestantism in an Indian Village in the Western Highlands of Guatemala," *Alpha Kappa Delton* (Winter 1960): 53.
61. Tax and Hinshaw, "Panajachel a Generation Later," 181–82.
62. Ibid., 182.

63. Annis, *God and Production*, 85.

64. Ibid., 98.

65. Sexton, "Protestantism and Modernization," 295.

66. Sexton and Woods, "Development and Modernization," 169.

## Chapter 4

1. Jorge E. Maldonado, "Building 'Fundamentalism' from the Family in Latin America," in *Fundamentalisms and Society: Reclaiming the Sciences, the Family, and Education,* ed. Martin E. Marty and R. Scott Appleby (Chicago: University of Chicago Press, 1993), 235.

2. In developing my survey questionnaire, I drew from a variety of sources by authors who have previously conducted public opinion research in the United States and Latin America. For a listing of these sources, please refer to the bibliography and the note in Appendix A.

3. This question was originally used in a survey of U.S. Evangelicals conducted on behalf of the Villars Committee on Relief and Development by the Center for Survey Research at the University of Virginia in February 1992.

4. Several criteria helped me decide which communities to survey: I wanted a sample that was geographically and linguistically diverse, that included towns of differing levels of ethnic and religious heterogeneity, and included isolated as well as relatively integrated towns. I'd hoped to include Chajul in the sample, but the research firm I hired felt that it would be too dangerous to conduct public opinion research in the Ixil Triangle.

5. Since I was primarily interested in comparing individuals of differing religious beliefs, I wanted to ensure that I had a usable number of Evangelical as well as Catholic respondents. Consequently, the interviewers were instructed to interview a minimum number of Evangelicals. To accomplish this, villages were divided into sectors and homes in those sectors were randomly chosen for interviews according to the standardized procedures of the research firm. If the required number of Evangelicals was not found in these residences, a standardized system for selecting additional houses was followed until the minimum number of desired interviews had been conducted. Following such procedures, the final sample was 49.9 percent Catholic and 43.8 percent Evangelical.

6. Other researchers have utilized reading or writing tests to measure respondents' proficiency. I decided against this principally because of the time it would have added to the interview, which already required, on average, about 45 minutes. I was concerned that if the interviews themselves took even longer than three-quarters of an hour, the rejection rate would be unacceptable. Without additional information from such tests, it is certainly possible that the literacy rate my survey revealed is overestimated, since respondents may have been unwilling to admit illiteracy.

7. All these differences are statistically significant at the 95 percent confidence level.

8. These procedures were principally cross-tabulations and tests of means.

9. In most cases when such intervening variables had influence, the significance of the connection between religious worldview and a dependent variable

dropped to a level beneath the 95 percent confidence level but maintained statistical significance at the 80 percent confidence level.

10. The pattern was not totally "pure," however, since more "Weak" Evangelicals than "Moderate" Evangelicals accepted the merit-based system.

11. The Foster Index is my own theoretical construction; that is, these variables seem to have a logical, *prima facie* connection to each other, and they flesh out various aspects of Foster's important thesis. Formal statisticians, however, might criticize this index because it does not have a significantly high inter-item correlation coefficient. Consequently, I created another index composed of four variables that clustered together on one factor in a rotated factor analysis. I call this index the Initiative Index and it is composed of the variables "school," "profit," "achieve," and "just economy," (four out of the six in the Foster Index). I labeled this factor cluster "initiative" because this seemed to be the underlying theme connecting these four items. "Profit" and "just economy" measure the legitimacy of an unequal, merit-based distribution of economic resources. These attitudes suggest that initiative can and should be rewarded. The variables "school" and "achieve" further measure the legitimacy and encouragement of initiative.

The results of the analysis of mean scores by worldview groups on this index are very similar to those resulting from analysis of the Foster Index and thus provide additional credibility to the arguments I make based on the Foster Index scores. For example, more individuals in the orthodox Evangelical group than in any other group scored in the highest category on the index (52.8 percent of orthodox Evangelicals scored high on the Initiative Index compared to only 28.4 percent of Cristo-pagans and 31.4 percent of traditional Catholics). Orthodox Catholics did nearly as well: 48.4 percent of them scored high. These differences are significant at $p = .05$. The test of means on the Initiative Index indicated similar results. The mean for orthodox Evangelicals was 3.33, compared with a Cristo-pagan mean of 2.82 and a traditional Catholic mean of 2.98. These differences also were significant at $p = .05$. Orthodox Catholics, at 3.34, had virtually the same average as orthodox Evangelicals. Similar patterns held up when "faith" rather than "cosmovision" was used as the independent variable, though under this scheme traditional Catholics scored higher. In this test, 45.7 percent of traditional Catholics scored in the highest initiative category and their mean score on the index was 3.26.

Chapter 5

1. The lighting of candles reference is to the practice common in the making of various costumbres—where lit candles and incense are offered up to the gods or dueños with special prayers and petitions. I interviewed Gaspar Mendosa at his home in Chajul, Guatemala, 5–6 January 1993.

2. *Alcalde* is the Spanish word for mayor. In this context, it signifies one of the special "year-bearer" days in the 260-day Mayan calendar. Traditionalists believe these days are particularly powerful. For an excellent discussion of the Mayan calendar, see chapter 4 in Barbara Tedlock, *Time and the Highland Maya* (Albuquerque: University of New Mexico Press, 1982).

3. Gaspar Laynes (pastor, Iglesia Elim), interview with author, Chajul, Guatemala, 6 January 1993.

4. This information was imparted to me in interviews with Pablo Chub (pastor, Iglesia Presbiteriano) and others, La Tinta, A.V., Guatemala, 20 November 1992.

5. Not his real name.

6. Liliana Goldin and Brent Metz, "An Expression of Cultural Change: Invisible Converts to Protestantism among Highland Guatemalan Mayas," *Ethnology* 30 (October 1991): 327.

7. Liliana Goldin, "Comercializacion y cambio en San Pedro Almolonga: un caso Maya-Quiche," *Mayab* (Madrid) 5 (1989), 45.

8. Goldin and Metz, "Cultural Change," 336.

9. Ibid., 326.

10. Ibid., 329.

11. Ibid.

12. Margot McMillan (SIL linguist), interview with author, Las Pacayas, Uspantan, Guatemala, 25 November 1992.

13. Perfecto Gonzales (pastor, Assemblies of God Evangelio Completo), interview with author, El Pinal, Guatemala, 26 November 1992.

14. Margot McMillan, interview with author, 25 November 1992.

15. Pablo Chub, interview with author, 20 November 1992.

16. Ray and Helen Elliott, interview with author, Nebaj, Guatemala, 6 January 1993.

17. Dr. Bayron Aquino, interview with author, Fundacion Contra El Hambre, Guatemala City, Guatemala, 6 October 1992.

18. Elder Cano, interview with author, El Pinal, Guatemala, 26 November 1992.

19. This same church also warns against the danger of too much education. While admitting that education is important for development, the elders caution that too much education can "lead one away from God. If a person gets too much education, he can fall away." The Apostle Paul, they note, was a highly educated man, but he "counted it all as rubbish."

20. David Stoll, "Between Two Fires: Dual Violence and the Reassertion of Civil Society in Nebaj, Guatemala" (Ph.D. diss, Stanford University, 1992), 166.

21. Ibid., 264, emphasis mine.

22. Not her real name.

23. Not her real name.

24. Silvano Diaz, interview with author, Centro de Salud, Almolonga, Guatemala, 23 March 1993.

25. Dr. Otto Raul Hernandez (chief physician at the Zunil Health Post), interview with author, Zunil, Guatemala, 13 July 1993.

26. Goldin and Metz, "Cultural Change," 334.

27. Pablo Chub, interview with author, 20 November 1992.

28. Tomas Pop Ich (elder, Iglesia Lluvias de Gracia), interview with author, La Tinta, Guatemala, 20 November 1992.

29. Marcelino Cu Cul (pastor, Iglesia Principe de Paz), interview with author, La Tinta, Guatemala, 19 November 1992.

30. The survey was conducted by FUNDEQI, a private, nonprofit Guatemalan agricultural development organization, and sponsored by FONAPAZ, the Guatemalan National Foundation for Peace. Interviewing was completed in the counties of Uspantan, Chicaman, and Cunén in August 1992. Fifty-seven communities were surveyed, representing a population of 14,055 individuals. I am grateful to Stan McMillan, member of the FUNDEQI board of directors and author of the FUNDEQI survey report, for sharing his data with me.

31. Victoriano Poou Xo (pastor, Assemblia de Dios Pentecostal), interview with author, La Tinta, Guatemala, 19 November 1992.

32. Anastacio Caso (pastor, Church of God "Bethsaida"), interview with author, Chimaltenango, Guatemala, 18 March 1993.

33. Mariano Riscayche Cotoc (pastor, Templo Evangelical El Calvario), interview with author, Almolonga, Guatemala, 24 March 1993.

34. Marcelino Cu Cul, interview with author, 19 November 1992.

35. Pablo Chub, interview with author, 20 November 1992.

36. This pattern holds when controlled for ethnicity and years of education. Income and occupation have some influence on the relationship: the statistical significance of the relationship is diminished when respondents in the highest income category only are considered or when respondents in the two highest paying occupational categories only are considered.

37. Antonio Rivera (acting director, Chajul Health Post), interview with author, Chajul, Guatemala, 11 June 1992.

38. Dr. Ezequiel Urizar, interview with author, Chajul, Guatemala, 24 November 1992.

39. Ibid.

40. Stoll, "Between Two Fires," 247.

41. Ibid.

42. Ibid., 247. The figures do not add up to 100 because most people are involved in more than one occupation.

43. Interestingly, nearly two thirds of the Evangelicals reported that they became owners of their own businesses *after* their conversion to Protestantism. This may possibly suggest either an increased sense of initiative enjoyed by converts or improved capital accumulation following their adoption of a Protestant ascetic ethic that enabled them to invest in their businesses.

44. Stoll, "Between Two Fires," 244.

45. Ray and Helen Elliot (linguists with the Summer Institute of Linguistics), interview with author, Nebaj, Guatemala, 6 January 1993.

46. Nevertheless, literacy rates remain low in the Ixil Triangle. In 1984, the health center in Nebaj reported a 25 percent literacy rate; the center in Chajul estimated 28 percent. [Cited in Stoll, "Between Two Fires," 178.] This figure for Chajul may be exaggerated. According to data from the Supreme Electoral Tribunal in 1990, which reports voter registration for literate and illiterate voters, Chajul's literacy rate is closer to 15 percent. The voter registration records in Nebaj compare more favorably with the estimate given by its health center: they show a 24 percent literacy rate. [Report of the Tribuno Suprema Electoral, Section on the Department of Quiche, *Memoria Elecciones 1990/ 1991*.] I have no quantitative data for literacy rates according to religious

affiliation for Chajul. Some Ixil Evangelicals insist that literacy rates are higher within their community; outside observers contend that illiteracy remains a formidable problem.

47. The figures are similar when women only are considered. Of Evangelical women, 80.5 percent claim to be able to read and write, compared to 67.8 percent of Catholic women.

48. Isaias Miranda (pastor, Iglesia Nazarena), interview with author, Uspantan, Guatemala, 27 November 1992.

49. Lilia Ninette Ogaldez y Vasquez, interview with author, Chajul, Guatemala, 11 June 1992.

50. Marcelino Cu Cul, interview with author, 19 November 1992.

51. While this difference is not statistically significant at the 90 percent confidence level, it may be suggestive. The pattern holds for both indígenas and Ladinos. Among respondents in the lowest income category, though, the propensity to use fertilizer is roughly equal. But the pattern of difference emerges when respondents in all the other income categories are considered. Education has some influence on the relationship as well. Among respondents with no education, few of either faith use fertilizer. The expected difference appears, however, among respondents with one to three years of education, four to six years of education, or a junior high level education, but is mitigated among respondents who have completed a high school education.

52. Dwight Jewett (linguist with the Summer Institute of Linguistics), interview with author, Chajul, Guatemala, 7 June 1992.

53. Ray and Helen Elliot, interview with author, 6 January 1993.

54. Vilma Avila Alvarado (Summer Institute of Linguistics), interview with author, Chajul, Guatemala, 8 June 1992.

55. Ray and Helen Elliot, interview with author, 6 January 1993.

56. Vilma Avila Alvarado, interview with author, 8 June 1992.

57. Ethnicity has some effect on this relationship; it is stronger for Ladinos than for indígenas.

58. Not his real name.

Chapter 6

1. See David Stoll and Virginia Garrard-Burnett, eds., *Rethinking Protestantism in Latin America* (Philadelphia: Temple University Press, 1993).

2. Quoted in Paul Lewis, "With Bible in Hand, Evangelicals Come Marching In," *New York Times*, 15 June 1989, A4.

3. Kenneth Freed, "Christianity's Holy War in Guatemala," *Los Angeles Times*, 13 May 1990, A1:1.

4. Peter Berger, *The Capitalist Revolution: Fifty Propositions About Prosperity, Equality and Liberty* (New York: Basic Books, 1986), 81.

5. For a critical commentary on liberation theology, see Cardinal Joseph Ratzinger, "Instruction on Certain Aspects of the 'Theology of Liberation'" in *Theology and the Church*, Juan Luis Segundo (Minneapolis: Seabury, 1984), 169–88 (appendix).

6. David Stoll, "Evangelical Awakening," *Hemisphere* (Winter/Spring 1990): 35.

7. David Stoll, *Is Latin America Turning Protestant?* (Berkeley: University of California Press, 1990), xviii.

8. Christian Smith, "The Spirit of Democracy: Base Communities, Protestantism, and Democratization in Latin America," *Sociology of Religion* 55 (Summer 1994): 119–43.

9. David Martin, *Tongues of Fire: The Explosion of Protestantism in Latin America* (Oxford: Basil Blackwell, 1990).

10. See Smith, "Spirit of Democracy," 134.

11. Ibid.

12. Martin, *Tongues of Fire*, 239 and 236. A recent review essay by David E. Dixon also highlighted the diversity of Evangelical political attitudes, citing studies from a variety of Latin American countries. See David E. Dixon, "The New Protestantism in Latin America: Remembering What We Already Know, Testing What We Have Learned," *Comparative Politics* 27 (July 1995): 479–92.

13. Martin, *Tongues of Fire*, 236–37.

14. Alan Wisdom (research director, Institute on Religion and Democracy), interview with author, Washington, D.C., 1 December 1990.

15. Alan Wisdom, interview with author, 1 December 1990.

16. Francisco Bianchi (senior pastor, Iglesia Verbo) and Carlos Velasquez (Foundation for Christian Education), interview with author, Guatemala City, Guatemala, 23 June 1992. Fernando Leal and Renan Quinonez (former advisors to President Rios Montt), interview with author, Guatemala City, Guatemala, 12 October 1992.

17. Efrain Rios Montt (former president of Guatemala), interview with author, Guatemala City, Guatemala, 16 July 1993.

18. For a succinct discussion of Kuyper's political thought, see his lecture, "Calvinism and Politics," in *Lectures on Calvinism*, Abraham Kuyper (New York: Fleming H. Revell Company, 1899), 98–142.

19. Rios Montt, interview with author, 16 July 1993.

20. Marco Tulio Cajas, interview with author, Guatemala City, Guatemala, 23 June 1992.

21. Conde's tragic personal history seems to symbolize the tumults of Guatemalan politics and perhaps has especially suited him to the task of peacemaker. His father was a congressman who was assassinated by the military; his grandfather had served as president of the Congress until he was killed by the guerrillas.

22. Manuel Conde, interview with author, Guatemala City, Guatemala, 23 July 1993.

23. Or "Church of the Word," in English. This large neo-Pentecostal church has close ties with its mother church, the Church of the Word in Eureka, California. Rios Montt became a member of the church during its early years, became an active lay leader in it, and turned to his fellow congregants for guidance during his 18-month tenure as president. The central Verbo church in the capital was established in 1977 following the arrival of U.S. missionaries from the mother church the preceding year; these missionaries came to provide relief aid in the wake of the earthquake. This congregation in Guatemala City now boasts some 6,000 members; Verbo has also established churches in other

areas, and the total membership in these congregations is an additional 6,000. Thirty percent of the Verbo churches have begun their own private, Evangelical elementary schools. A neo-Pentecostal church, Verbo teaches often on the church's role in society and sees its educational curricula as developing the country's future political, business, and cultural leaders. Francisco Bianchi (senior pastor, Verbo Church) and Rafeal Pontufa (director of FUNDESEDI, Verbo's educational foundation), interview with author, Guatemala City, Guatemala, 9 October 1992.

24. Manuel Conde, interview with author, 23 July 1993.

25. Marco Antonio Rodriguez (president, Alianza Evangelica), interview with author, Guatemala City, Guatemala, 23 July 1993.

26. Interview with Rafael Escobar Arguello (editor, *Hechos* Magazine), Guatemala City, Guatemala, 8 October 1992.

27. Manuel Conde, interview with author, 23 July 1993.

28. Marco Tulio Cajas, interview with author, 23 June 1992.

29. Fernando Solarez (senior pastor, Iglesia de JesuCristo Familia de Dios), interview with author, Guatemala City, Guatemala, 30 March 1993.

30. Harold Caballeros (senior pastor, Iglesia El Shaddai), interview with author, Guatemala City, Guatemala, 31 March 1993.

31. Edmundo Madrid (senior pastor, Iglesia Lluvias de Gracia), interview with author, Guatemala City, Guatemala, 13 January 1993.

32. Stan Herod (SEPAL), interview with author, Guatemala City, Guatemala, 8 October 1992.

33. Steven Sywulka (director, Radio TGN), interview with author, Guatemala City, Guatemala, 6 October 1992.

34. Estuardo Salazar (regional coordinator for Latin America, Association of Christian Schools International), interview with author, Guatemala City, Guatemala, 12 October 1992.

35. Stoll, "Latin America," 175.

36. Lucas Mendosa (president of the Casa de la Cultura), interview with author, Chajul, Guatemala, 4 January 1993.

37. Paul Townsend, personal correspondence, 2 November 1993.

38. Robert Moffitt (president, Harvest Foundation, Tempe, Arizona), interview with author, 26 January 1994. Harvest Foundation helps train Protestant pastors in low-income areas throughout Latin America.

39. Martin, *Tongues of Fire*, 239.

40. Richard Millett, "Limited Hopes and Fears in Guatemala," *Current History* 90 (March 1991): 125.

41. "Polls Reflect Electoral Ambivalence," *Central America Report* 27 (August 1990): 248.

42. Martin, *Tongues of Fire*, 22.

43. Peter Berger in the foreword to Martin, *Tongues of Fire*, ix.

44. Stoll, "Evangelical Awakening," 35.


Chapter 7

1. Alfred Kaltschmitt (director, AGROS Foundation), interview with author, Guatemala City, 30 September 1992.

2. Paul Townsend, interview with author, Guatemala City, 5 June 1992.

3. George M. Foster, "Peasant Society and the Image of Limited Good," in *Peasant Society: A Reader*, ed. Jack M. Potter, May N. Diaz, and George M. Foster (Boston: Little, Brown, 1967), 311.

4. Ibid., emphasis mine.

5. May N. Diaz, "Economic Relations in Peasant Society," in *Peasant Society: A Reader*, ed. Jack M. Potter, May N. Diaz, and George M. Foster (Boston: Little, Brown, 1967), 50.

6. Ibid., 54.

7. Foster, "Limited Good," 305. Foster explains that the Limited Good idea pertains not only to economic goods, but to other things as well. For example, the mindset applies to friendship: "The evidence that friendship, love, and affection are seen as strictly limited in peasant society is strong." The perception that love is limited informs the way peasants interpret sibling rivalry: often the belief is that the older child becomes jealous of the mother's attention to the new, nursing infant. In Guatemala if an older child becomes ill at this time, he or she is diagnosed with *chipe*, meaning "jealousy." In parts of Guatemala, *chipe* is also used to refer to the husband's jealousy of an adolescent son's attention from his mother: the more attention the son receives, the less there is for the father. Similarly, there is widespread evidence that peasants believe blood, like affection, is limited. Peasants believe that the more blood one has, the more healthy one will be and that the loss of blood is nonregenerative. According to Foster, this is one reason why Latins are reluctant to donate blood. See Foster, "Limited Good," 308–309).

8. Ibid., 315.

9. Ibid., 311.

10. Cesar Menjivar Cartegena (Pastor, Iglesia de Dios de la Profeción Universal), interview with author, Almolonga, Guatemala, 23 March 1993.

11. Liliana Goldin and Brent Metz, "An Expression of Cultural Change: Invisible Converts to Protestantism Among Highland Guatemalan Mayas," *Ethnology* 30 (October 1991): 327.

12. Sol Tax and Robert Hinshaw, "Panajachel a Generation Later," in *The Social Anthropology of Latin America: Essays in Honor of Ralph Leon Beals*, ed. Walter Goldschmidt and Harry Hoijer (Los Angeles: University of California at Los Angeles, 1970), 184.

13. J. Burdick, "Rethinking the Study of Social Movements," in *The Making of Social Movements in Latin America*, ed. A. Escobar and S. Alvarez (Boulder, Colo.: Westview Press, 1992), 180.

14. David Stoll, "Evangelical Awakening," *Hemisphere* (Winter/Spring 1990): 243.

15. The abatement of ethnic tensions is also due to the years of war. According to Stoll, the town had a sense of being caught "between two fires"—the persecution practiced by the Guatemalan army and the Guerrilla Army of the Poor (EGP). These external pressures brought Nebaj's two ethnic communities together.

16. Stoll, "Evangelical Awakening," 256.

17. Goldin and Metz, "Cultural Change," 334.

18. David Martin, *Tongues of Fire: The Explosion of Protestantism in Latin America* (Oxford: Basil Blackwell, 1990), 231.

Conclusion

1. Not her real name.
2. Not his real name.
3. A qualification is necessary: I found Evangelicals to be generally active in community life in the Ixil Triangle and in Chimaltenango but less so in the other case study communities.
4. Ronald Inglehart, "Modernization and Postmodernization: The Changing Relationship Between Economic Development, Cultural Change, and Political Change" (Paper delivered at the Conference on Changing Social and Political Values, Complutense University, Madrid, 27 September–1 October 1993), 8, emphasis mine.
5. Jane Schneider, "Spirits and the Spirit of Capitalism," in *Religious Orthodoxy and Popular Faith in European Society*, ed. Ellen Badone (Princeton: Princeton University Press, 1990), 27.
6. Ibid., 28.
7. Ibid., 29.
8. Ibid., 31.
9. Ibid., 34.
10. David Martin, *Tongues of Fire: The Explosion of Protestantism in Latin America* (Oxford: Basil Blackwell, 1990), 33.
11. Amy L. Sherman, *Preferential Option: A Christian and Neo-Liberal Strategy for Latin America's Poor* (Grand Rapids: Eerdmans, 1992).
12. Lawrence Harrison, *Who Prospers? How Cultural Values Shape Economic and Political Success* (New York: Basic Books, 1992), 229–30.

# Bibliography

Adams, Richard, ed. *Political Changes in Guatemalan Indian Communities.* New Orleans: Middle American Research Institute of Tulane University, 1957.

Almond, Gabriel A., and Sydney Verba. *The Civic Culture: Political Attitudes and Democracy in Five Nations.* Princeton: Princeton University Press, 1963.

Annis, Sheldon. *God and Production in a Guatemalan Town.* Austin: University of Texas Press, 1987.

Berger, Brigitte, ed. *The Culture of Entrepreneurship.* San Francisco: Institute for Contemporary Studies, 1991.

Berger, Peter L. *The Capitalist Revolution: Fifty Propositions About Prosperity, Equality & Liberty.* New York: Basic Books, 1986.

———. *The Sacred Canopy.* Garden City, N.J.: Doubleday, 1967.

Brusco, Elizabeth. "The Household Basis of Evangelical Religion and the Reformation of Machismo in Colombia." Ph.D. diss., City University of New York, 1986.

Cancian, Frank. *Economics and Prestige in a Maya Community.* Stanford: Stanford University Press, 1965.

Carlson, Ruth, and Francis Eachus. "The Kekchi Spirit World." In *Cognitive Studies of Southern MesoAmerica,* edited by Helen Neuenswander and Dean E. Arnold. Dallas: Museum of Anthropology, Summer Institute of Linguistics, 1981.

Colby, Benjamin N., and Lore M. Colby. *The Daykeeper: The Life and Dis-*

*course of an Ixil Diviner.* Cambridge, Mass.: Harvard University Press, 1981.

Colby, Benjamin N., and Pierre L. van den Berghe. *Ixil Country.* Berkeley: University of California Press, 1969.

Critchfield, Richard. *Villages.* New York: Doubleday, 1981.

Diaz, May N. "Economic Relations in Peasant Society." In *Peasant Society: A Reader,* edited by Jack M. Potter, May N. Diaz, and George M. Foster. Boston: Little, Brown, 1967.

Diener, Paul. "The Tears of St. Anthony: Ritual and Revolution in Eastern Guatemala." *Latin American Perspectives* 5 (Summer 1978): 92–116.

Early, John D. "Education via Radio Among Guatemalan Highland Maya." *Human Organization* 32 (Fall 1973): 221–29.

Edgerton, Robert B. *Sick Societies: Challenging the Myth of Primitive Harmony.* New York: Free Press, 1992.

Etzioni, Amitai. "Entrepreneurship, Adaptation, and Legitimation: A Macro-Behavioral Perspective." *Journal of Economic Behavior and Organization* 8 (1987): 175–89.

Fillol, Tomas Roberto. *Social Factors in Economic Development: The Argentine Case.* Cambridge: MIT Press, 1961.

Foster, George M. "Peasant Society and the Image of Limited Good." In *Peasant Society: A Reader,* edited by Jack M. Potter, May N. Diaz, and George M. Foster. Boston: Little, Brown, 1967.

Freed, Kenneth. "Christianity's Holy War in Guatemala." *Los Angeles Times,* 13 May 1990.

Gerth, H. H., and C. Wright Mills, eds. and trans. *Max Weber: Essays in Sociology.* New York: Oxford University Press, 1964.

Goldin, Liliana. "Comercializacion y cambio en San Pedro Almolonga: un caso Maya-Quiche." *Mayab* (Madrid) 5 (1989): 45.

———. "Work and Ideology in the Maya Highlands of Guatemala: Economic Beliefs in the Context of Occupational Change." *Economic Development and Cultural Change* 41 (October 1992): 103–23.

Goldin, Liliana, and Brent Metz. "An Expression of Cultural Change: Invisible Converts to Protestantism among Highland Guatemalan Mayas." *Ethnology* 30 (October 1991): 325–38.

Goldschmidt, Walter, and Henry Hoijer, eds. *The Social Anthropology of Latin America: Essays in Honor of Ralph Leon Beals.* Los Angeles: Latin American Center at the University of California, 1970.

Greenberg, Linda. "Illness and Curing Among Maya Indians in Highland Guatemala: Cosmological Balance and Cultural Transformation." Ph.D. diss., University of Chicago, 1984.

Halévy, Élie. *The Liberal Awakening 1815–1830.* Vol. 2 of *A History of the English People in the Nineteenth Century.* Translated by E. I. Watkin. New York: Barnes & Noble, 1961.

Harrison, Lawrence E. *Underdevelopment Is a State of Mind.* Lanham, MD: Madison Books, 1985.

———. *Who Prospers? How Cultural Values Shape Economic and Political Success.* New York: Basic Books, 1992.

Hunter, James Davison. *Culture Wars: The Struggle to Define America*. New York: Basic Books, 1991.

Inkeles, Alex, and David H. Smith. *Becoming Modern: Individual Change in Six Developing Countries*. Cambridge, Mass.: Harvard University Press, 1974.

Jongkind, F. "The Agrarian Colonies of Dutch Calvinists in Praná, Brazil." *International Migration* (Geneva) 27 (September 1989): 467–86.

Kelsey, Vera, and Lily de Jongh Osborne. *Four Keys to Guatemala*. New York: Funk and Wagnalls, 1943.

Lewis, Paul. "With Bible in Hand, Evangelicals Come Marching In." *New York Times*, 15 June 1989.

Maldanado, Jorge E. "Building 'Fundamentalism' from the Family in Latin America." In *Fundamentalisms and Society: Reclaiming the Sciences, the Family, and Education*, edited by Martin E. Marty and R. Scott Appleby. Chicago: University of Chicago Press, 1993.

Martin, David. *Tongues of Fire: The Explosion of Protestantism in Latin America*. Oxford: Basil Blackwell, 1990.

McClelland, David. *The Achieving Society*. New York: Irvington Publishers, 1976.

McClosky, Herbert, and John Zaller. *The American Ethos: Public Attitudes toward Capitalism and Democracy*. Cambridge, Mass.: Harvard University Press, 1984.

Myrdal, Gunnar. *Asian Drama: An Inquiry into the Poverty of Nations*. New York: Pantheon, 1968.

Nash, June. *In the Eyes of the Ancestors: Belief and Behavior in a Maya Community*. New Haven: Yale University Press, 1970.

———. "Protestantism in an Indian Village in the Western Highlands of Guatemala." *Alpha Kappa Deltan* (Winter 1960): 49–53.

Nelson, Wilton M. *Protestantism in Central America*. Grand Rapids: Eerdmans, 1984.

Neuenswander, Helen, and Dean Arnold, eds. *Cognitive Studies of Southern MesoAmerica*. Dallas: Museum of Anthropology, Summer Institute of Linguistics, 1981.

Nida, Eugene A. *Communication of the Gospel in Latin America*. Cuarnavaca, Mexico: Centro Intercultural de Documentación, 1969.

Novak, Michael. *Will It Liberate?* New York: Paulist Press, 1986.

Oakes, Maud. *The Two Crosses of Todos Santos: Survivals of Mayan Religious Ritual*. New York: Pantheon Books, 1951.

Paul, Lois, and Benjamin Paul. "Changing Marriage Patterns in a Highland Guatemalan Community." *Southwestern Journal of Anthropology* 19 (Nov. 1963): 131–48.

Potter, Jack, May N. Diaz, and George M. Foster. *Peasant Society: A Reader*. Boston: Little, Brown, 1967.

Redfield, Robert. *A Village That Chose Progress*. Chicago: University of Chicago Press, 1950.

Saler, Benson. "Religious Conversion and Self-Aggrandizement: A Guatemalan Case." *Practical Anthropology* 12 (May/June 1965): 107–14.

Schneider, Jane. "Spirits and the Spirit of Capitalism." In *Religious Orthodoxy and Popular Faith in European Society*, edited by Ellen Badonne. Princeton: Princeton University Press, 1990.

Schumpeter, Joseph A. *Capitalism, Socialism, and Democracy*. New York: Harper Brothers, 1950.

Seligson, Mitchell. *Peasants of Costa Rica and the Development of Agrarian Capitalism*. Madison: The University of Wisconsin Press, 1980.

Seligson, Mitchell, and John Booth, eds. *Political Participation in Latin America*, Vol. II. New York: Holmes & Meier, 1979.

Sexton, James D. "Education and Innovation in a Guatemalan Community: San Juan la Laguna." *Latin American Studies* 19. Los Angeles: Latin American Center at the University of California, 1972.

———. "Protestantism and Modernization in Two Guatemalan Towns." *American Ethnologist* 5 (May 1978): 280–301.

———, ed. *Son of Tecún Umán: A Maya Indian Tells His Life Story*. Tuscon: University of Arizona Press, 1981.

Sexton, James D., and Clyde Woods. "Development and Modernization among Highland Maya: A Comparative Analysis of Ten Guatemalan Towns." *Human Organization* 36 (Summer 1977):156–72.

Sherman, Amy L. *Preferential Option: A Christian and Neoliberal Strategy for Latin America's Poor* Grand Rapids: Eerdmans, 1992.

Sieber, Sam D. "The Integration of Fieldwork and Survey Methods." *American Journal of Sociology* 78 (May 1973): 1335–59.

Smith, Christian. "The Spirit of Democracy: Base Communities, Protestantism, and Democratization in Latin America." *Sociology of Religion* 55 (Summer 1994): 119–43.

Smith, Waldemar. *The Fiesta System and Economic Change*. New York: Columbia University Press, 1977.

Sowell, Thomas. *The Economics and Politics of Race*. New York: Quill, 1983.

Stoll, David. "Between Two Fires: Dual Violence and the Reassertion of Civil Society in Nebaj, Guatemala." Ph.D. diss., Stanford University, 1992.

———. "Evangelical Awakening." *Hemisphere* (Winter/Spring 1990): 34–37.

———. *Is Latin America Turning Protestant?* Berkeley: University of California Press, 1990.

Stoll, David, and Virginia Garrard-Burnett, eds., *Rethinking Protestantism in Latin America*. Philadelphia: Temple University Press, 1993.

Tax, Sol, and Robert Hinshaw. "Panajachel a Generation Later." In *The Social Anthropology of Latin America: Essays in Honor of Ralph Leon Beals*, edited by Walter Goldschmidt and Henry Hoijer. Los Angeles: Latin American Center at the University of California, 1970.

Tedlock, Barbara. *Time and the Highland Maya*. Albuquerque: University of New Mexico Press, 1982.

Thompson, Richard. *The Winds of Tomorrow: Social Change in a Maya Town*. Chicago: University of Chicago Press, 1974.

Townsend, Paul G., ed. *Ritual Rhetoric From Cotzal*. Guatemala City, Guatemala: Instituto Linguistico de Verano, 1980.

Warren, Kay B. *The Symbolism of Subordination: Indian Identity in a Guatemalan Town*. Austin: University of Texas, 1978.

Wattenberg, Daniel. "Gospel Message of Getting Ahead Inch by Inch." *Insight* (16 July 1990): 15–17.

Weber, Max. *The Protestant Ethic and the Spirit of Capitalism*. Translated by Talcott Parsons. London: Unwin Paperbacks, 1976.

Woods, Clyde M., and Theodore D. Graves. *The Process of Medical Change in a Highland Guatemalan Town*. Los Angeles: Latin American Center of the University of Los Angeles, 1973.

Wuthnow, Robert. "Understanding Religion and Politics." *Daedalus* (Summer 1991): 1–20.

# Index